Nation-Building

Forum on Constructive Capitalism
Francis Fukuyama, *Series Editor*

Nation-Building

Beyond Afghanistan and Iraq

• •

Edited by

Francis Fukuyama

The Johns Hopkins University Press
• BALTIMORE •

© 2006 The Johns Hopkins University Press
All rights reserved. Published 2006

Printed in the United States of America on acid-free paper

9   8   7   6   5   4   3   2   1

The Johns Hopkins University Press
2715 North Charles Street
Baltimore, Maryland 21218-4363
www.press.jhu.edu

Library of Congress Cataloging-in-Publication Data

Nation-building : beyond Afghanistan and Iraq / edited by Francis Fukuyama.
    p.   cm.
    "Product of a conference held at the Paul H. Nitze School of Advanced International
Studies (SAIS), the Johns Hopkins University, in April 2004"—Ack.
    Includes bibliographical references and index.
    ISBN 0-8018-8334-2 (hardcover : alk. paper) — ISBN 0-8018-8335-0 (pbk. : alk. paper)
    1. Nation-building—Congresses.   I. Fukuyama, Francis.
JZ6300.N38   2006
327.73′009′0511—dc22   2005019347

A catalog record for this book is available from the British Library.

Contents

Acknowledgments　　*vii*
List of Abbreviations　　*ix*

INTRODUCTION
Nation-Building and the Failure of Institutional Memory　　*1*
Francis Fukuyama

Part I · The Historical Experience of Nation-Building

· CHAPTER 1 ·
From Consensus to Crisis: The Postwar Career of Nation-Building
in U.S. Foreign Relations　　*19*
David Ekbladh

· CHAPTER 2 ·
Nation-Building in the Heyday of the Classic Development
Ideology: Ford Foundation Experience in the 1950s and 1960s　　*42*
Francis X. Sutton

· CHAPTER 3 ·
Building Nations: The American Experience　　*64*
Minxin Pei, Samia Amin, and Seth Garz

· CHAPTER 4 ·
Nation-Building: Lessons Learned and Unlearned　　*86*
Michèle A. Flournoy

Part II · Afghanistan

• CHAPTER 5 •

Sovereignty and Legitimacy in Afghan Nation-Building   *107*
S. Frederick Starr

• CHAPTER 6 •

Rebuilding Afghanistan: Impediments, Lessons, and Prospects   *125*
Marvin G. Weinbaum

• CHAPTER 7 •

The Lessons of Nation-Building in Afghanistan   *145*
Larry P. Goodson

Part III · Iraq

• CHAPTER 8 •

What Went Wrong and Right in Iraq   *173*
Larry Diamond

• CHAPTER 9 •

Striking Out in Baghdad: How Postconflict
Reconstruction Went Awry   *196*
Johanna Mendelson Forman

• CHAPTER 10 •

Learning the Lessons of Iraq   *218*
James Dobbins

• CONCLUSION

Guidelines for Future Nation-Builders   *231*
Francis Fukuyama

Contributors   245
Index   251

Acknowledgments

THIS BOOK is the product of a conference held at the Paul H. Nitze School of Advanced International Studies (SAIS), the Johns Hopkins University, in April 2004, titled "Nation-Building: Beyond Afghanistan and Iraq." This conference was part of the Bernard L. Schwartz Forum on Constructive Capitalism, and this book is the first in the Forum on Constructive Capitalism series. I thank Bernard Schwartz, chairman and CEO of the Loral Corporation, for his generous support of both the conference and the forum since the latter's founding in 2001. The forum is dedicated to understanding the global economy and the opportunities and dangers associated with technology and economic development. Clearly, the way that we think about these issues has shifted dramatically since September 11, 2001, and I appreciate the flexibility with which the forum has been allowed to address the turns in international events.

Many people contributed to the success of the conference, and comments both official and informal helped shape this book's chapters. The Honorable Said Jawad, ambassador of Afghanistan, was kind enough to serve as the conference's keynote speaker. Thomas Carothers of the Carnegie Endowment for International Peace, Reuel Gerecht of the American Enterprise Institute, and Kenneth Pollack of the Brookings Institution made presentations that were not included in this volume. I give special thanks to Abdulwahab Alkebsi, Ryan Crocker, Amitai Etzioni, Barbara Haig, and

Stephen Hosmer for serving as commentators, and to Charles Doran, Tom Keaney, and Tom Mahnken for their work as panel chairs. Jessica Einhorn, dean of SAIS, introduced the conference and was, as always, supportive of the project as a whole.

Conferences of this sort do not happen without a great deal of behind-the-scenes administrative work. Most of this happened flawlessly, due to the efforts of my program assistant, Cynthia Doroghazi, who also did a tremendous amount of work in pulling this volume together. Felisa Klubes and Katrine Petkova provided great assistance in setting up publicity for the event. In addition, Björn Dressel, Carlos Hamann, Jikang Kim, Rima Kohli, Matt Miller, Trita Parsi, and Matt Tocks helped with the running of the conference. I also thank Henry Tom of the Johns Hopkins University Press for his help in bringing out this volume.

Abbreviations

AIOG	Afghan Interagency Operating Group
ARG	Afghan Reconstruction Group
CFC-A	Combined Forces Command–Afghanistan
CJTF	Commander of the joint task force
CPA	Coalition Provisional Authority
DDR	Disarmament, demobilization, and reintegration
FAO	United Nations Food and Agriculture Organization
IATF	Interagency task force
ISAF	International Security Assistance Force
IVS	International Voluntary Service
KDP	Kurdistan Democratic Party
MLAT	Mutual Legal Assistance Treaty
MNF	Multinational Force
NATO	North Atlantic Treaty Organization
NGO	Nongovernmental organization
NSC	National Security Council
NSP	National Solidarity Program
OAS	Organization of American States
OEF	Operation Enduring Freedom
OPIC	Overseas Private Investment Corporation
ORHA	Office of Reconstruction and Humanitarian Assistance

PDD	Presidential Decision Directive
PRT	Provincial reconstruction team
PUK	Patriotic Union of Kurdistan
SCAP	Supreme Commander of the Allied Powers
SCIRI	Supreme Council for the Islamic Revolution in Iraq
SEADAG	Southeast Asian Development Advisory Group
TVA	Tennessee Valley Authority
UNDP	United Nations Development Program
UNESCO	United Nations Educational, Scientific, and Cultural Organization
UNICEF	United Nations Children's Fund
UNMOVIC	United Nations Monitoring, Inspection, and Verification Commission
USAID	United States Agency for International Development

Nation-Building and the Failure of Institutional Memory

Francis Fukuyama

I don't think our troops ought to be used for what's called nation-building. I think our troops ought to be used to fight and win war. (October 11, 2000)

We meet here during a crucial period in the history of our nation, and of the civilized world. Part of that history was written by others; the rest will be written by us. (February 26, 2003)

I sent American troops to Iraq to make its people free, not to make them American. Iraqis will write their own history, and find their own way. (May 24, 2004)

GEORGE W. BUSH

GEORGE W. BUSH has gone through a striking transformation on the subject of nation-building: from opponent of the very concept as candidate for president, to grandiose social engineer on the eve of the Iraq war, to chastened supporter of indigenous Iraqi nation-building a year later. These changes track the profound ambivalence felt by the American public to this activity. Conservatives have always been skeptical about nation-building as a kind of international social welfare, whereas liberals have seen the effort to create a democratic Iraq as an extension of the American empire. Yet both ends of the political spectrum have come to support nation-building efforts at different times—conservatives as part of the "war on terrorism" and liberals for the sake of humanitarian intervention.

The frequency and intensity of U.S. and international nation-building efforts have increased since the end of the Cold War, which, as Michael Ignatieff has pointed out, left a band of weak or failed states stretching from North Africa through the Balkans and the Middle East to South Asia.[1] In addition, parts of sub-Saharan Africa, East Asia, Central America, and the Caribbean have been the loci of state failure in recent decades. These failures have produced refugees, human rights abuses, inter- and intrastate wars, drug and human trafficking, and other problems that crossed international borders. And after September 11, 2001, it became clear that weak or failed states could sponsor terrorism that threatened the core security interests of the world's sole superpower, the United States.

Although conventional military power was sufficient for some purposes, such as expelling Serbian military forces from Kosovo or defeating Saddam Hussein's army, the underlying problems caused by failed states or weak governance could only be solved through long-term efforts by outside powers to rebuild indigenous state institutions. Security problems in earlier times centered around strong states that could maintain a monopoly of force over their own territory, but many post–Cold War crises involved an internal absence of state power that necessitated outside intervention and long-term receivership by the international community. Thus the ability of outside powers to provide governance and control the internal behavior of failed or weak states has become a key component of their national power.

As the chapters by David Ekbladh, Francis X. Sutton, and Minxin Pei, Samia Amin, and Seth Garz demonstrate, nation-building has a long history in American foreign policy, yet it is clear that the United States and the international community have taken on new nation-building efforts at an increased rate since 1989. The authors of a RAND study on the U.S. experience with nation-building point out that there has been roughly one new nation-building intervention every two years since the end of the Cold War.[2] In their chapter, Minxin Pei and colleagues provide a list of American efforts at nation-building over the past century that indicates this increasing tempo.

There is a certain amount of controversy as to what constitutes nation-building, and the rate of new nation-building activities is affected by which cases one counts. The authors of the RAND study argue that South Korea and South Vietnam should not be considered nation-building exercises because they were simply meant to reinforce an existing status quo in a divided society, or else did not have the creation of a democracy as a final goal.[3] The logic of this argument is not clear: it is true that the United States intervened in South Korea and South Vietnam to protect those countries from communist aggression, but, as David Ekbladh points out in his chapter, the United States very self-consciously initiated aid programs designed to promote both political and economic development in both places to counter communist political influence. The Vietnam War was seen, as Ekbladh makes very clear, as a struggle between two competing visions of nation-building—communist and Western. And although democracy is increasingly seen as a necessary component of nation-building, the United States and the international community have supported efforts to promote political and economic development quite independently of explicit efforts to advance democracy in the target country. Following its toppling of the Taliban regime in Afghanistan, the United States was relatively modest in its claims to be constructing a fully democratic political order.

Some Definitions

Europeans often criticize Americans for the use of the term *nation-building,* reflecting as it does the specifically American experience of constructing a new political order in a land of new settlement without deeply rooted peoples, cultures, and traditions. Nations—that is to say, communities of shared values, traditions, and historical memory—by this argument are never built, particularly by outsiders; rather, they evolve out of an unplanned historical-evolutionary process. What Americans refer to as *nation-building* is rather state-building—that is, constructing political institutions, or else promoting economic development.

This argument is largely true: what Americans mean by *nation-building* is usually state-building coupled with economic development. However, the flat assertion that foreigners have never succeeded in nation-building is not true. Many imperial powers have sought to build nations within their colonies, and some have succeeded. The most notable case is the British in India. As Sunil Khilnani demonstrates in *The Idea of India,* the notion of India as a nation-state was something that was invented under British rule.[4] Prior to Britain's arrival, the subcontinent was a hodgepodge of princely states, languages, ethnic groups, and religions, with the Mogul Empire's writ limited only to parts of northern India. Under the British, India got a sense of itself as a single, unified political space (even if that space was carved into Muslim and Hindu areas at Partition) and acquired a common language, a civil service and bureaucratic tradition, an army, and other institutions that would be critical to the emergence of a democratic India in 1947.[5]

But the British legacy on the subcontinent is in many ways unique; few colonial powers had such a large and durable effect on their subject peoples. For all practical purposes, what passes for nation-building is a much more limited exercise in political reconstruction or re-legitimation, or else a matter of promoting economic development. Outside powers can succeed at negotiating and enforcing ceasefires between, say, rival ethnic groups; it is seldom that they can make these groups understand that they are part of a larger, nonethnic identity.

Even in the cases of postwar Germany and Japan—often taken as models of successful nation-building—the influence of outside powers on the political development of these countries is exaggerated or misunderstood. The United States and other occupying powers did relatively little state-building in either country: both Germany and Japan possessed powerful state bureaucracies that survived the war weakened but structurally intact. The occupation authorities conducted political purges of both bureaucracies, but the exigencies of the postwar reconstruction forced them to bring back many former Nazis or senior bureaucrats with ties to the prewar regimes. In Japan in particular, General Douglas MacArthur succeeded in purging only the top couple of layers of officials in the powerful economics ministries; as recent Japanese revisionist historians have shown, the postwar economic planning ministries that became known as "Japan, Inc." had their origin in the 1940 credit-allocation and munitions production system.[6]

What did occur in both Germany and Japan was the re-legitimation of the new governments on a democratic basis, with the drafting of democratic constitutions. (In the Japanese case, the political system was democratized without forcing abdication of the Emperor, a decision of MacArthur's that eased the postwar transition but made the break with the prewar past much less clear than in Germany.) And in both countries, the Allied occupations eventually got around to promoting economic reconstruction, once the Soviets had finished stripping their occupation zones of equipment as war reparations. But in both cases, what went on under the rubric of nation-building looked quite different from more recent efforts in such failed states as Somalia, East Timor, or Afghanistan, where the state itself had ceased to exist.

Reconstruction versus Development

Nation-building encompasses two different types of activities, reconstruction and development. Although the distinction between the two is often blurred, it was always present to nation-builders of earlier generations dealing with post-conflict situations. The official title of the World Bank is, after all, the International Bank for Reconstruction and Development, and most of its early activity fell under the first heading. *Reconstruction* refers to the restoration of war-torn or damaged societies to their preconflict situation. *Development,* however, refers to the creation of new institutions and the promotion of sustained economic growth, events that transform the society open-endedly into something that it has not been previously.

There is a huge conceptual difference between reconstruction and development. Reconstruction is something that outside powers have shown themselves historically able to bring about. Japan, Germany, Italy, and postwar Western Europe more generally were all examples of successful American reconstruction efforts. Similarly, although the postconflict reconstruction efforts in Bosnia and Kosovo were late, poorly coordinated, and politically confused, they did, in fact, manage to meet their goal of stabilizing fragile postconflict situations and returning the target countries to an economic state close to what they had been prior to conflict. Reconstruction is possible when the underlying political and social infrastructure has survived conflict or crisis; the problem is then the relatively simple matter of injecting sufficient resources to jumpstart the process, in the form of supplying food, roads, buildings, infrastructure, and the like.

Development, however, is much more problematic, both conceptually and as a matter of pragmatic policy. As the chapters in this book by David Ekbladh and Francis X. Sutton demonstrate, the self-confidence of Americans in their ability to help poor countries develop was quite high soon after World War II and then fell sharply during and after the Vietnam War. This early confidence was based in large measure on the experience of domestic state-building in New Deal projects, such as the Tennessee Valley Authority (TVA), which were seen at that time as huge successes in eliminating poverty in the rural South. There was a great deal of enthusiasm for state-led development at this time, with multilateral agencies like the World Bank and private nongovernmental organizations (NGOs) like the Ford Foundation providing technical training to help developing country governments do economic planning—understandably, perhaps, as this was the norm in most developed countries at the time. On the economic side, aid came in the form of large infrastructure projects or poorly thought-out industrialization projects.

The early American self-confidence in its ability to promote development came crashing down under the pressure of a variety of factors in the 1970s and 1980s. State-building, done (as Sutton indicates in his chapter) without regard for the democratic legitimacy of the governments involved, implicated foreign donors in the human rights abuses of recipients and failed to prevent coups, revolutions, and wars that led to political breakdown. Pakistan, an early target of foreign development efforts, is a prime example. Economic planning fell out of favor intellectually with the Reagan-Thatcher revolution in the late 1980s and was replaced by orthodox economic liberalism as the dominant conceptual framework. But most importantly, none of the approaches popular in any given decade proved adequate to promote sustained long-term growth in countries with weak institutions or where local elites were uninterested or incapable of managing the development process themselves. The record is particularly horrendous in the world's poorest region, sub-Saharan Africa, many of whose countries have experienced negative per capita growth in gross domestic product (GDP) and regression in institutional development, even though some 10 percent of the entire region's GNP is provided by outside donors.[7] Where sustained economic growth did occur, particularly in East Asia, it tended to come about under the leadership of domestic elites and not as a result of the efforts of foreign donors, lenders, or allies.[8]

To the extent that there has been intellectual progress in this area, it lies in an appreciation for the complexity and multidimensionality of the development problem. In the 1950s and 1960s, under the influence of the Harrod-Domar and neoclassical growth models, it was common to think about less-developed countries as if they were simply developed countries minus the resources and could be set on a path to self-sustaining growth through the infusion of sufficient investment capital. This approach was followed in later decades by emphases that shifted in turn to education, population control, debt relief, and structural adjustment as panaceas for development. In recent years, a great deal of attention has been paid, appropriately, to institutions and governance as critical factors in development.[9] But any honest appraisal of where the "state of the art" lies in development today would have to conclude that, although institutions may be important, we know relatively little about how to create them; they are, in any case, only one part of a much more complicated set of necessary strategies.

In light of this record, it is tempting to say that nation-builders should stick to reconstruction and eschew the development function. The problem is that this bifurcation is usually not possible in developing countries with weak or absent state sectors. In many cases, conflict has destroyed basic institutions, obliterating the distinction between reconstruction and development. In Somalia, Afghanistan, and Iraq after the United States–led invasion, no state infrastructure existed to provide security or to distribute state services, as it did in postwar Japan or Europe. These societies had fallen into chaos or warlordism, and new central government institutions had to be created virtually from scratch. To get them back to where they were prior to the outbreak of conflict thus required development as well as reconstruction.

The development function is a critical nation-building skill for another reason: it is only the ability to create and maintain self-sustaining indigenous institutions that permits outside powers to formulate an exit strategy. A lack of conceptual clarity on how to promote institutional development makes it extremely difficult to transition out of the reconstruction phase of nation-building. For example, Gerald Knaus and Felix Martin have described the office of the High Representative in Bosnia as a kind of European Raj.[10] Nearly a decade after the signing of the Dayton Accord, the Bosnians are incapable of governing themselves. The international community, in the person of the high representative, overturns the results of democratic elections, unseats officials, and otherwise takes on governance functions in place of local authorities, all in the name of eliminating corruption and promoting good governance and human rights. But this approach undercuts the Bosnian capacity for self-government by making the Bosnian state dependent on outside support; most observers would agree that an exit by the international community anytime soon would land Bosnia back in the same tangle of internal conflicts that prompted outside intervention in the first place.

In certain respects, reconstruction can even become the enemy of development over the long run. Reconstruction requires rapid, massive outside intervention to stabilize conflicts, rebuild infrastructure, and deal with humanitarian issues. The local government is, by definition, unable to provide these functions itself, and it is often completely bypassed as foreign military forces, aid agencies, and NGOs flood into the country. Capacity-building must take a back seat to service delivery; more often than not, what little capacity exists is undermined by the presence of foreigners richly endowed with both resources and capabilities. In Afghanistan, a driver for a foreign media company makes several times the salary of a government minister; who, under these circumstances, would prefer to continue working for a disorganized and feckless local bureaucracy?

The development phase, by contrast, requires the eventual weaning of local actors and institutions from dependence on outside aid. This is conceptually straightforward, but extremely difficult to implement in practice. First, it is seldom the case that local institutions are actually strong enough to do all of the things that they are intended to do. Weaning them from outside support at times means that a particular governmental function simply is not performed. Second, the outside nation-builders get into the habit of ruling and making decisions, and they are reluctant to allow their local protégés to make their own mistakes. American officials' reluctance to cede decisionmaking power to a new Iraqi government was glaringly evident, as Larry Diamond points out in his chapter, in the early months of the U.S. occupation. And third, nation-builders often lack clarity about their own impact on local populations. They chant the mantra of institution- or capacity-building, and they fail to understand how their continued presence in the country tends to weaken precisely those institutions they are seeking to strengthen.

The Failure of Institutional Memory

None of these problems is new or unfamiliar to anyone who has been in the reconstruction or development business in times past. The United States plunged into its first big nation-building exercise during the reconstruction of the South in the aftermath of the Civil War, and it undertook numerous new projects in the Philippines and Caribbean during the period leading up to World War II.[11]

What is remarkable about this entire experience is how little institutional learning there has been over time; the same lessons about the pitfalls and limitations of nation-building seemingly have to be relearned with each new involvement. This became painfully evident during the American occupation and reconstruction of Iraq after April 2003. James Dobbins and Michèle A. Flournoy both contend that a fair degree of learning actually did take place within the U.S. government in the course of its various nation-building projects in the 1990s.[12] The reconstruction of Bosnia, for example, was marked by substantial confusion and lack of coordination both within the U.S. government and between the United States and its European allies. But the Kosovo reconstruction went much more smoothly because the same players tried to avoid the problems of the earlier crisis. In her chapter, Michèle Flournoy describes the history of Presidential Decision Directive (PDD) 56 (reproduced in its entirety at the end of her chapter), which was the Clinton administration's effort to codify its learning about how to organize postconflict reconstruction operations. PDD 56 was adopted in the wake of Somalia and Haiti; it was first applied during the Kosovo reconstruction, and it was one of the reasons why that nation-building operation went more smoothly than did previous ones.

Unfortunately, much of this knowledge was lost after the Bush administration took office. PDD 56 was supposed to have been replaced by a new, comprehensive framework for organizing the interagency nation-building process, but persistent objections from the Pentagon prevented that framework's final approval by the president prior to the 9/11 attacks. Thus when the United States embarked on a new nation-building exercise in Afghanistan in the wake of its December 2001 defeat of the Taliban regime, there was no agreed-upon internal U.S. government framework for organizing the reconstruction efforts there.

The first year of the Afghan reconstruction saw numerous problems, both with overall U.S. strategy (as the chapter by S. Frederick Starr explains) and in the on-the-ground coordination of United States and international relief efforts (see the chapters by Marvin G. Weinbaum and Larry P. Goodson). This strategic confusion resulted from a mistaken emphasis on sovereignty over the legitimacy of the new Afghan government. The reasons for the lack of coordination are complex and rooted, in part, in the absence of a preexisting framework for interagency coordination. It is clear, however, that the Pentagon and the vice president's office interpreted the problem as one of mismanagement on the part of the lead agencies on the civilian side—namely, the State Department and the U.S. Agency for International Development (USAID). This circumstance set the stage for the peculiar way in which planning for Iraq's reconstruction was organized.

President Bush signed the PDD authorizing full-scale war planning for an invasion of Iraq in August 2002.[13] Every individual agency—Defense, USAID, Justice, and State (with the massive State Department "Future of Iraq" plan)—had been planning for the postwar period since the spring of 2002. What did not exist, however, was an overall effort to coordinate across the U.S. government, or a single point of authority for the postwar period comparable to the command position occupied by General Tommy Franks on the military side.

This type of planning did not get started until January 20, 2003—with the appointment of former Lieutenant General Jay Garner as head of a new Office of Reconstruction and Humanitarian Assistance (ORHA)—less than two months before the start of the war. The reason for this delay was ostensibly a fear on the part of the Bush administration that revelation of extensive planning for the postwar period would undercut diplomatic efforts in the United Nations by indicating that the administration had already decided on war. This argument is less than plausible, however, because the United States had already begun massive deployments of forces to the Persian Gulf in preparation for war, a deployment that could be reversed only at significant cost. The real reason had to do with a fight that took place within the administration over control of the reconstruction process.[14]

In every previous nation-building exercise in which the United States was involved after General MacArthur in Japan, there were always two lines of authority—one on the civilian side, going through the ambassador and the State Department, and a second through the field commander via the military chain of command; these two lines of authority were generally coordinated through a country team, usually chaired by the ambassador. The Iraq reconstruction was wholly directed by the Pentagon, breaking this precedent. President Bush was apparently persuaded by Defense Secretary Donald Rumsfeld's argument concerning the need for unity of command in the reconstruction. The lesson that Rumsfeld drew from Bosnia was that split authority on the U.S. side tends to tie U.S. forces down, because the civilian side is always good at devising reasons why U.S. troops are politically necessary and thus cannot be withdrawn. In addition, a poisonous level of distrust had developed between the Pentagon and the vice president's office, on the one hand, and the State Department and the intelligence community on the other. The former had pushed strongly for the war and felt that the latter was only grudgingly on board, hence the argument for Pentagon ownership of the entire reconstruction effort. Interagency distrust was greatly exacerbated by the dispute over the role to be played by Ahmed Chalabi, the Iraqi émigré who headed the Iraqi National Congress and was the Pentagon's favorite to lead a provisional government.

The Afghan reconstruction influenced the nature of the Iraq reconstruction. The former was run in the traditional way, with two lines of authority and a country team headed by an ambassador. The Pentagon argued that the State Department and USAID were handling the job incompetently; President Bush was evidently furious at the lack of progress on the Kabul-to-Kandahar highway that was to be the centerpiece of the U.S. nation-building effort. This interpretation strengthened the Pentagon's case for sole ownership of the Iraq reconstruction.

Unfortunately, this analysis of the Afghan experience was only partly correct. The early problem with the Afghan reconstruction was not the dual lines of authority or State Department involvement, but rather one of personalities. By 2003, when these problems had largely been fixed, the Afghan reconstruction proceeded much more smoothly than its counterpart in Iraq. Civil-military cooperation worked well both at the level of the ambassador and the local military commander as well as in the field, with the development of provincial reconstruction teams (PRTs) that combined security and reconstruction personnel in a single integrated package. (On the PRTs and on-the-ground coordination efforts, see the chapters by Marvin G. Weinbaum and Larry P. Goodson.)

In principle, unity of command is a good idea; Rumsfeld was right in observing that Bosnia had been marked by continuing squabbles between the civilian and military authorities and an overall lack of coordination. The international division of labor in the Balkans did indeed create overlapping and poorly coordinated national teams that wasted time and money. The problem in Iraq, however, was that the Pentagon office put in charge of organizing the reconstruction (the Office of the Undersecretary of Defense for Policy) had no prior experience with this kind of operation and had limited institutional capacity for setting up the kind of organization needed. The interagency coordination necessary for postconflict reconstruction is among the most complex tasks of any that the U.S. government attempts to undertake. Defense, State, USAID, Justice, Treasury, and a host of other agencies all have roles to play, many of them defined by statute; just knowing how all of these moving parts fit together is a major task. The problem was compounded by ORHA's late start (itself a result of the interagency fight over who should control the reconstruction) and by General Garner's relatively low level of authority. Garner and ORHA went from a staff of six at the end of January to seven hundred by the time they shipped out to Kuwait and then Iraq in mid-March. ORHA had no organic logistics capabilities and was dependent on military commanders with other priorities for transporting its own staff; simply getting the reconstruction team into the theater was a major undertaking.

The chapter by Johanna Mendelson Forman details at length the failures of the Bush administration's planning process before the occupation and its poor execution of the reconstruction effort thereafter. This failure has, in fact, become the topic of a growing literature.[15] According to Bob Woodward, the final war plan briefed by then-commander of Central Command Tommy Franks to Bush administration principals did not include a so-called "Phase IV" plan—that is, instructions to commanders on how to employ their forces after the end of active combat.[16] It is equally astonishing that Franks could give such a briefing and that none of his civilian bosses asked him about where the missing Phase IV plan was.

The administration did plan for a number of contingencies that did not occur, such as a humanitarian/refugee crisis and oil well fires; however, it was completely blindsided by the collapse of state authority in Iraq and the chaos that followed. This omission is a perfect example of institutional memory failure. Almost every postconflict reconstruction during the previous decade and a half, from Panama to East Timor, had been characterized by the collapse of local police authority and the ensuing disorder. Consequently, a great deal of thought and effort had been given to improving the so-called "civ-pol" function through the early deployment of constabulary forces.[17] Unfortunately, few of the officials responsible for the Iraq reconstruction had personal experience with these earlier efforts, and they evidently expected that the post-Saddam transition would look like those in Eastern Europe in 1989.[18] That misjudgment would prove extremely costly, as looters stripped government ministries bare and Iraq's infrastructure crumbled.

L. Paul Bremer replaced Jay Garner in mid-May 2003, and ORHA was replaced by the Coalition Provisional Authority (CPA). It is an unfortunate but common perception that Garner was fired because of incompetent management of the reconstruction; in reality, the administration had planned on this shift from before the war. A full history remains to be written, but, even at this early juncture, the very structure and mission of the CPA raise a number of interesting questions from the standpoint of the proper institutional approach to nation-building.

Two Models of Occupation

The Iraq occupation represented a very different model from that of the country team used in Afghanistan. In the latter case, there was an early return of sovereignty to an interim government led by Hamid Karzai, as established by the Bonn Accord in December 2001.[19] The United Nations and its special envoy, Lakhdar Brahimi, played a large role in organizing and legitimating the transition, and other North Atlantic Treaty Organization allies were given specific roles and missions early on. Although the United States remained the predominant outside military power in Afghanistan, and for all practical purposes could act as if it were sovereign in its pursuit of al-Qaeda and Taliban forces, U.S. military forces remained capped at approximately 10,000 through mid-2003 (increased thereafter to 23,000) and did not initially seek to provide domestic order anywhere but in Kabul. There was, in other words, a deliberate decision to go into Afghanistan with a light footprint. The long-term political goal was modest, moreover: the United States never promised that it would turn Afghanistan into a model democracy. The objective, rather, was to end the country's legacy as a haven for terrorists and to bring a modicum of stability to its population.

The situation was much different in Iraq: The goals were more ambitious and the footprint much heavier. President Bush had stated before the war that Iraq was to be made a democracy and that the war would be the opening phase of a much larger plan to transform the politics of the greater Middle East. The country was invaded by coalition forces without the help of any indigenous actors, as there had been in Afghanistan. With the fall of Saddam Hussein's regime, the CPA became the sovereign authority in Iraq, and the United States held that authority for more than 13 months until its transfer back to an interim Iraqi government on June 28, 2004. The CPA replaced the government of Iraq in toto, moving symbolically into the old Republican Palace once occupied by Saddam. Although the United States established a 25-member Iraqi Governing Council in the summer of 2003, Iraqi participation in the actual governance of the country was minimal for the first year of the occupation.

Afghanistan and Iraq thus represent two very different models for managing a reconstruction. The Afghan model used modest means in pursuit of relatively modest objectives (an initial disbursement of only $192 million, increased subsequently to $1.6 billion; see figures in the chapter by

Goodson) and sought wherever possible to offload responsibility onto local actors (e.g., the Northern Alliance militias), the United Nations, or other allies. The Iraqi model put very substantial resources in the service of very ambitious objectives, with an emphasis on U.S. control of as much of the reconstruction effort as possible. Although the United States sought to involve more outside countries in the Iraqi reconstruction, particularly as its costs began to escalate, those countries were not given nearly the same sorts of responsibilities that allies were allowed in Afghanistan (e.g., the Germans rebuilding the Afghan police).

There were many disadvantages to proceeding in the latter fashion. The CPA was, in effect, a massive new bureaucracy, created on the fly and in the field, under adverse and (as came to be seen) deteriorating security conditions. Unlike the situation with a country team, there was no existing cadre of professionals ready for this kind of overseas duty. The entire staff had to be recruited on the spot, many on 90-day temporary duty assignments that limited their effectiveness and ability to establish relationships with local Iraqis. Throughout its entire existence, the CPA was understaffed and had to spend considerable energy building up its own organization rather than providing governmental services to Iraqis. Given the novelty of this organization, lines of authority were confused. Although Bremer nominally worked for and reported to Defense Secretary Rumsfeld, he increasingly dealt directly with the White House staff and bypassed the Pentagon bureaucracy. Relationships with the local U.S. military command were reportedly both strained and confused. The massive U.S. military presence and its role in providing law and order were regarded as increasingly oppressive by the Iraqi people, and this perception played a role in stimulating violent resistance. And then, with the transfer of sovereignty in June 2004, this entire, large bureaucracy had to be dismantled and its functions handed back either to Iraqi ministries or to the new embassy/country team. This once again created substantial confusion as roles and missions were reassigned to a different bureaucracy.

It is interesting to speculate whether the small-footprint Afghan model could have been used in Iraq. Certain officials in the Pentagon would, in fact, have preferred such a strategy. It would have involved appointing a provisional government of Iraqis and transferring sovereignty to it early on. For all practical purposes, this government would have to have consisted primarily of "externals" like Chalabi, based outside Iraq prior to the war. The United States would then have offloaded as much responsibility to this new government as possible, as quickly as possible, drawing down its own military forces and retaining influence through an embassy.

It is of course impossible to know what would have happened under such a counterfactual scenario, but it is extremely doubtful that anything like it could have materialized. The United States was able to go into Afghanistan with light forces because it had a powerful internal ally, the Northern Alliance, and because it had strong support from an Afghan population exhausted by 30 years of civil war. The émigré groups that would have formed the core of an interim Iraqi administration, by contrast, had no forces of their own (apart from a small militia and intelligence service controlled by Chalabi), no administrative capacity, and significantly less legitimacy than Afghan president Karzai. A weak, sovereign Iraqi interim government would not have been able to control the massive looting that took place in the summer of 2003 or restore domestic order in cities throughout Iraq, and, in all likelihood, it ultimately would have been subject to the same insurgency the U.S. occupiers faced. It would not have been capable, on its own, of restoring electrical power or oil production. Needless to say, it could not have undertaken a search for Saddam Hussein's weapons of mass destruction. There is little likelihood that the United States could have drawn down its forces substantially or avoided a preeminent role in providing domestic security.

The Afghan model thus was not one that could have easily been applied to Iraq, unless U.S. goals there had been dramatically lower (e.g., simply the elimination of weapons of mass destruction). However, the United States could have made a much earlier effort to find a way to return sovereignty to an interim Iraqi government, one not based on externals like Chalabi with a great deal of political baggage. (That ultimately happened with the selection of Iyad Alawi as interim prime minister.) The United States could have sought to keep as much of the old regime's state structure in place, particularly the army, a move that would have required a much more restricted de-Ba'athification effort. And it could have avoided the overcentralized CPA model altogether by adhering to a more traditional, country team approach.

The first lesson of the Iraq occupation ought to be the need for the United States to be far more cautious in undertaking such ambitious projects in the first place. But given the genuine problems posed by failed states, it is unlikely that the United States or the international community more broadly will be able to avoid nation-building in the future. If we are to avoid making the same mistakes, we must come to understand what went wrong and what could be done better in the nation-building exercises that the United States undertakes in the twenty-first century.

Notes

1. Michael Ignatieff, "The Burden," *New York Times Magazine,* January 5, 2003, 22–27, 50–54.

2. James Dobbins, Keith Crane, Seth Jones, et al., *America's Role in Nation-Building: From Germany to Iraq* (Santa Monica, Calif.: RAND, 2003).
3. Ibid.
4. Sunil Khilnani, *The Idea of India* (New York: Farrar, Straus, and Giroux, 1999).
5. Similarly, the Japanese did not create modern Korean nationhood during their rule over the peninsula, but their oppressive rule certainly strengthened Korean nationalism and left behind some durable institutions (e.g., the bank-centered industrial group) that would be the foundation for South Korea's postwar economic miracle. On the Japanese colonial legacy in economic policy, see Jung-En Woo, *Race to the Swift: State and Finance in Korean Industrialization* (New York: Columbia University Press, 1991).
6. Eisuke Sakakibara, *Beyond Capitalism: The Japanese Model of Market Economics* (Lanham, Md.: University Press of America, 1993).
7. Nicholas van de Walle, *African Economies and the Politics of Permanent Crisis, 1979–1999* (Cambridge: Cambridge University Press, 2001).
8. As the chapter by David Ekbladh shows, South Korea is an interesting partial example. The United States regarded the Republic of Korea as a showcase for its Cold War development efforts, both before and particularly after the Korean War, and pumped substantial money and technical advice into the country. But Korea's economic takeoff under Park Chung-hee, although benefiting from U.S. largess, was mostly an indigenous effort.
9. See, for example, Douglass C. North, *Institutions, Institutional Change, and Economic Performance* (New York: Cambridge University Press, 1990); World Bank, *World Bank Development Report 1997: The State in a Changing World* (Oxford: Oxford University Press, 1997); Francis Fukuyama, *State-Building: Governance and World Order in the 21st Century* (Ithaca, N.Y.: Cornell University Press, 2004).
10. Gerald Knaus and Felix Martin, "Lessons from Bosnia and Herzegovina: Travails of the European Raj," *Journal of Democracy* 14 (July 2003): 60–74.
11. See John D. Montgomery and Dennis A. Rondinelli, eds., *Beyond Reconstruction in Afghanistan: Lessons from the Development Experience* (New York: Palgrave Macmillan, 2004).
12. Dobbins et al., *America's Role in Nation-Building*. See also the chapters by Michèle A. Flournoy and James Dobbins.
13. Bob Woodward, *Plan of Attack* (New York: Simon and Schuster, 2004).
14. Francis Fukuyama, "Nation-Building 101," *Atlantic Monthly*, January/February 2004, 159–62.
15. James Fallows, "Blind into Baghdad," *Atlantic Monthly*, January/February 2004, 52–77; Kenneth M. Pollack, "After Saddam: Assessing the Reconstruction of Iraq," Saban Center Analysis Paper no. 1 (Washington, D.C.: Saban Center, 2004).
16. Woodward, *Plan of Attack*.

17. Robert M. Perito, *The American Experience with Police in Peace Operations* (Clementsport, Canada: Canadian Peacekeeping Press, 2002).
18. This was not true of Garner himself, who had led Operation Provide Comfort in Kurdistan in 1991. Unfortunately, lack of local police authority was not a problem in Kurdistan; much of the emphasis of Garner's planning reflected his experiences there, which proved to be atypical both of reconstructions more generally and of what would unfold in the rest of Iraq in 2003.
19. See Antonio Donini, Karen Wermester, and Nora Niland, et al., *Nation-Building Unraveled? Aid, Peace and Justice in Afghanistan* (Bloomfield, Conn.: Kumarian Press, 2003).

Part I · The Historical Experience of
Nation-Building

CHAPTER 1

From Consensus to Crisis

The Postwar Career of Nation-Building in U.S. Foreign Relations

David Ekbladh

IF, AS MARK TWAIN SAID, history never repeats itself but at best rhymes, then we are undoubtedly hearing some verse in Iraq and Afghanistan. These nation-building efforts recall the policies of the Cold War, when the United States was invested in the development of new states for strategic purposes in the context of a larger global struggle. But what is happening in Iraq and Afghanistan is not a literal translation of the past. During the Cold War, nation-building gained a prominent position in U.S. strategy. Rooted in collaborative action by a host of actors, the concept of nation-building was based on a broad consensus on the methods and goals of economic and social development. Although it held sway for nearly a generation, this formulation did not survive new pressures that emerged in the 1960s, particularly the stresses of the Vietnam War. The shattering of the consensus reshaped development strategies and influenced the idea of nation-building in ways that can be felt to the present day.

Nation-building in the years after World War II was understood by a spectrum of U.S. policymakers and international actors to be a collective activity. The nation-building energy expended during the Cold War was not solely that of state agencies. Nongovernmental, international, and, particularly, private business organizations were involved in the complex task of reconstructing and developing nations. The efforts in Iraq and Afghanistan, however, diverge from their Cold War progenitors. Cooperation by non-governmental and international organizations in Iraq has been hesitant at best. And even though policymakers and administrators encourage coordination and strategic thinking both there and in Afghanistan, the central or state planning considered instrumental to nation-building after World War II is no longer seen as a necessary part of the development equation.

These situations are a distinct change from earlier efforts. At the height of the Cold War in the 1950s and 1960s—which, not coincidentally, was the apex of the influence of development on the world stage—the U.S. government could reference a broad consensus on what development (or modernization) was to accomplish. Many observers generally accepted that the construction of viable nation-states was the basic goal of economic and social development and that the state should be the pivot for this process. Such thinking was popular with states as well as with the international and nongovernmental bodies committed to development. This shared view helped the U.S. government forge relationships with nonstate actors and utilize them as important adjuncts in nation-building efforts that served Cold War grand strategy in Iran, South Korea, and South Vietnam.

This cooperative approach to nation-building depended on the consent of nonstate groups to such projects. Not only the means and ends of U.S. foreign policy came under attack during the Vietnam War, but also the idea of development itself. During the 1960s, many basic assumptions of the development concepts that lay at the heart of nation-building were challenged from a variety of perspectives. Nation-building, particularly those programs of development guided by state planning, fell out of favor.

The distrust brought about by the war in Southeast Asia and the fraying of development ideology altered the relationships that the U.S. government had fostered with nonstate actors. It also rearranged institutional capacities to perform development tasks inside and outside the American state. Indeed, the crisis that shook the aid community in the 1960s bequeathed many of the institutional arrangements and concepts that continue to shape the outlines of nation-building today.

Constructing a Postwar Approach to Development

The type of development that became a staple of American foreign policy during the Cold War was not sired by that global struggle. Many of its concepts had their roots in the interwar period, particularly in the New Deal (which itself was connected to contemporaneous international trends of progressive reform).[1] These ideas were not considered synonymous with modernization or universally accepted as something the United States should export. Nevertheless, these concepts had broad support and they became pervasive in U.S. foreign policy after World War II. A number of scholars have noted the international career of the New Deal in the Marshall Plan and the U.S. postwar occupation of Japan.[2]

The New Deal's example did not stop with the postwar occupations and other immediate aftereffects of World War II. Many supporters eagerly embraced development programs, as these efforts promised to raise the standards of living in poorer areas. The enthusiasm of advocates was not based solely on humanitarianism. As the Cold War became a global struggle, Americans inside and outside the government saw colonial and newly independent areas of the globe as key areas of competition with the Soviet Union. Arthur Schlesinger Jr. saw the best examples of New Deal reform—particularly the model of economic and social development embodied in the Tennessee Valley Authority (TVA)—as "a weapon." With such armaments, the United States had the means to "outbid all the social ruthlessness of the communists for the support of the peoples of Asia" and developing nations elsewhere.[3]

But these programs were conceived of differently than those of the Marshall Plan in Europe. Experts believed that nations in such regions as East and Southeast Asia, unlike the countries in Western Europe, lacked the accoutrements of a modern economy and society. This observation was not limited to the technological infrastructure of factories, power plants, and transportation that were the most obvious signs of modernity, but also applied to the absence of the necessary engineers, managers, and assorted technocrats responsible for building and maintaining such systems.

Developmental questions were not limited to technological issues. Successful modernization (a term just coming into use in the 1940s and 1950s) required the construction not only of new technological systems but also of new social and political relationships. In Asia—a key theater of Cold War confrontation at that time, and therefore a focal point for development activity—Americans felt that poor societies would have to rely on the state to cultivate these changes. John King Fairbank, a sinologist and leading commentator on Asian affairs, was among those who articulated such views. Most newly independent nations were assumed to lack strong civil societies. At best, they had stunted educational, entrepreneurial, and other structures believed to be central to economic growth and the social change that came with it in many parts of the West. Fairbank was among those who thought such nations would be well served in their development efforts if they imbibed the example of New Deal agencies like the TVA, in which government capital was put to work on tasks the private sector would not or could not perform.[4] This view reflected the larger assumption of the time that states built nations.

These development agendas were necessarily broad. From the end of World War II onward, the American state understood that the task of reconstructing societies on modern lines was not something it could implement alone. During the war, it turned to a gamut of nongovernmental organizations (NGOs) to assist in relief programs, coordinating their activity. In the years following the war, there was a strong understanding in the U.S. government of the indispensable capacity of various charities, voluntary organizations, universities, missionary groups, businesses, and foundations as relief and reconstruction blurred into economic and social development.

Mobilization of such private resources by the U.S. government was a key part of the evolution of numerous U.S. foreign aid programs after the war. Importantly, many nongovernmental groups actively sought the government's engagement, coordination, and regulation in this transitional period.[5] These organizations did not always agree with government policy and certainly were not uniform in their outlooks, but there was a wide-ranging acceptance of the view that modernization was a positive force and a general consensus on how it should proceed.

This capacity building for overseas development carried over into the United Nations. The United Nations had a general orientation toward development in its charter, but in the 1940s the United States urged the creation of a number of bodies and commissions invested with development missions. One example, the Technical Assistance Program, mirrored many U.S. plans and would later be a foundational element of the United Nations Development Program.

By the end of the 1940s, the U.S. government had greatly contributed to the cultivation of a diverse set of institutional resources oriented toward the basic task of building modern nations, and the American state had evolved its own new capacities for this task. In 1949, President Truman made his "Point Four" declaration promising U.S. technical assistance for development on a global scale, which many supporters saw as an extension of New Deal potential to the international arena.

One of the first times this set of relationships was put to prominent use was during the reconstruction of South Korea in the 1950s. Since 1945, the United States had been involved in state-building in Korea, a task initially assigned to the U.S. Army. Many of the programs undertaken went far beyond simple reconstruction and stabilization tasks. Education, agriculture, industry, and other programs aimed to enhance or improve capacities that had existed under Japanese colonial rule. These efforts even included attempts to "modernize" the Korean language to include new scientific and technical terms.

Such efforts were continued after the U.S. Army departed, following the creation of the Republic of Korea in 1948. They were handed off to the Economic Cooperation Administration, the body initially created to administer the Marshall Plan in Western Europe, which was given a global writ to foster development in the late 1940s.

Following the outbreak of war on the peninsula in 1950, the "reconstruction" of South Korea became a massive, marquee event. U.S. Secretary of State Dean Acheson went to the United Nations in September and described Korea as a "vast opportunity," a country where the United States along with "the United Nations and the specialized agencies can demonstrate to the world what they have learned."[6] South Korea was the largest development effort in the world during the 1950s. In this period, the United States alone pumped more than $2 billion in economic aid into Korea. All of these efforts had a larger plan behind them, which was best articulated by Robert R. Nathan, a New Dealer and founding member of Americans for Democratic Action. Issued in 1954, Nathan's huge report laid out a five-year plan to create a self-sustaining Korean economy and society through foreign aid and technical assistance.[7]

To achieve this goal, the American government tapped its preexisting relationships with U.N. bodies and NGOs. The United Nations Korean Reconstruction Agency (initially seen as the prime mover in Korea's postwar development) sponsored the Nathan report. Other segments of the U.N. family, particularly the United Nations Educational, Scientific, and Cultural Organization and the Food and Agriculture Organization, were directly involved in development aid and planning after the war. Nongovernmental groups were enthusiastic collaborators. They not only brought their own financial resources to the operation but also served as conduits for tens of millions of dollars of official aid and reservoirs of expertise. NGOs saw themselves as more flexible and creative than the government and multinational bodies but nevertheless invested in a cooperative relationship to further the wider project of nation-building.[8]

The Nathan plan—which was seen by those working in Korea during the 1950s and 1960s as the basic document on Korean development—appeared after the Eisenhower administration had taken power. Republicans, in general, had been suspicious of a New Deal for the globe, and the administration took office promising to focus on "trade not aid" as the basis of overseas economic policy.[9] This general policy tack would be altered in the later 1950s, but it never applied to South Korea. There was never an assumption that markets and trade alone would ensure that a modern, stable, and noncommunist state and society would take hold on the southern end of the Korean peninsula.

Generally, the planning ideas that Nathan and others in the U.S.-U.N. aid community deployed on the Korean peninsula were in line with contemporary international thinking on how economic development should proceed. A consensus emerged in the 1950s that national economic planning should be the focal point of development and that the state was the best institution in poor nations to push development forward. In the 1950s and 1960s, influential thinkers in international economics like Gunnar Myrdal, W. Arthur Lewis, Alexander Gerschenkron, and John Kenneth Galbraith emphasized this point of view. Echoing the earlier opinions of Fairbank and others, such thinking held that governments had to perform certain economic and social tasks best done through state planning, as critical sectors of civil society were often too weak to perform the tasks alone.[10] Planning was therefore widely accepted in the United States and internationally as an integral part of effective nation-building in the postwar period. In fact, the *International Encyclopedia of the Social Sciences* that appeared in the 1960s would not give "development" its own entry, instead listing it in a subsection under "economic planning."[11]

Creation of a Development Community

Despite reservations within the Eisenhower administration toward foreign aid, there was enthusiastic support for development in the United States at large through the 1950s and into the 1960s. Outside the government, there was considerable activity to galvanize resources for what was seen as a critical means of guiding global change and containing Russian and Chinese influence in the Third World. Large foundations, particularly the Ford and Rockefeller Foundations and the Carnegie Corporation of New York, committed themselves to supporting a variety of programs that nurtured development domestically and overseas. For example, among a host of other international programs, Rockefeller and Ford joined forces to set up the International Rice Research Institute at Los Baños in the Philippines, which would eventually incite key parts of the "Green Revolution." The triad of big foundations ladled out generous sums to a collection of universities to support education in international affairs and area studies.

Foundations were also instrumental in cultivating university capacity and agitating for better coordination of U.S. government aid efforts through the 1960s. In addition, the large foundations supported programs that tapped academic knowledge to be placed in the direct service of overseas development projects.[12] One of the best examples of the increasingly direct links between scholarly expertise on regional studies and development and pressing policy matters was the Southeast Asian Development Advisory

Group (SEADAG). Established by the Asia Society in 1966, SEADAG funneled the expertise of academicians in fields related to Southeast Asia directly to policymakers.[13]

Universities in the United States, particularly the land-grant colleges, had a long heritage of work overseas that predated the Cold War, but the spectrum of U.S. university involvement in foreign affairs in general and development in particular underwent a transformation in the 1950s and 1960s whose consequences are felt to this day. Calls by government aid agencies were answered by a variety of schools across the country that were soon sending their own missions around the globe.[14]

One of the U.S. universities most active on this front was Michigan State University (MSU). A land-grant college with a history of extension work in the United States itself, MSU was quick to capitalize on the demand for technical assistance overseas. In the early 1950s, for projects with the U.S. government, it sent technical assistance missions to the Ryukyu Islands, Colombia, and Brazil.[15] Its greatest exertions, however, would be in the intense nation-building efforts in South Vietnam.[16] MSU put considerable effort into building the local institutions seen as essential to the construction of stable, modern societies. In South Vietnam, a U.S. government–funded team of experts from MSU provided the technical assistance to construct schools to train a new civil service and oversaw the formation of a national police force.[17]

MSU also worked with a variety of NGOs in its international programs, cooperation that illustrates how private voluntary groups fit into the equation. During the 1950s, there was an expansion of the already significant numbers of voluntary organizations involved in development. Emblematic was the International Voluntary Service (IVS), formed in 1953. Like other NGOs, IVS highlighted its cooperation with government programs. The group proudly announced that it had "been a mechanism for coordinating governmental and private agency efforts at village levels" in South Vietnam. One of its key goals was to provide the government with a "cadre of trained [American] specialists who had demonstrated a capacity to engage in development under alien conditions."[18] IVS quickly earned a reputation as an exemplar of community-level development through its programs in Africa and Asia. When the formation of a "Peace Corps" was mooted in the early months of the Kennedy administration, IVS was referenced by supporters of the idea to suggest that a youth program sponsored by the government could work.[19] Part of this confidence was forged by IVS in the years after 1956 through its work to support various aspects of rural development under contract with the U.S. government in South Vietnam.[20]

American businesses also invested in overseas development. Private companies had long been involved in work seen as developmental in one form or another. However, following World War II, a number of firms focused directly on overseas development. Robert Nathan's work in Korea had been done under the auspices of an eponymous economic consulting firm. David Lilienthal, former head of the TVA and the Atomic Energy Commission, formed an engineering and consulting firm, Development and Resources (D&R), that would carry out regional development projects from Iran to Colombia and even train Peace Corps volunteers. Existing firms like Bechtel, which had a long history of furthering economic development in the United States (having been one of the "Five Companies" that built the Hoover Dam), set their sights on overseas development contracts. Among Bechtel's foreign projects was a set of infrastructure programs in South Korea during the 1950s.

Seeking to understand this burgeoning development community, the Carnegie Corporation funded a series of studies from 1956 to 1960 under the direction of Harlan Cleveland, a veteran of aid programs during the 1940s and 1950s. The "Carnegie Project" provided a detailed snapshot of the interaction of these multiple actors at the apogee of the importance of development on the international scene.

In explaining "overseasmanship," the study's authors also discussed the continuity and multifaceted nature of modernization. The postwar period had seen dramatic changes in the magnitude of American overseas activity. This trend was shown through the numbers of Americans who ventured overseas in the decade and a half following World War II. The military had seen a dramatic increase in its foreign deployments. In 1957, there were 1.12 million American servicemen posted outside the United States. More significantly, more than 1.5 million American civilians were living abroad by 1959. Of these, more than 100,000 were working on projects with U.S. organizations (excluding those in the U.S. military and the Foreign Service). They were split among government, missionary, business, educational, and voluntary groups. Much of this work was directly related to modernization brought about by a new world order.[21]

From the perspective of the Carnegie Project, these Americans were all operating in an altered world, one that was defined politically by nationalism and economically by industrialization. In the countries only recently freed from colonial rule, there were rising expectations for a better life and the desire of leaders to cultivate modern economies and industry. It was logical that the United States should have a role in this process, as "the potentialities of large-scale industrialization have been demonstrated most vividly by the United States." In the contemporary world, "international affairs were now internal affairs," as modernization required direct activity by Americans inside these countries to foster the deep changes required. The Soviet threat to "isolate the West from its former dependencies in Africa and Asia" through activities in the Third World forced a critical competition on Americans. The speed with which these "operations on a global scale in military, economic, social, [and] psychological fields" expanded was a result of this Soviet challenge.[22]

The Carnegie Project reports accurately described the growing collection of private and voluntary groups that made up important parts of the diverse nation-building community. The U.S. government was assumed to be at the center of the web of development activities in foreign nations.[23] At home, one of the basic suggestions by the study's authors was that the U.S. government establish a National Foundation for Overseas Operations, with representatives from civil organizations to coordinate education and other efforts by the government and NGOs to prepare Americans for foreign work.[24]

The capacity of the U.S. government to lead these efforts had expanded for the task. Through the 1950s, a variety of administrative and program changes had led to a veritable alphabet soup of agencies responsible for U.S. foreign aid—the Economic Cooperation Agency, the Technical Cooperation Administration, the Mutual Security Administration, the Foreign Operations Administration, and the International Cooperation Administration. As the "New Frontiersmen" of the Kennedy administration took the reigns in 1961, the government aid program was again reformed into the U.S. Agency for International Development (USAID). In the early 1960s, USAID was at the pinnacle of its influence as an organization. Total U.S. foreign aid commitments stood at well over $2.9 billion in 1962. This influence was due in part to the importance accorded development by the Kennedy administration. Such senior advisors as Dean Rusk, Chester Bowles, and Walt Rostow made modernization a focal point of U.S. foreign relations toward the Third World and in the policies of the Cold War in general. Kennedy himself would go to the United Nations in 1961 to convince that body to declare the 1960s the "Decade of Development." Major initiatives like the Peace Corps and the Alliance for Progress show the prominent position held by development. Modernization was also inseparable from another growing U.S. effort during the Kennedy years—Vietnam.

The Crucible of Vietnam

Vietnam would pull in all components of this diverse and interconnected collection of nation-builders. Modernization was integral to the war effort in Southeast Asia from the earliest moments of U.S. involvement. Aid from the Eisenhower administration onward emphasized the construction of a viable noncommunist state in South Vietnam. But developmental ideas also became intertwined with the military side of the effort. Counterinsurgency tactics that came into vogue as the conflict accelerated in the early 1960s saw coordinated development activity as integral to the overall project of pacifying a conflict zone.

An example of this interconnection was the "strategic hamlets" program attempted from 1961 to 1963. The construction of defended villages and the arming of their inhabitants were emphasized as important elements of the total program of social engineering. By replacing traditional ways with the infrastructure of modern life, such as new roads, electrification, better communication, and new agricultural techniques, peasants would not only experience material gains but also develop an outlook based on the idea of progress. Americans hoped that these changes would foster greater loyalty to the South Vietnamese regime while immunizing the population against the appeals of the National Liberation Front (the NLF, or Viet Cong). The intention was to eventually isolate the NLF from its sources of support and fatally undermine it.[25]

Overall, the strategic hamlets program was a failure, but some of its underlying assumptions would live on in other aspects of U.S. "pacification" efforts in Vietnam—programs that made up what U.S. government officials referred to as the "other war," such as the "revolutionary development" program and the later Civilian Operations and Revolutionary Development Support (CORDS) program. Each assumed that defeating the communist threat in the countryside was not solely a military question; they supported agricultural, educational, public health, and related programs, along with the construction of local institutions to support them. The end goal, again, was to turn villagers into modern citizens and away from the enticements of the Viet Cong.[26]

USAID was heavily and directly involved in these and other programs. To carry out these tasks, the mission to South Vietnam grew from 732 Americans on staff in 1965 to 1,856 in 1967. Added to the latter tally were 293 employees from other U.S. agencies involved in aid programs, plus 474 from U.S. contractors, as well as some 1,395 foreign nationals and 3,537 Vietnamese—a total of 7,575 personnel. USAID's total expenditures in Vietnam increased as the military conflict heated up, rising to $495 million in 1967 and remaining close to that level through the end of the decade.[27]

If development ideas were intimately tangled with the day-to-day waging of the war, they also held an important public and strategic position. The Johnson administration took great care to emphasize that the American commitment to the region brought more than intensified conflict. Johnson's 1965 speech at the Johns Hopkins University, which is often seen as a firm commitment to U.S. military support of South Vietnam, was also a promise to "improve the life of man in that conflict-torn corner of our world." Development was linked to regional efforts to harness the Mekong River, in which Johnson saw the promise of such New Deal programs as the Rural Electrification Administration and the TVA.[28]

The need to show that U.S. engagement in the region could be constructive led to a further effort at development. In 1966, the Johnson administration turned to David Lilienthal, with his strong cachet in the development community, to head a high-profile commission to plan the postwar reconstruction and development of South Vietnam. Lilienthal brought D&R to bear on the issue as well. Working with South Vietnamese counterparts, the Joint Development Group (JDG) that Lilienthal headed was a variant of the planning theme already seen in South Korea.

Like the Nathan group, the JDG was to produce a comprehensive planning document that covered the most important aspects of Vietnamese development. (Noticeably absent was any involvement by the United Nations in the project.) The work of the JDG, which drew on resources created by SEADAG, was connected to the national economic planning in which the Republic of Vietnam was already engaged—it had already sponsored two five-year plans.[29] The JDG started work in 1967 and issued its report in 1969, but, even in that short time, the assumptions underpinning the concept of nation-building had started to crumble.

The Crisis of Development

Outside the context of U.S. involvement in Vietnam, there were already solid outlines of what we would today call "donor fatigue" by the mid-1960s. Within USAID, there was persistent concern that the American public was souring on the larger program of foreign aid. This sentiment did not bode well, considering that segments of the U.S. Congress had long been suspicious of aid.[30] During the mid-1960s, the place of foreign aid in U.S. global strategy was reconsidered at high levels. In 1966 and 1967, the Council on Foreign Relations convened a series of meetings on U.S. foreign assistance that drew in leading members of the mainstream development community.[31] By and large, they agreed that aid was facing great difficulties, not the least of which was a general disillusionment with the concept.[32]

These anxieties were shared internationally.[33] The unease was summarized in 1967 at a gathering of representatives of the United Nations, the World Bank, Barclays Bank, and the World Council of Churches. Their language was blunt: The participants felt there was "a clear and present danger, an emergency" on the question of development. There was broad agreement that assistance efforts were suffering from a "paralysis of leader-ship," which fed a belief that "at present everything is going wrong."[34]

The concerns of the international development community mirrored a wider dissatisfaction with the concepts of development and economic growth that had been broadly accepted after World War II. As the decade progressed, many politicians and commentators on the right honed their longstanding challenges to the dominant ideas of international develop-ment ranging from economic planning to foreign aid.[35] Equally important was a profound shift on the left. Feminism spurred a critique of many es-tablished assumptions of modernization.[36] The school of "dependency theory" that appeared in the 1960s asked whether the global capitalist economy was resulting in the underdevelopment of many poor countries rather than raising standards of living.[37] A reborn environmental move-ment began to question Western models of growth, asking whether these ideas should be exported to poor nations. Connected to this movement was an increasing awareness that many hallmarks of postwar develop-ment—particularly large infrastructure projects, such as dams—adversely affected local environments and their human populations.

President Kennedy's ambitious call to action had given way to dis-appointment and, in some sectors, recrimination. There was increasing skepticism that development could deliver on all its promises as quickly as had been predicted. Many problems came to be seen as intractable barriers, whereas others struck at the basic ideas underpinning modernization.

Mainstream supporters did not sit passively as the established ideas of development unraveled. Advocates rallied behind the concept of a "de-velopment house" that would serve as a focal point for research and ad-vocacy on development ideas. The Ford and Rockefeller Foundations signed on to underwrite the organization, which eventually emerged as the Over-seas Development Council. Its authority came in part from its prominent membership, which included David Lilienthal, Eugene Black, Edward Ma-son, and David Rockefeller, with James P. Grant at the helm.[38] Grant's spectrum of development experience ranged from work with the United Nations in China after World War II to high-level positions in U.S. gov-ernment aid agencies that had culminated in his heading USAID's Vietnam office. (He would later head the United Nations Children's Fund.) This experience made him an authoritative voice on an increasingly fractious subject. A further sign that the consensus on development was fraying was a move in 1968 by the president of the World Bank, George Woods. Ob-serving rampant inertia and strife across the development community, Woods issued an unprecedented call for a "grand assize" to review the pre-ceding 20 years of development assistance.[39]

"New Directions" in Foreign Aid

Established ideas regarding development were facing effective critiques by the mid-1960s. However, these challenges cannot be divorced from the American involvement in Vietnam. The conflict in Southeast Asia shook all aspects of international affairs, and international development was not exempt. One of the most obvious effects was the reordering of the U.S. budget. As the war devoured an increasing share of the federal budget, the "Great Society" and foreign aid were starved of funds. Under these pressures, U.S. foreign aid actually declined (when adjusted for inflation) over the course of the "Development Decade."[40]

The war's impact on the role of development in U.S. foreign policy was not confined to the federal budget. The cumulative effects of the stresses of the 1960s were expressed by the broad reformulation of the national security posture of the United States, the "Nixon Doctrine,"[41] whose central thesis was that the United States "cannot—and will not—conceive all the plans, design all the programs, execute all the decisions, and undertake all the defense of the free nations of the world."[42]

The status of foreign assistance was shifted by this wider turn in U.S. strategy. In line with his doctrine, President Nixon called for "New Directions" in foreign aid in May 1969. The president envisioned revised programs of technical assistance and the cultivation of private enterprise in developing nations. An even more important departure was the call for greater emphasis on multilateral aid through such organizations as the United Nations and the World Bank.[43]

The call for aid to be redirected appeared at a time when official Washington was palpably disenchanted with foreign aid policy and in particular with its main executor, USAID. In October 1971, the Senate—for the first time ever—voted down the president's foreign aid request.[44] This action was the result of a number of factors, including increasing discomfort with the military elements of foreign aid and the yawning credibility gap around the executive branch. Many observers came to believe that development assistance sired political and military commitments that would end in mire like Vietnam.[45]

Tied to this sentiment was a general dissatisfaction with USAID itself. In its most visible theater of action, Vietnam, USAID's programs were increasingly seen as yoked to the corrupt and often incompetent government of South Vietnam. Money was frittered away on ineffective projects, eroding the agency's status. Indeed, there was a backlash against cooperation with the South Vietnamese government within USAID itself. But more fundamental problems loomed. Veterans of aid work recalled that the "best and brightest of AID went to Vietnam" only to be humbled by almost insurmountable obstacles, not the least of which was that "there was no way anyone could do development in that war zone."[46]

Across official Washington, demands were made for deeper reforms to foreign aid than Nixon had suggested. In 1971, Senator J. W. Fulbright called the overall aid program a "shambles."[47] The rejection of the president's aid budget in 1971 was a sign that Congress would no longer accept the premises that had underpinned U.S. foreign aid activity for the previous generation and that drastic reforms were required. Congress kicked off a major policy review examining the place and purpose of aid. Although the origins of the debate lay in a power struggle between the executive and legislative branches, it was waged with the intellectual ammunition that was the product of the crisis surrounding development in the 1960s.

James Grant and other influential individuals involved in this debate saw that development was in a "growing crisis" even as a "major rethinking" of development was taking place. Among advocates of development there was an increasing distrust of bureaucracies in development in the period that pointed away from national planning.[48] This suspicion of state apparatus segued into an environmental critique that was often opposed to the broadly conceived and widely implemented technological and infrastructure policies that national planning had tended to fund.

Grant, as part of a growing chorus of critics, asserted that the postwar approach to development placed too much emphasis on economic indicators. He aligned with those who agitated for the alleviation of poverty to be placed at the center of the development mission. Those working on reforming aid felt that most postwar development programs had a tendency to assume that national economic growth would eventually "trickle down" to improve the living standards of the poor. With the appreciation that inequalities were actually increasing in the developing world, this approach was deemed inadequate.[49] Out of the critiques, a new formulation for the goals of development appeared, demanding that development turn away from planning and big programs and emphasize "appropriate technology" to meet "basic human needs" and focus directly on attacking poverty.[50]

Grant's critique and the intellectual milieu from which it emerged had considerable impact on the restructuring that followed the "New Directions" legislation of 1973. The effects on USAID were immediate and dramatic: worldwide staff declined from a high of 18,030 in 1968 to just 8,489 by 1975.[51]

However, reform within "New Directions" was not merely belt tightening, but a fundamental change to the philosophy that guided USAID. John Hannah, former MSU president and Nixon's appointee to head the embattled organization, put forward a new program in line with Congressional demands. It reoriented the agency to concentrate on providing for the basic needs of people in developing countries. USAID would "become less of general purpose assistance organization and more of a specialized agency. It will seek to combine . . . resources to address a relatively limited group of basic human problems."[52]

At the core of these "priority problems" that Hannah and others outlined was poverty. Instead of "impersonal measures of GNP growth" or "rising national income," both staple elements of national economic planning, development in USAID's vision was now conceived of as "better food, more education, improved health, and more jobs for all people." Rather than emphasize large programs, USAID would focus on smaller, more discrete programs to foster development.[53] "New Directions" fundamentally changed the orientation and capacities of the agency, and its effects were lasting—it endured as a basic policy well into the 1980s. Many observers, particularly critics of U.S. aid policy, have seen the structural changes caused by this policy as fundamentally determining the institutional capacities and worldview of USAID in the decades following Vietnam.[54]

Equally deep were the changes wrought by the crisis years of the 1960s and 1970s on the interconnected development community that had evolved in the postwar years. NGOs became increasingly wary of working in such close conjunction with the government as adjuncts of its larger plans to build nations. An example of this unease was the break-up of relations between IVS and USAID in Vietnam. IVS had been one of the largest and most effective contractors with USAID, with 151 volunteers working on various village-level programs at the height of its commitment in 1968.[55] As the U.S. military commitment grew, staff grew increasingly critical of policies that created masses of refugees, damaged farmland, and left people to navigate "free fire" zones in the countryside. In 1967, this bubble of resentment burst. Calling the war an "overwhelming atrocity," some of the most experienced IVS Vietnam staff resigned en masse. Considering the exposure and reputation of IVS as a leading development NGO, this action grabbed considerable media coverage and inspired tough questions on the state of American development policy in Vietnam.[56]

Nor were private businesses committed to development spared the effects of Vietnam. Lilienthal's report on postwar Vietnam, although broad in scope and yet detailed, in the best traditions of development planning, was not well received by Congress or the executive branch.[57] When the JDG's final report was issued in 1969, it quickly disappeared into the shadow of an apparently unending conflict.[58]

Symptomatic of the change in attitudes was the 1971 broadside by the magazine *The Nation* on Lilienthal and D&R. It savaged Lilienthal for his involvement in a development system that worsened rather than lessened global inequities and poverty. Years before, *The Nation* had been a staunch supporter of the New Deal planning and development ideas that Lilienthal had exemplified. As perceptions of development and its place in world affairs changed, the corporation and its chairman were cast as "agents of the new empire." Lilienthal became emblematic of elites whose "passion for development and . . . fascination with technology" drew the United States into dubious overseas commitments. D&R had made profits from its development work in these American adventures, as well as by training members of a further "agency of empire," the Peace Corps.[59]

The place of universities within the postwar development structure also came under fire. The 1960s saw powerful campus protests against university involvement in programs connected with the war in Southeast Asia. In 1966, Michigan State University was subjected to a critical exposé in *Ramparts* magazine for its work in South Vietnam for the U.S. government and was forced to endure the fallout.[60]

This sort of criticism stressed the close relationships between universities and the government forged over the preceding decades. In an odd twist, the pressures of the Vietnam period reoriented part of SEADAG's research agenda. With the same analytical brio that its participants had turned on Asian development, SEADAG assessed the impact of the war in Southeast Asia on domestic American institutions.[61] That SEADAG went outside its area of focus to investigate the fallout of the war within the United States is a sign of how deeply the conflict affected the nation-building community. SEADAG itself had to deal with perceptions that it was a toady to a U.S. government policy that was massively unpopular on most campuses by the late 1960s. This situation led a number of scholars to sever their ties with the group.[62] SEADAG itself did not long outlive the U.S. commitment to the region, ceasing operations in 1976.[63]

The collaborative ethos that had knit together the activities of universities, business, and voluntary groups under the banner of state-coordinated development programs had unraveled. The relationship of the U.S. government with NGOs would never be the same. Even as many NGOs became leery of working too closely with state-sponsored projects, a significant element of "New Directions" was a commitment to work not only with but also through voluntary agencies.[64] However, NGOs were no longer treated as adjuncts for the planning or implementation of projects but as the "programmers of whole segments of development action."[65] They were given considerably more initiative in forming and shaping projects by a smaller USAID. On one level, it was an acknowledgement of the expanding capacity and diversity of the NGO community. Importantly, foreign policy experts thought that this increased discretion would allow for greater flexibility and, in some respects, credibility for scaled-down development projects.

Changes came at other levels as well. The increased emphasis on funneling development aid through multilateral institutions that began in the Nixon years eventually pushed the World Bank into its present position as the largest single source of development aid. Robert McNamara, himself a sort of refugee of the debacle in Vietnam, took the reigns of the Bank in 1968 and fundamentally changed its global role. By the time he left the institution in 1981, its portfolio of loans had increased from $800 million to more than $12 billion, and it had turned into a full-fledged development agency.

Taken as a whole, the Vietnam era was the "perfect storm" to rearrange not only the key institution in U.S. aid policy but also the basic goals of development aid. The war was part of a global shift that fractured the existing consensus on what development was to accomplish. The belief in broadly conceived development planning centered on the state broke down under critiques emerging from every quarter. Ideas that placed faith in smaller-scale, "sustainable" projects that were aimed directly at people and at alleviating poverty moved to center stage. Nation-building as a basic goal of development aid became suspect on the political left even as those on the right accelerated their attacks on the role of the state in economic policy in the 1980s, after the Latin American debt crisis. Even before the Soviet empire's collapse, ebbing tensions between the superpowers denied advocates of development assistance the Russian specter as a justification for their programs.[66] Trapped between two unwelcoming ideological poles and with few friends and strong rationales, the concept of nation-building withered.

The Return of Nation-Building

After the Cold War, beliefs stemming from the crisis of the 1960s continued to hold sway. Through the 1990s, many players across the political spectrum pinned great hopes on NGOs and civil-society bodies to carry out development and other tasks on the world stage that had once been the province of the state.[67] Although there were reflections of nation-building in the composition of various interventions during the 1990s (in Bosnia, Somalia, East Timor, and Haiti), these forays were rarely advertised as pure nation-building exercises, as the concept remained politically unpalatable. Nevertheless, many of the institutions involved, ranging from the World Bank to the smallest NGOs, saw the need for development aid to build state capacities and strengthen civil society—elements found in all post–World War II nation-building—in troubled areas as a means to prevent conflict and build peace.[68] In other reforms, the World Bank, from its position as the most influential institution in the development community, proposed a "Comprehensive Development Framework" in 1999 to integrate the government, international groups, and civil-society organizations involved in development work in particular countries. It was an acknowledgement of the diversity of actors involved in the process and of the need for a "holistic long-term strategy" to effectively implement programs. At the same time, the Bank was extraordinarily careful to declare that it was not advocating a return to development planning.[69]

These and other trends show that constituent parts of the nation-building ethos were still important and, at times, indispensable for international actors. Yet the sort of nation-building that had fallen into disrepute after Vietnam remained something to be avoided, in name as well as content. George W. Bush squeezed political gain out of attacking the still unpopular concept in his 2000 presidential campaign.

The ready return of the term *nation-building* to the international lexicon following wars in Afghanistan and Iraq is a sign of the concept's endurance. However, its reappearance has not meant a reconstruction of the structures, assumptions, and relationships that drove nation-building efforts during the Cold War. In part, this failure is a reflection of the development community's continuing wariness of large-scale programs. In the struggle by the United States to build a new and viable state in Iraq after the demolition of the Hussein regime in 2003, many specialists and policymakers maintain an overt hostility to the idea of state planning and control. Even among the recent converts to nation-building in the Bush administration and the Coalition Provisional Authority, reflexive references remained for the need for privatization in the reconstruction. A blunt American policy in Iraq has also served to alienate many nonstate institutions whose forerunners were regular participants during the Cold War. As a result, capable organizations have given Iraq a wide berth. Although private contractors have been quick to jump into the Iraq project, they represent only one side of the diverse selection of institutions involved in nation-building's earlier variations.

After World War II, nation-building was not performed solely through government action but also through the use of the abilities of NGOs and international institutions. From the 1940s on, the U.S. government understood that private and international bodies, and particularly private voluntary organizations, have the knowledge, resources, and commitment to carry out many of the tasks that are vital to all stages of nation-building. These actors are extremely valuable in terms of the abilities they bring, as well as the credibility they can instill. However, their participation in such operations is contingent on the perception that the development program they are being asked to participate in is just. As Vietnam and the collapse of the postwar consensus on development demonstrate, when nongovernmental and international actors are wary of or opposed to the nation-building agenda of a state, not only is the state's particular project likely to suffer, but the larger concept of nation-building and the broader strategies in which it is enmeshed may also come undone.

Notes

1. Daniel T. Rodgers, *Atlantic Crossings: Social Politics in a Progressive Age* (Cambridge, Mass.: Belknap Press, 1998).
2. On Japan, see Theodore Cohen, *Remaking Japan: The American Occupation as New Deal* (New York: Free Press, 1987); on the Marshall Plan, see Michael J. Hogan, *The Marshall Plan: America, Britain and the Reconstruction of Western Europe, 1947–1952* (New York: Cambridge University Press, 1987).
3. Arthur M. Schlesinger, Jr., *The Vital Center: The Politics of Freedom* (Boston: Houghton Mifflin, 1949), 233.
4. John K. Fairbank, "Communist China and the New American Approach to Asia," in John K. Fairbank, ed., *Next Step in Asia* (Cambridge, Mass.: Harvard University Press, 1949), 13–21.
5. See, for example, McFall to Knowland, April 27, 1950, Decimal File, 1950–54, 800.49, RG 59, box 4378, National Archives, College Park, Md.; Gates to Wood, April 22, 1946, Decimal File, 1950–54, 800.49, RG 59, box 4147, National Archives, College Park, Md.
6. Remarks of Dean Acheson, U.N. General Assembly, Fifth Session, Plenary Meetings, vol. I, *Official Records,* 279th meeting, September 20, 1950, 26–27.
7. Robert R. Nathan Associates, "An Economic Programme for Korean Reconstruction" (Washington, D.C.: U.N. Korean Reconstruction Agency, 1954).
8. "The Voluntary Agency—What Is It?" May 22, 1957, reel 21, Records Relating to the Internal Affairs of Korea, 1955–59, RG 59, National Archives, College Park, Md.
9. Burton I. Kaufman, *Trade and Aid: Eisenhower's Foreign Economic Policy, 1953–1961* (Baltimore: Johns Hopkins University Press, 1982).
10. Gunnar Myrdal, *Development and Underdevelopment: A Note on the Mechanism of National and International Economic Inequality* (Cairo: National Bank of Egypt, 1956), 62; W. Arthur Lewis, *The Theory of Economic Growth* (Homewood, Ill.: Richard D. Irwin, 1955); Alexander Gerschenkron, *Economic Backwardness in Historical Perspective* (Cambridge, Mass.: Harvard University Press, 1962); John Kenneth Galbraith, *Economic Development* (New York: Houghton Mifflin, 1962).
11. W. Arthur Lewis, "Development Planning," in *International Encyclopedia of the Social Sciences,* vol. 12 (New York: Macmillan, 1968), 118–25.

12. John W. Gardner, *Aid and the Universities* (New York: Education and World Affairs, 1964).

13. "Evaluation of the Southeast Asia Development Advisory Group," USAID Library doc. 1 (Washington, D.C.: USAID Library, 1972).

14. John Ernst, *Forging a Fateful Alliance: Michigan State University and the Vietnam War* (East Lansing: Michigan State University Press, 1998), 7.

15. Ibid., 7–8.

16. David L. Anderson, *Trapped by Success: The Eisenhower Administration and Vietnam, 1953–1961* (New York: Columbia University Press, 1991).

17. Ernst, *Forging a Fateful Alliance*, 41–84.

18. Winbun T. Thomas, "The Vietnam Story of International Voluntary Service, Inc.," USAID Library Docs. 49, 55, 77 (Washington, D.C.: USAID Library, June 1972)

19. "Youth Corps Idea Popular Abroad," *New York Times,* January 12, 1961, 11; Gertrude Samuels, "A Force of Youth as a Force for Peace," *New York Times,* February 5, 1961, SM26.

20. Thomas, "The Vietnam Story of International Voluntary Service, Inc.," 113–14.

21. Gerard J. Mangone, "Dungaree and Grey-Flannel Diplomacy," in Harland Cleveland and Gerard J. Mangone, eds., *The Art of Overseasmanship* (Syracuse, N.Y.: Syracuse University Press, 1957), 11–29.

22. Harland Cleveland, Gerald J. Mangone, and John Clarke Adams, eds., *The Overseas Americans* (New York: McGraw-Hill, 1960), 4–7.

23. Harland Cleveland, "Introduction: The Essence of Overseasmanship," in Cleveland and Mangone, *The Art of Overseasmanship*, 1–7.

24. Cleveland et al., *The Overseas Americans*, 303.

25. For the modernization ideas behind the strategic hamlets program, see Michael E. Latham, *Modernization as Ideology: American Social Science and "Nation-Building" in the Kennedy Era* (Chapel Hill: University of North Carolina Press, 2000), 167–207. See also Douglas S. Blaufarb, *The Counterinsurgency Era: U.S. Doctrine and Performance, 1950 to the Present* (New York: Free Press, 1977), 116–18.

26. Memorandum Komer to the president, "The Other War in Vietnam: A Progress Report," NSF, Files of Robert Komer, box 1–2 (Austin, Tx.: Lyndon Baines Johnson Library, September 13, 1966).

27. Agency for International Development, Program Presentation to the Congress, Proposed FY 1969 Program, H-5 (Washington, D.C.: USAID Library, 1969).

28. Lyndon Johnson, "Address at the Johns Hopkins University: 'Peace Without Conquest,'" April 7, 1965, in *Public Papers of the Presidents of the United States, Lyndon B. Johnson, 1965,* vol. 1 (Washington, D.C.: U.S. Government Printing Office, 1966), 398.

29. Asia Bureau, "Development Planning," *Vietnam Terminal Report,* USAID Library doc. 2 (Washington, D.C.: USAID Library, December 31, 1975).

30. "Memo for Administrator: Memorandum on the Foreign Aid Studies," box 23, David Bell Papers (Boston: John F. Kennedy Presidential Library, September 22, 1965).
31. Kaysen to Bell, box 11, David Bell Papers (New York: Ford Foundation Archives, November 11, 1966).
32. Discussion Meeting Report, Foreign Aid Policy, First Meeting, box 11, David Bell Papers (New York: Ford Foundation Archives, November 29, 1966); Discussion Meeting Report, Foreign Aid Policy, Second Meeting, box 11, David Bell Papers (New York: Ford Foundation Archives, February 1, 1967); Discussion Meeting Report, Foreign Aid Policy, Fourth Meeting, box 11, David Bell Papers (New York: Ford Foundation Archives, April 4, 1967); Discussion Meeting Report, Foreign Aid Policy, Fifth Meeting, box 11, David Bell Papers (New York: Ford Foundation Archives, May 2, 1967).
33. Davidson Summers, "Report on Trip to Europe," box 13, David Bell Papers (New York: Ford Foundation Archives, June 6, 1967).
34. Summary of Discussions, Meeting on Aid and Development, box 13, David Bell Papers (New York: Ford Foundation Archives, April 20, 1967).
35. For a discussion of the discontent with modernization on all sides of the political spectrum in this period, see Howard Brick, *Age of Contradiction: American Thought and Culture in the 1960s* (New York: Twayne, 1998), 44–65.
36. Ester Boserup, *Woman's Role in Economic Development* (New York: St. Martin's Press, 1970).
37. Andre Gunder Frank, *Capitalism and Underdevelopment in Latin America* (New York: Monthly Review Press, 1967).
38. "Overseas Development Council Prospectus," June 1968, box 2507, RG 2, RAC; Rockefeller to Harrar, box 2507, RG 2, RAC (North Tarrytown, N.Y.: Rockefeller Archive Center, October 7, 1968).
39. Address by George Woods to the U.N. Conference on Trade and Development, box 483, David E. Lilienthal Papers (Princeton, N.J.: Princeton University Seely G. Mudd Manuscript Library, February 9, 1968). The "Pearson Report" that emerged called for increased aid to the developing world to maintain high levels of economic growth. However, these conclusions were sharply criticized from a variety of positions.
40. Charles R. Frank and Mary Baird, "Foreign Aid: Its Speckled Past and Future Prospects," *International Organization* 29 (Winter 1975): 140.
41. William Bundy, *A Tangled Web: The Making of Foreign Policy in the Nixon Presidency* (New York: Hill and Wang, 1998), 67–68.
42. Richard M. Nixon, "U.S. Foreign Policy for the 1970s: A New Strategy for Peace," in *Public Papers of the Presidents: Richard Nixon, 1970* (Washington, D.C.: U.S. Government Printing Office), 116–90.
43. President Nixon's Message to Congress, "New Directions in Foreign Aid," USAID Library doc. (Washington, D.C.: USAID Library, May 28, 1969).

44. Felix Belair, Jr., "Foreign Aid Bill Beaten," *New York Times,* October 30, 1971, 1.
45. Vernon W. Ruttan, *United States Development Assistance Policy: The Domestic Politics of Foreign Economic Aid* (Baltimore, Md.: Johns Hopkins University Press, 1996), 102.
46. Reminiscences of John H. Sullivan, Foreign Affairs Oral History Project (Washington, D.C.: USAID Library, October 29, 1996).
47. Felix Belair, "Foreign Aid Setup Called 'Shambles' by Senate Group," *New York Times,* April 26, 1971, 1.
48. Ruttan, *United States Development Assistance Policy,* 105.
49. James P. Grant, "Beyond Economic Growth or SEADAG's Unique Opportunity," Asia Society Papers (North Tarrytown, N.Y.: Rockefeller Archive Center, August 1972); James P. Grant, "Growth from Below: A People Oriented Development Strategy," Overseas Development Council, December 1973; Unprocessed materials (North Tarrytown, New York: Rockefeller Archive Center); James P. Grant, "Development the End of Trickle Down?" *Foreign Policy* 12 (Fall 1973): 43; Reminiscences of John H. Sullivan.
50. Edgar Owens and Robert Shaw, *Development Reconsidered: Bridging the Gap Between Government and People* (Lanham, Md.: Lexington Books, 1972); Ruttan, *United States Development Assistance Policy,* 107.
51. Agency for International Development, "Introduction to the FY 1974 Development Assistance Program Presentation to Congress," USAID Library doc. 6 (Washington, D.C.: USAID Library, 1974).
52. Agency for International Development, "Introduction to the FY 1973 Development and Humanitarian Assistance Program Presentation to Congress," USAID Library doc. 1 (Washington, D.C.: USAID Library, 1973).
53. Ibid., 1–2.
54. See, for example, Nicholas Eberstadt, *Foreign Aid and American Purpose* (Washington, D.C.: American Enterprise Institute, 1988), 50–52.
55. Thomas, "The Vietnam Story of International Voluntary Service, Inc.," 17.
56. Bernard Weinraub, "Volunteer Aides in Saigon Dispute," *New York Times,* September 15, 1967, 1; Bernard Weinraub, "4 Chiefs of Volunteer Unit in Vietnam Quit over War," *New York Times,* September 20, 1967, 1; "I Have Seen the 'Destruction of a People I Love,'" *New York Times,* September 24, 1967, 24; "Are We Losing the 'Other War'?" *New York Times,* September 25, 1967, 44; Thomas, "The Vietnam Story of International Voluntary Service, Inc.," 37–38.
57. Felix Belair, Jr., "Plan for South Vietnam Recovery Scored in House," *New York Times,* May 16, 1969, 3.
58. Joint Development Group, *The Postwar Development of South Vietnam: Policies and Programs* (New York: Joint Development Group, 1970).
59. Marshall Windmiller, "Agents of the New Empire," *Nation,* May 10, 1971, 592–96.
60. Ernst, *Forging a Fateful Alliance,* 115–16.

61. McAlister Brown, "The Impact of the Indochina Involvement on American Political Institutions," SEADAG Paper, USAID Library doc. PN-ABI-180 (Washington, D.C.: USAID Library, May 1971).
62. Eric R. Wolf and Joseph G. Jorgensen, "Anthropology on the Warpath in Thailand," *New York Review of Books,* November 19, 1970, 26–35; "Evaluation of the Southeast Asia Development Advisory Group," 2.
63. Bordonaro to Boylan, Asia Society Papers (North Tarrytown, N.Y.: Rockefeller Archive Center, June 15, 1977).
64. Agency for International Development, "Introduction to the FY 1973 Development and Humanitarian Assistance Program," 2.
65. J. W. Gilmore, "AID's New Directions with Private and Voluntary Organizations," USAID Library doc. 9 (Washington, D.C.: USAID Library, March 11, 1977).
66. Overseas Development Council, "U.S. Development Cooperation Assistance and the Third World: Issues and Options for the 1990s," box 1318, (New York: Carnegie Corporation of New York Archives, Rare Book and Manuscript Library, Columbia University, November 1988).
67. Jessica T. Matthews, "Power Shift," *Foreign Affairs* 76 (January/February 1997): 50–66.
68. USAID, "The Role of Foreign Assistance in Conflict Prevention," USAID Conference Report, (Washington, D.C.: USAID Library, January 8, 2001).
69. World Bank, "Overview and Background of the CDF" (Washington, D.C.: World Bank, 1999); James Wolfensohn, "Discussion Paper on the Comprehensive Development Framework" (Washington, D.C.: World Bank, 1999).

CHAPTER 2

Nation-Building in the Heyday of the Classic Development Ideology

Ford Foundation Experience in the 1950s and 1960s

Francis X. Sutton

THE FORD FOUNDATION'S roots lay in alarm over FDR's 1935 request to Congress for an inheritance tax or a steeply progressive estate tax, which brought subsequent legislation and led promptly to the foundation's establishment on January 15, 1936. The deaths of Edsel Ford in 1943 and Henry Ford Sr. in 1947 brought it great potential wealth, because their wills made the foundation heir to about 90 percent of the Ford Motor Company. By January 1951, the trustees calculated a corpus of $447 million. That figure, although unrealistically low in relation to contemporary dividends, was unprecedentedly large. It dwarfed the endowments of the previous philanthropic giants, Rockefeller and Carnegie, and exceeded the combined endowments of the three richest American universities (Harvard, Yale, and the University of Texas). Ford remained for decades the largest foundation in the world, and it kept growing such that by 1960 its endowment was about three-fifths that of all the American institutions of higher education.[1]

Paul Hoffman, who in 1950 became Ford's first president, thus had resources that did not look derisory in the face of many national and international problems. Even as the foundation continued to grow, its annual budget around 1960 was larger than the regular budgets of the United Nations and all its specialized agencies. Having come to the foundation from heading the administration of the Marshall Plan for the reconstruction of Europe, it was hardly surprising that Hoffman quickly put the foundation into overseas development programs in Asia and the Near East (as the Middle East was then called). In his characteristically enthusiastic way, Hoffman believed that the development of poor nations was the key to successful competition with the attractions communism had for them and was critical to the maintenance of world peace. Others around him in the foundation's first leadership (like George Kennan) did not share his beliefs, but Hoffman prevailed and set the foundation on a commitment to underdeveloped countries that it has kept, in varied forms, until today. In the 30 years to 1981, the foundation committed about $2 billion in current dollars to international efforts of various kinds, of which about $1.5 billion concerned developing countries.

The way in which Ford took up its commitment to overseas development was certainly shaped by the prevailing doctrines and ideologies of the time, as well as, of course, by the nervous state of the world around 1950. The pattern of development assistance that Hoffman and his colleagues set for the foundation in 1951 put it firmly in the business of nation-building under principles and in styles it shared with many other organizations at the time. There are methods of engaging in development assistance that are rather different from nation-building and that came to be more important in later years, and we can trace a decline of nation-building efforts by Ford in more recent years. But first we must recall how the concept was once central to Ford's development efforts, and how the emergence of new nations at that time shaped the definition of development.

The Burst of New Nation-Building after World War II

We have been reminded of the terrible destructiveness of World War II in recent months as we have looked back for precedents to the challenges of rebuilding Iraq and Afghanistan. The Ford Foundation, wealthy by some measures, was certainly a poor thing in the face of such vast and widespread destruction as that found in postwar Japan and Germany. In some places in Southeast Asia, where the foundation would make nation-building efforts, there had been destruction and disorder left after the initial Japanese conquests and the struggles that followed. Burma, one of the first places the foundation undertook a development program, had been subjected to protracted fighting after the Japanese occupation in 1942, and there were continuing struggles, including incursions of Chinese Nationalists, after independence in 1948. Similarly, when the foundation started in Indonesia in 1952, it encountered the effects of Japanese occupation and years of armed struggle against the Dutch colonials before independence in 1949.

But most of Ford's efforts in nation-building did not come amid the wreckage of war, or in the sort of collapsing or failing states as those that concern us now. There were the wounds of Partition on the Indian subcontinent, but in most of the places it ventured, the foundation could focus on development rather than reconstruction; it came mostly into new sovereignties that had emerged more or less peacefully in an upsurge of values and aspirations that were changing the world.

The Second World War brought a great flowering of egalitarian sentiments, aspirations, and demands. Perhaps the most conspicuous manifestation of the newly vigorous and expanded egalitarianism after World War II came in what Abba Eban saw by the early 1980s as the "astonishing emergence of some 90 new sovereignties."[2] Indeed, the acquisition by previously subordinated peoples of control of their governments was the most dramatic expression of a new era in human equality. Because most of Africa and a large part of Asia had been under colonial power before World War II, the majority of the new sovereignties formed on ex-colonial territories. As such, they became the main focus of Ford's development and nation-building efforts (as they did for other organizations).

The colonial devolution inaugurated in Asia in the 1940s spread to Africa in the 1950s and swelled into the remarkable burst of African independence in 1960. The new states brought into existence were put by Ernest Gellner in his famed essay, *Nations and Nationalism,* in a special category.[3] They initially were dependencies established by external powers on territories that typically embraced diverse peoples, "lacking common positive traits," as Gellner wrote, but were held together by the administration and control of a colonial government that imposed a language, laws, and regulations, so that there came to be a social identity distinctive to that territory.

There was a broadly common character to the institutional structure of the colonial societies. They had a governmental structure based on European patterns, built on bureaucracies, civil and military, with the higher positions in them filled mostly or entirely by European whites, the lower levels filled by "natives" of various sorts. A kind of caste system prevailed, in which social behavior and authority were predicated on skin color and racial origin, in both governmental and nongovernmental affairs. The famous sparseness of the colonial ruling elite was based on more than the control of firearms, indirect rule, and the calculated accommodation of subjects to power.

This structure of colonial societies meant that the apparatus of government was both the most conspicuous and prestigious expression of their hierarchical social structures, and in a time of rising egalitarian values, their Achilles' heels. In the heyday of colonialism, the majesty of the government could not be attacked openly by its subjects without severe consequences;

hostility and alienation were indirectly expressed—notably through religion. But the breakdown of deference and the authority that had been based on it was widespread and rapid in the wake of World War II. In some places, as in Indochina or Indonesia, this revolutionary change of authority came with violent and protracted struggles. But in many places, notably in Africa, a remarkably nonviolent negotiated transfer took place of the control of government from external, colonial to native hands.

It has been said that the apparatus and habitations of government were the great prizes for the leaders of national independence movements. Government was one part of a colonial society that could be quickly appropriated and used as an ultimate reward for effort and suffering; it was a natural base for launching visions of new futures, and it also had jobs for the boys. In some situations, the winning of the government, its powers, and its dignities occurred after profound disruptions of the old regimes, as in Indonesia and Malaya, where the Japanese had unseated and humiliated colonial powers, bringing back Sukarno from his exile in Flores and conquering Singapore. In other places, much remained as before, certainly outside government, and even within it.

The international development movement, which the Ford Foundation joined in 1951, arose in the context of this historic collapse of white, European world dominance. The collapse was a process hastened and intensified by the East-West division of the world after World War II—a division itself rooted in conflicts of status and culture, within the West and beyond, with the Soviet Union and then China posing revolutionary challenges to the West. The conception that Lenin and Mao had found the historically ordained path to the future was a fearful and menacing challenge to a retreating Europe and an emerging America. Both had to devise responses to this challenge that would concede national independence but did not turn over new nations to the ambitions of their Cold War foes. Development assistance was an ideology and practice designed to meet the challenge.

Development as Nation-Building in the 1950s and 1960s

Development in the sense I am using the word here was an ideological phenomenon that emerged as a major element in international affairs during and after World War II, and has persisted in evolving forms to the present.[4] There has, of course, always been development (and decay) in other senses, but in recent times, development has been an ideology guiding the actions of governments, private organizations, and people of many sorts. The Ford Foundation adopted this ideology wholeheartedly when it began its overseas development programs in 1951. In its initial forms, development was directed at the progress and well-being of nation-states, and not primarily at the melioration of individual lives or the relief of poverty, as it has recently been commonly understood.

The ideology of development declared that aid must be free of the cultural restrictions that imperialism and colonialism had imposed, and that it should not bring new strictures. Aid in its various forms—financial, physical, and other—was to be culturally neutral, and generous conceptions of the neutrality of technical knowledge and skills helped broaden what was admissible.[5] In the prevailing political setting around 1950 and under the leadership of men deeply experienced in public affairs, Ford followed the orthodoxies that were emerging in the United Nations and U.S. government policy. Paul Hoffman was accustomed to negotiating with national leaders, and when he started the foundation's development program, he traveled to Karachi and New Delhi to talk with Liaquat Ali Khan and Jawaharlal Nehru to explore what Ford might do to help their countries.

The rationale for the Ford Foundation's development programs sprang from its presumed contribution to "the maintenance of the peace," the first of its objectives and the one that attracted the most public interest. The conception that development promoted world peace was reinforced by the fear—strongly felt by Hoffman and his colleagues—of the competition with the communists for the "minds of men" in the emerging new nations. The world was in the midst of a process of decolonization that indeed the United States was prodding along, but that could hardly be stopped. The question was not whether independence should come, but when, and what the competence and maturity of the fledgling states would be. New nations were to be economically viable and capable of running their own affairs in an acceptable manner. They were not to be abandoned, nor launched prematurely, nor held in tutelage too long. The metropolitan power and other countries and organizations assumed responsibility for helping and hastening this process.[6]

The initial period of development policy was thus wrapped in concerns about the viability of new nation-states. Whether from the calculations of realpolitik or from the fresh surge of moralistic concerns, the development of new nations became not only their own concern, but a concern of the more affluent and powerful nations as well. And the willingness of the latter was reinforced by optimistic assessments of their institutional capacities to assist effectively. When the Ford Foundation entered the development business, President Truman's "Point Four" in his 1949 inaugural was very recent encouragement; he had said, "For the first time in history, humanity possesses the knowledge and the skill to relieve the suffering of more than half the people of the world . . . living in conditions of misery." And the spread of democratic independence would "supply the vitalizing force to stir the people of the world into triumphant action, not only against their human oppressors, but also against . . . hunger, misery, and despair."[7] The new Ford Foundation under Paul Hoffman was eager to take a place in this action.

Strategies of Assisting Nation-Building

The nation-states that emerged from colonial pasts therefore had (1) a bureaucratic governmental apparatus that usually could be carried over in some form to the new, independent state and under the control of its political leadership, and (2) a society that had a typical diversity of peoples, ethnically, religiously, and tribally, and was generally heavily rural and much under private control of various kinds. Two principal foci for the achievement of freedom were thus before these new nations: (1) to build viable and effective governments and (2) to weld diverse peoples into a common nationhood. There were many other aspects of development, but these two goals became principal foci of Ford's efforts, too.

Working with and Building Governments

The authority of government as the legitimate voice of a nation's people made government the natural point of entry of those, like the Ford Foundation, purveying development assistance. The practice that Paul Hoffman established in his initial foray into the Indian subcontinent in the summer of 1951 became the standard practice of Ford's development program for decades. There were initial, formal approaches to the national leadership followed quickly by more extended relations with administrators and technical officers. This pattern of day-to-day interactions with the civil service, augmented occasionally with relations with the political leadership, became standard in Ford's practice. It had several advantages. The European heritage of the colonial bureaucracy involved principles of nonpolitical bureaucrats working with different political ministers and leaders. This principle of political neutrality in the civil service fit the requirement that development assistance should be technical and culturally neutral. The conception that these countries should have democratic governments, representing all their people, implied that they must be served by civil and military services that were not politicized. Leaving the military side to national agencies, the Ford Foundation made the civil service the normal and principal point of contact with these new nations.

When Hoffman left the foundation in 1953, the new president, Rowan Gaither, put Don Price in charge of the foundation's overseas activities. Price was already a distinguished figure in the history of public administration in the United States. He made a long tour in Asia in 1954 to see the programs on the ground and concluded that they worked best where there were civil services Ford could "brace against." The success of the programs in India and a hopeful start in Pakistan owed much to the heritage of the famous "steel frame," the Indian civil service. The weakness of the government bureaucracy was one reason Price (and later, his successor, Forrest Hill) saw for the weakness of the program that had been started in Burma. The same was true for the even slower start of the program in Indonesia, where Price had to get a new representative before he could see much activity. In both Burma and Indonesia, the disruptions of war and occupation had broken the established forms of the old colonial bureaucracy and weakened it with bloated numbers and other inefficacies.

The importance of a colonial bureaucratic heritage was particularly evident to Price when he came to Iran in 1954. The Ford representative for the Near East had been given a $500,000 "blank check" by the trustees in the excitement at the overthrow of Mossadeq's government in 1953. He decided to put it into rural development and soon had an energetic American planning a program for the Iranian government. Price was distressed to find that the Iranian officials in the Ministry of Agriculture were "completely without experience" and "had no idea how to start a training program or what to train people for." They wanted the foundation simply to come in and do the job, which it refused to do; this was not the kind of cooperation development was supposed to involve. A similar effort to engage with the government of Iraq in a rural development program was foundering on the lack of technical expertise in the government when the revolution in 1958 further discouraged the foundation.

Making Effective Independent Governments

The successful launching of new nation-states depended critically on the viability and effectiveness of their governments. Even in India, where the foundation found the kind of civil service it needed, there was a quick appeal for its help in analyzing what kind of a government independent India should have. Sunil Khilnani, in his thoughtful reflections on the emergence of India from the British Raj, recalls that the British were skeptical about any unity outlasting their reign; he argued that although Congress "inherited the undamaged coercive and bureaucratic powers of the British Raj, . . . the circumstances were ones of uncertainty and crisis," and that Nehru's dominance was always "tenuous," since he had to act against "inclinations of both his party and the state bureaucracy" throughout his time as prime minister.[8] It was thus not surprising that Nehru's first request to the foundation's representative for technical assistance was for a consultant to write a report on (1) the functions of a minister, (2) the new role of administrative officers beyond the keeping of law and order, and (3) the relations of ministers and secretaries.

Such requests for ideas on basic questions of governmental structure later became fairly numerous as the foundation became involved in the process of African independence. Beginning its African program in 1958, before most of the sub-Saharan African countries were independent, Ford was drawn into the momentous debates over forms of government, constitutions, and the reshaping and restaffing of the civil services. The foundation provided funding and recruited some of the participants for a 1960 conference in Lagos on a federal constitution for Nigeria. It provided a series of consultants on the planning and preparation of governments for independence, the reorganization of ministries and services, manpower surveys, and crash training programs. Such technical assistance continued after independence in the provision of so-called "staff development advisors," usually accompanied by job analysts and other specialists, in such places as Nigeria, Tanzania, Kenya, Zambia, and Botswana.

Such examples of the foundation's engagement in building, sustaining, or transforming governments as they evolved from colonial bureaucracies into new states could be greatly expanded. Assistance to training institutions both in the host countries and overseas; technical assistance of many kinds in governmental organizations, procedures, and techniques; conferences; and support to relevant academic resources became a regular and extensive business of the foundation. There were sometimes rude challenges to this work, even by Americans, as when the foundation sponsored a conference on public administration in Colombia that was bleakly told by Professor Frank Tannenbaum that conditions in Latin American made "personal government unavoidable" with "loyalty and friendship taking precedence over efficiency, training, and public service" that the conference technocrats were planning.[9]

In short, however smooth the transition from colonial control to independence and however intact the civil service of familiar structure, the independent government was differently led, had different relations to its citizenry, and was seeking a different character and responsibilities than its colonial predecessor.

Familiar phrases like "the failed export of Westminster democracy" are gropings toward understanding the deep discontinuities across the independence divide in the nature of governmental authority. The new, independent nation-state thus needed to be reformulated at its apex, the state, as well as in other aspects. It is perhaps not obvious that foreign agencies could have significant roles in such a sensitive process. But some of the needs were clearly technical matters requiring specialized expertise, which technical assistance might be able to supply. And the Ford Foundation had the advantage of its private status; it was not—not officially at least—representing some foreign power. In addition, the new national governments were remarkably accessible to outsiders, at least in the first years of independence.

One particular sort of assistance to national governments became especially prominent in Ford programs, and sometimes was quite consequential. The fledgling independent governments wanted their countries to develop rapidly in their new-found freedom, even to "take-off," as Walt Rostow told them they could do. They would have to do the right things with their resources and potentials, and the faith of the time was that this required national planning, through which governments—and those who were helping them—would guide their societies toward the progress they sought. The capacity of governments to mount such national planning became an urgent matter of nation-building, and a preferred focus of Ford's development programs.

The Ford Foundation and National Planning

Nearly everywhere the Ford Foundation went to explore what it might do in overseas development, it encountered the desire of nations to plan new futures. Thus, Hoffman's initial engagement in India with Nehru centered on the Planning Commission that Nehru chaired. This encounter led to Ford's largest initial development project, the Indian community development program (discussed later).

When Hoffman reached Karachi in 1951, Pakistan was not yet organized for planning and seemed chiefly interested in Islamic economics, but by 1953 it had established a planning board, and asked Ford to supply a group of advisors who would assist it in preparing a five-year plan. The Ford Foundation representative in Pakistan went to Harvard and secured the services of economist Edward Mason, beginning the foundation's commitment in Pakistan that would last until 1965. Mason set about organizing the Harvard Development Advisory Service, which subsequently branched out to many other countries, usually with funding from the Ford Foundation.

The foundation had been urged to supply economists and fiscal experts to Indonesia before it had anyone in the country exploring what it might do, as Paul Hoffman and John Cowles heard in Hong Kong in 1951 on their way home from India. When the foundation later responded to proposals to finance the Center for International Affairs at the Massachusetts Institute of Technology (MIT), it enabled MIT to make early links with Indonesian economists and planning. In the years of Sukarno's confrontations, the foundation could not do much directly for Indonesian national planning. But between the mid-1950s and 1965, it financed enough Indonesian economic competence in training abroad to bring forth the famed "Berkeley mafia" after Suharto took power in 1966; the state planning agency, BAPPENAS, was financed directly soon thereafter.

The foundation's initial doubts about working with the governments that it encountered in the Near East made for a slow start in national planning there. The first project to develop was in Iran, following a 1957 visit of Abolhassan Ebtehaj, Iran's plan organization director, to Edward Mason at Harvard. This visit began an engagement, from 1959 to 1962, of Harvard and the Ford Foundation, which committed $1.2 million to an Economic Bureau devising uses of Iran's oil income and drawing up a national plan. The foundation hesitated in engaging with Egypt's embryonic planning organization prior to 1958, when the arrival from India of a manpower specialist, John Hilliard, as the foundation's representative in Cairo quickly brought grants in 1959 and 1961 of some $450,000 to an Institute of Economic Planning. Support to this organization continued, with vicissitudes, during the 1960s. And under the new policies of the Sadat regime in the 1970s, support for planning was resumed. Jordan also received several planning grants in the 1960s, both for manpower and economic planning.

The governments encountered by the foundation in Africa when it began development programs there in 1958 were as enamored of national planning as other governments had been, and their great educational needs brought special demands for manpower surveys and planning. Within a few years, the foundation was supporting planning organizations in Ghana, Nigeria, Kenya, and Tanzania, and somewhat later, in Botswana.

For various reasons, the close relations with governments through their civil services, which became foundation practice in Asia and Africa, did not develop in a similar way in Latin America. There was, nevertheless, support of planning organizations in Colombia and Argentina beginning in 1963 (again in conjunction with Harvard), the former lasting longer than the latter.

Developing countries manifested greater appetites for national plans than the economists and other experts in these countries could satisfy. The capacity of the foundation to find and supply experts who could be entrusted with helping nationals in these countries make the desired plans became not only an asset, but also at times a constraint on what it could do. For example, a Ugandan government request for planning assistance had to be rejected not on its merits or promise (and indeed, in the face of hazards of "Eastern" competition), but because the foundation's recruiting powers were overstretched at the time. Despite such constraints, the foundation saw the nurturing of planning organizations as of such high importance that it directed considerable financial and administrative resources to such assistance.[10]

From the perspective of several decades that badly tarnished the prestige of national planning, this sort of nation-building looks less important now than it did. Even at the time, there were serious doubts about the utility of many of the plans that were produced.[11] But it would be unduly narrow to assess these efforts solely on the merits of economic planning in promoting development. The need of new governments for economic and other technical competences was clear, and planning agencies were then a preferred way of introducing them. In the case of Pakistan, after a decade of Ford-Harvard assistance, the Planning Commission, in the judgment of the historian Khalid bin Sayeed, had achieved expertise "vastly superior to any other government department" and exerted a corresponding influence on economic decisionmaking; and a proud foundation representative a little earlier found its influence "so profound . . . that it is impossible to overstate the import of this project."[12] Mixed judgments prevailed in the case of Iran, but they were firmly positive on the quality and performance of the Harvard teams and the "creative and enthusiastic Iranian staff" the teams worked with and taught.[13] Foundation experts and other observers also claim that important contributions were made by the Kenyan, Indonesian, and Botswanan projects.

In addition to providing economists and other experts in technical assistance to planning organizations, the foundation supported a broad array of training opportunities for present and prospective planners. Some of these training programs were established within the host countries; others were in such places as the World Bank, Harvard, and Williams College. In some instances, such training could be a supplement to a technical assistance team. In others, as in the cases of Indonesia and Latin America, competence was being prepared for a future day, in what was known as capacity-building.

Development for All the People: Rural Development and Agriculture

I have argued that the nation-building that was the business of development in the wake of World War II was concerned on the one hand with making viable and effective governments and on the other with welding diverse peoples into common nationhood. Much goes into the making of nations, and much was tried in the burst of nation-building after World War II. For a foundation heavily engaged with education (especially higher education) at home, it was natural for Ford to help build the educational resources of new nations. It was not notably active in such integrative efforts of the new nations as universal education, the spread of literacy campaigns, and cultural creations and revivals. But rural community development had a particular prominence among these integrative efforts, and certainly it was prominent for the Ford Foundation.

The Ford Foundation's first major overseas development program was its support of Indian community development, a program that was planned and worked out in 1951 and subsequent years, in conjunction with the Indian Planning Commission chaired by Prime Minister Nehru. It was a program of rural development and nation-building that was initially much admired and imitated, with help from Ford, in other countries. India was by no means alone in steering the foundation to rural development; similar priorities were encountered elsewhere, as governments and their civil servants typically presented this great concern to the foundation.

That Prime Minister Nehru and Paul Hoffman and his companions in 1951 quickly focused on the community development program demonstrated the concern on both sides for the stability and success of India. Leading a nation that had had a traumatic birth at Partition, Nehru had acute concerns over the divisions of language, religion, class, and caste within India. And he once wrote, "Personally, I feel the biggest task of all is not only the economic development of the people of India as a whole, but even more so the psychological and emotional integration of the people of India." His biographer, Sarvepalli Gopal, maintained that Nehru's first great hope for the integration of India lay in community development.[14]

The community development program was inspired by a vision that there were untapped reservoirs of motivation and capacity in common people (rather like Harry Truman's belief, recalled earlier in this chapter, in a "vitalizing force" he thought could bring people to "triumphant action"). The community development movement was to be big enough to transform the 500,000 villages that constituted most of India. The initial Ford scheme involved 1,500 villages and five training centers across India, and its first costs were about $3.5 million; but U.S. Ambassador Chester Bowles arrived in India shortly after Hoffman and the Ford group with $50 million to spend, and community development was vastly extended. It looked big enough to matter even on India's daunting scale.

Grants for community development in other countries followed the Indian model. Pakistan started the Village Agricultural and Industrial Development (V-AID) program in 1953, which the Ford Foundation supported, along with Burma's Mass Education Council.

This spread of foundation support for rural development programs came not simply because such programs were on Ford's agenda. The foundation was responding to new and urgent concerns of national governments. The reach of government into rural areas had typically been limited for centuries, not only in South and Southeast Asia but also in such places as Iraq, Iran, and much of Africa; this neglect was often not overcome by colonial governments. Newly independent governments, basing their legitimacy on representing all their people, had at least to try to reach them even beyond that. The impressive triumph of Mao's adherents in winning over China's peasant population spurred India and other countries across Asia and beyond to tackle the development of rural areas as well as the urban centers more noisily pressing on government. Governments unaccustomed to solicitous concerns for distant "little people" found themselves barraged with proposals for land reform and other benefits for peasants. By the 1950s, governments were trying to reverse long-held habits and were seeking international help from the Ford Foundation and others to improve the lives of their villagers.

During the 1950s, the Ford Foundation attempted to engage broadly with several of the ambitions for rural development of Near Eastern governments, including land reforms. Ford was substantially involved in efforts by the Iranian government at rural development from 1953, which lasted in varying forms until the foundation left Iran in 1964. But by 1958, community development in India was in serious trouble.

What had happened? The history of the flourishing and international celebration of Indian community development and its subsequent decline into doubts and discredit in the late 1950s is a familiar chapter in the annals of development. Increased food production had always been an important aim of the community development program. Rising crop totals in the mid-1950s garnered confidence in the program, but this confidence was rudely shaken by a bad monsoon. There was general alarm when, in 1957–58, India's food grain output declined by 10 percent, and the specter of starvation in a growing population loomed. The next decade was rife with drama for the Ford Foundation, India, and the international development community. The foundation struggled through bitter divisions over funding an Intensive Agricultural Districts Program (IADP), for which its representative, Douglas Ensminger, asked more than $20 million of special appropriations. However dramatic and absorbing these struggles were, their interest here lies not in the merits of the contenders or the outcome of the IADP program, but in the trumping by food production of the nation-building objectives of the community development program.

Ensminger never abandoned the faith that a government-sponsored and promoted program of rural development would cement national unity and alter the relations of government and its people through new types and behavior of public officials. But community development lost credibility not only in India but elsewhere. In his biography, Sarvepalli Gopal related that Nehru's hopes for bringing the rural masses into the Indian nation shifted from community development to the system of local government called *panchayati raj,* and then more vaguely to the spreading of education.

In neighboring Pakistan, the V-AID imitation of India's community development was floundering by the mid-1950s. Where the foundation was working with weaker governments, the hope of building nations through engaging local energies with governments fell away quickly. Thus, the foundation was quickly disillusioned by the Iranian government's hesitation over antagonizing large landlords and its unwillingness to multiply the pilot project Ford worked on at Gorgon, south of the Caspian; it withdrew permanently from the country in the early 1960s.

The Ford Foundation's Retreat from Nation-Building

From Nation-Building to Establishing Better Conditions for It: Food Production and Population Control

Although the prevailing conceptions of nation-centered development disposed the Ford Foundation in the 1950s to jump into efforts at building new nations, there were also growing hesitations and constraints. Large, "general purpose" foundations had by this time come to be called "research" foundations. Under Paul Hoffman—and with Ford's initial avoidance of scientific research as proper business at a time when the U.S. government was supporting it so strongly through defense research, the National Institutes of Health, and the National Science Foundation—this established disposition of foundations did not constrain Ford's plunge into development programs. But the emphasis on development began to be seriously questioned a few years later under the presidency of Henry Heald (1956–66), who was a former university president and thought the foundation should properly be devoted to research and education. This notion that it was better for a foundation to stick essentially to education and research rather than engage in building the institutional requisites of new nations grew in the Ford Foundation during the 1950s. It came to be a serious challenge to the concept of the overseas development program that Paul Hoffman had started.

Heald was convinced that Rockefeller, with its staff of agricultural scientists and its work on improved agricultural technology, had the "right end of the stick," and that Ford, with its elaborate training and extension

Table 2.1 Ford Foundation Expenditures on Rural Development and Agricultural Technology, 1950–1979

Years	Rural development	Agricultural technology
1950–59	13,846	339
1960–69	7,210	36,348
1970–79	5,317	49,205

Note: All figures in thousands of current dollars.

programs across India and in other countries, had the wrong end. And by 1960, there was an alternative at hand to what the foundation had been doing for rural development.

Forrest Hill, the Ford vice president, had for several years had an idea that Heald thought was on the right end of the stick. Hill believed that better agricultural technology was essential to any marked increase in production, and he was persuaded that this technology could be produced most promptly and efficiently by privately controlled, international institutions. In the Ford Foundation's coffers, he had the money to make institutions of the necessary size, and, by collaboration with Rockefeller, he could get the necessary expertise. The rapid and remarkable success of the International Rice Research Institute, miracle seeds, and the Green Revolution encouraged a new Ford leadership after 1966, under McGeorge Bundy and David Bell, to devote the large sums shown in table 2.1 to agricultural technology.

A similar trend took place in the field of population control, which, after inhibitions lasting until 1959, became a major focus of the foundation's development programs. Indeed, after a very feeble start in the 1950s, this part of the foundation's development expenditures amounted to 25 percent of the total by 1981, a larger fraction of the foundation's development efforts than went to agriculture and rural development (21%) or development planning and management (23%), and was only exceeded by education (31%). Some population programs were mounted with national governments, but the largest expenditures were the $114 million devoted to research and training on reproductive science and contraceptive technology. This 45 percent of the $252 million total spent on population problems in the 30 years to 1981 was spent in the world's leading research centers, as well as in developing countries. Like the effort to improve agricultural technology, programs in population control were attempts to improve the conditions under which nation-building could occur, rather than direct efforts at nation-building.

The Decline of Efforts to Build Governments and Planning Organizations

Perhaps the last burst of international enthusiasm for new governments came in Africa in 1960, the continent's great year of reaching independence. Confidence in the efficacy and beneficent intentions of governments began to decline thereafter and has continued to slide in subsequent decades in most parts of the world, as documented by public opinion polls. A basic theme in my chapter is that there was an organic connection between promoting the functioning of national governments and the classical ideology of development. With a decline of confidence in government, there was inevitably a disruption of this tie. The Ford Foundation's faith in an effective civil service as a condition of successful development assistance was not abandoned, but it came to be perceived more as a necessary than a sufficient condition for development.

The collapse of Ayub Khan's government in Pakistan was an especially traumatic experience for the Ford Foundation. The achievements of Pakistan's economic growth in the years of Ayub's dominance had been impressive, and a brilliantly led and prestigious Planning Commission won much credit for it. But unfortunately, the international admiration of the country's economic growth was not shared domestically, where the government displeased and lost control of a hostile populace. This course of events was particularly shocking to the Ford Foundation, which had been proud of much that it had done in Pakistan, not only in support of the Planning Commission through the Harvard Development Advisory Service, but also in stimulating the Green Revolution, promoting family planning, and much else.

Technical assistance was supposed to supply the expertise lacking in new countries; behaving according to the doctrine of proper technical assistance, experts were only to advise and train "counterparts" in the receiving service. They were not to make substantive decisions for the countries they were serving, but to act through their proper national counterparts. In actual practice, there were, of course, regular—sometimes massive—departures from this ideal of fastidiously careful restraint from telling the government of another country what it ought to do. Such radical departures from the ideal were common in poorly staffed Nepal under a series of Ford planning grants that ultimately amounted to some $1.6 million.

Today, the relevance of this experience of Ford in Pakistan and elsewhere lies in its illustration of the intrinsic difficulties in providing external assistance to nation-building through the building and maintenance of good governments. The needs of government at any given time inevitably include decisions on problems of the moment, and there are certainly many situations in which the national officers taxed with the responsibility for such decisions are ill-equipped to make them. An external advisor may come to feel a bit like André Gide, when the latter famously remarked that having observed wicked deeds in central Africa, he felt obliged to do something, however reluctantly, about these evils. The typical responsibility of planning organizations for drawing up multi-year plans was at a comfortable remove from the temptations of weighing in on the problems of the day. Sensible people regularly saw that there were more urgent tasks for consultants than the writing of multi-year plans, and undoubtedly more such plans were produced than were heeded or used. But the production of such plans may have been a necessary condition for sustainable relationships.

Assessment of the effects of foundation and other assistance to the governments of developing countries is complicated by the multiplicity of determinants of these governments' fates. It is obvious that what Zulfikar Ali Bhutto and General Zia ul Haq did to the civil services of Pakistan had more consequence for the evolution of Pakistan's governments than what the Ford Foundation did through its large array of grants and technical assistance. And similar observations may be made for Egypt, sub-Saharan Africa, and elsewhere. Foundation officers were discouraged by the difficulty in achieving detectable results from their dealings with governments. But the resultant loss of confidence was less obvious and serious than a decline in the faith in the capacity and will of governments to lead and guide development that had been essential to the old orthodoxy. Writing toward the end of the 1980s on this old orthodoxy, John P. Lewis noted, "The conventional view is that governments overreached. The acceptance of responsibility [for change and development] far exceeded their capacity to perform."[15]

The decline of confidence in the capacity of governments was paralleled by a disillusionment with their benevolent intentions. By the end of the 1960s, the issue of how closely the foundation should associate with governments that were clearly oppressive or exploitative was seriously considered in the Ford Foundation. Ford had indeed from the first assessed whether governments were seriously committed to development, but initially, indulgence prevailed. Such latitude declined in the 1960s and thereafter, as human rights became a forceful issue in the foundation, as it did for many other organizations—including, in time, many governments.

The financial records I have been using show continuing engagements with governments in developing countries. But, as John Lewis reminded us, it became the conventional view that too much was expected of them, and a new era arrived in which nation-building, if it was seriously intended at all, had to be sought in new ways through the diversity and many addresses of civil society.

Nation-Building in an Era of Unusual Access and Trust: What Is Left Decades Later

I have depicted development in its classic and original form after World War II as a process willed and guided by governments that were committed to the advancement of their peoples and were to be assisted by the more advanced and affluent nations in unintrusive and culturally neutral ways. This was to be nation-building in which external sources of technical knowledge and other resources were not representing their own interests, but seeking genuinely to serve their host nations. These were of course ideal principles, but there were exemplifications in actual practice. Douglas Ensminger prided himself that he was not regarded as a foreigner by the Indians with whom he worked, and many staffers and experts supplied by the foundation were proudly loyal to their host countries. This "disloyalty," if you will, to their own organizations and countries of origin, was a loyalty to the ideology of development; it was also much facilitated by the exceptional intimacies that were possible between nationals and the purveyors of assistance from abroad in those years.[16]

We are now in an era of caution and pessimism about nation-building, and the ideology of development that had something like universal assent from the post–World War II years into the 1960s has been variously abandoned, transformed, or enveloped in passionate contention. There has been ample reason to judge as heady and inflated the optimism about the improvability of human life and societies everywhere that prevailed after World War II. The twin faiths—that progress and prosperity for all could be effectively planned by governments and that these governments would be devoted to the genuine service of their people—look particularly innocent after the Soviet collapse and the rise of kleptocracies elsewhere. Painful recent experience has made nation-building look dangerous, difficult, and costly, particularly for outsiders who may dare to venture into it.

Unquestionably, a great deal has gone wrong in the historic dissolution of colonialism and the resulting multiplication of sovereignties. Parts of the world, notably Africa, have experienced the cessation or reversal of development. Dismaying instabilities and conflicts—concentrated, above all, in poor places—have deprived multitudes of their livelihoods and, in such places as the Congo and Sudan, have taken the very lives of too many individuals. It is easy to assume that the vision and practice of development that inspired new and old nations, the United Nations, and private enthusiasts like the Ford Foundation were thus misguided or, at best, pathetically ineffectual.

Such a pessimistic assessment of the recent past neglects the remarkable achievements brought to rich and poor and amply shared by the developing countries. Growth in the gross domestic product is too limited a measure of this era's gains for less-developed countries; another indicator, average life expectancies, increased from 40.7 to 62.4 years over the four decades from 1950–55 to 1990–95 in these countries.

As an old colleague liked to remark, we should be modest about our failures as well as our successes; much that we could not foresee or control has affected what is left from deliberate effort. But some things were seen and done right. The doctrines of technical assistance emphasized professional knowledge and skills that were indispensable. And in some circumstances, this training did have striking effects, as when a Gideon's band of the "Berkeley mafia," after years of Ford fellowships, brought macroeconomic stability to Indonesia to end the wildness of the final Sukarno years. This sort of capacity-building by training cadres of professionals is evidently a necessary part of development strategy and nation-building at any time, as is the institution-building that can put such capacity to work.

There is, alas, much more to development than infusing necessary knowledge and techniques. The path to the rational conduct of affairs lies through the nonrational establishment of values and institutions that are not easy to reach and affect. In the universalistic and egalitarian enthusiasms that prevailed in the era after World War II, there was a disposition to minimize the cultural differences of peoples, and hence, the need to affect them. But a not-unreasonable optimism prevailed about the leveling out of cultural difference into necessary uniformities of modernism. And there was undoubtedly too little regard for the stubborn persistence of the particularisms of personal ties in kinship, locality, and ethnicity that would emerge in corruption and contentions, crippling the state and other institutions that were left when colonialism fell in Asia and Africa.[17]

I have made the era of nation-building after World War II somewhat special historically, in that the experience of colonialism had lingering effects and eased the way for outside assistance and presumed expertise. But I do not mean to suggest that the up-welling of enthusiasm for development at that time was unique or transitory. Conceptions of development have changed with the rise of a new emphasis on civil society and nongovernmental institutions. But the embracing egalitarianism that brought a concern for human beings everywhere has not changed, and the emphasis on whole populations that led developers to formerly disregarded peasantries has not. It has often been remarked that what Akhter Hameed

Khan called "the cosmopolitan cult of community development" may have passed into history, but its aims and methods live on in the work of myriad nongovernmental organizations and their helpers. Certainly, in this country, there is remarkable evidence that we continue to be ready to undertake brave ventures to bring democracy—and its necessary condition, hope for prosperity—to distant and troubled places. Whatever the declared mistrust of nation-building and the common pessimism that we do not know how to do it, we find our government committed to formidable ventures in it. An example of this tendency can be seen in as sober a body as a study group from the Council on Foreign Relations, which has recently espoused the radicalism of land reform in the Andes.[18]

This vocation to universal progress, if one may so describe it, is not new. I have been reminded by the new Library of America collection of John Greenleaf Whittier's poetry that the hopeful, egalitarian vision that drove us after World War II was alive in this country in 1866, when he published his *Snowbound*. Whittier foresaw how seemingly "careless boys":

> Shall Freedom's young apostles be,
> Shall every lingering wrong assail;
> The cruel lie of caste refute,
> Old forms remould, and substitute
> For Slavery's lash, and freeman's will,
> For blind routine, wide-handed skill;
> A school-house plant on every hill,
> Stretching in radiate nerve-lines thence
> The quick wires of intelligence;
> Till North and South together brought
> Shall own the same electric thought.

Not just a vision of post–Civil War reconciliation, but a prefiguration of the twentieth-century vision of Harry Truman and others of a world of shared development, and perhaps now of a twenty-first-century vision of democracy for all?

Notes

1. See Francis X. Sutton, "The Ford Foundation: The Early Years," *Daedalus* 116 (1, 1987): 41–91.
2. Abba Eban, *The New Diplomacy: International Affairs in the Modern Age* (New York: Random House, 1983), xii.
3. Ernest Gellner, *Nations and Nationalism* (Oxford: Blackwell, 1983), esp. p. 83.
4. Francis X. Sutton, "Development Ideology: Its Emergence and Decline," in Francis X. Sutton, ed., *A World to Make: Development in Perspective* (New Brunswick, N.J.: Transaction, 1990), 33–58, takes this view.

5. In the article "Technical Assistance" in the *International Encyclopedia of the Social Sciences* (New York: Macmillan, 1968), I viewed it as an ideology.
6. Lord Hailey's *African Surveys*, particularly the second, were gargantuan monuments from these efforts, now often viewed with critical skepticism. See, for example, Frederick Cooper, "Modernizing Colonialism and the Limits of Empire," SSRC *Items and Issues* 4 (Fall/Winter 2003/2004): 1–9, with numerous citations to relevant studies.
7. This famous inaugural is described at length in David McCullough, *Truman* (New York: Simon and Schuster, 1992): 723–34.
8. Sunil Khilnani, *The Idea of India* (New York: Farrar, Straus, and Giroux, 1999) 28–30.
9. See Frank Tannenbaum, "The Influence of Social Conditions," in Martin Kriesberg, ed., *Public Administration in Developing Countries* (Washington, D.C.: Brookings Institution Press, 1965), 33–42.
10. There is a category in the standard subject classification developed at Ford for its international grants, titled "34 Economic Planning and Development Advisory Services." It showed some $30 million in expenditures between 1950 and 1981 in current dollars, or about $77 million in 1982 dollars, with the largest amount in these constant dollars being $29 million in the decade from 1960 to 1969.
11. Edward Mason, *The Harvard Institute for International Development and Its Antecedents* (Cambridge, Mass.: Harvard University Press, 1980) is liberally endowed with such doubts.
12. Khalid bin Sayeed, *The Political System of Pakistan* (Boston: Houghton Mifflin, 1957), 149–50; Haldore Hansen in the Pakistan response to the internal Ford Foundation "Janus" survey, report no. 03070 (New York: Ford Foundation Archives, 1966), 79.
13. Mason, *The Harvard Institute for International Development and Its Antecedents,* 4–12 and reviews cited therein.
14. Sarvepalli Gopal, *Jawaharlal Nehru: A Biography,* vol. 3, 1956–64 (Cambridge, Mass.: Harvard University Press, 1984), 22; the quotation is from a 1957 letter.
15. John P. Lewis, "Government and National Economic Development," in Sutton, *A World to Make,* 70.
16. Similar intimacies also occurred with foreign researchers or with others showing nothing more than sympathetic interest in a new, developing country. Remarkable intimacies were common in the early years of African independence, and they also occurred in large countries with leading figures who would be thought to be too busy for any but the most important visitors. Thus, Indira Gandhi was known to be surprisingly accessible to visiting foreigners, even as aid organizations were finding her permanent secretaries less accessible.

17. It was a mark of the times that warnings from more than a century of Latin American independence were not taken to be relevant.
18. Council on Foreign Relations, "Andes 2020: A New Strategy for the Challenges of Colombia and the Region," report of an independent commission (New York: Council on Foreign Relations Center for Preventive Action, 2004), 134.

CHAPTER 3

Building Nations

The American Experience

Minxin Pei, Samia Amin, and Seth Garz

FEW NATIONAL UNDERTAKINGS are as complex, costly, and time-consuming as reconstructing the governing institutions of foreign societies. Even a combination of unsurpassed military power and abundant wealth does not guarantee success, let alone quick results. Historically, nation-building attempts by outside powers are notable mainly for their bitter disappointments, not their triumphs. Among the great powers, the United States is perhaps the most active and persistent nation-builder. Of the more than 200 cases of the use of force by the United States since 1900, 17 cases (including the occupation of Iraq) may be considered attempts at nation-building.[1]

To be sure, most U.S. military interventions abroad have consisted of major wars (e.g., the two world wars), peacekeeping missions (as in Bosnia), proxy wars (in Nicaragua and Angola in the 1980s), covert operations (the coup in Chile in 1973), humanitarian interventions (the Balkans in the 1990s), the rescue of American citizens; the defense of its allies under attack (in Korea in 1950), and one-time retaliatory strikes (the bombing raid against Libya in 1986). To distinguish ordinary military interventions from nation-building efforts, we apply three strict criteria.[2]

First, the practical effect, if not the declared goal, of U.S. intervention must be a regime change or the survival of a regime that would otherwise collapse. Regime change or survivability is the core objective of nation-building, because an outside power, such as the United States, must overthrow a hostile regime or maintain a friendly indigenous regime to be able to implement its plans. It is worth noting that the primary goal of early U.S. nation-building efforts was, in most cases, strategic. In its first efforts, Washington decided to replace or support a regime in a foreign land to defend its core security and economic interests, not to build a democracy. Only later did America's political ideals and its need to sustain domestic support for nation-building impel it to try to establish democratic rule in target nations.

The deployment of large numbers of U.S. ground troops is the second criterion of nation-building. As the case of Guatemala in 1954 demonstrates, a regime change may occasionally be accomplished without the deployment of U.S. ground forces. But nation-building generally requires the long-term commitment of ground forces, which are used either to depose the regime targeted by the United States or to maintain a regime that it favors. In many cases, U.S. ground troops are needed not only to fight hostile forces in target countries, but also to perform essential administrative functions, such as establishing law and order.

The use of American military and civilian personnel in the political administration of target countries is the third and quintessential criterion of nation-building. As a result of its deep involvement in the political processes of target countries, the United States exercises decisive influence in the selection of leaders to head the new regimes. Washington also restructures the key political institutions of a target country (e.g., rewriting the constitution and basic laws) and participates in the nation's routine administrative activities (e.g., public finance, the delivery of social services).

On the basis of these three criteria, we characterize 17 of more than 200 American military interventions since 1900, roughly 8 percent, as attempts at nation-building through the promotion or imposition of democratic institutions desired by American policymakers.

The most striking aspect of the American record on nation-building is its mixed legacy in establishing democratic regimes. Of the 17 target countries listed in the table 3.1, 2 (Iraq and Afghanistan) are ongoing projects. Two were unambiguous successes, Japan and West Germany, both of which were defeated Axis powers in World War II. Two other target countries, Grenada and Panama, may also be considered successes. However, Grenada is a tiny island nation with 100,000 inhabitants, and Panama's population is less than three million. Nation-building generally is less challenging in small societies. Conversely, American nation-building efforts failed to establish and sustain democracies in the other 11 cases (excluding Afghanistan and Iraq). Three years after the withdrawal of U.S. forces, democracy was considered to be functioning in only 5 of the 11 cases; 10 years after

Table 3.1 Nation-Building Efforts Led by the United States since 1900

Target country	Population	Period	Duration (years)	Multilateral or unilateral?	Type of interim administration	Democracy after 10 years?
Iraq	24 million	2003–present	1+	Unilateral	American for one year; surrogate regime afterward	?
Afghanistan	26.8 million	2001–present	2+	Multilateral	UN administration	?
Haiti	7.0 million	1994–96	2	Multilateral	Local administration	No
Panama	2.3 million	1989	<1	Unilateral	Local administration	Yes
Grenada	92,000	1983	<1	Unilateral	Local administration	Yes
Cambodia	7 million	1970–73	3	Unilateral	U.S. surrogate regime	No
South Vietnam	19 million	1964–73	9	Unilateral	U.S. surrogate regime	No
Dominican Republic	3.8 million	1965–66	1	Unilateral	U.S. surrogate regime	No
Japan	72 million	1945–52	7	Multilateral-unilateral[a]	U.S. direct administration	Yes
West Germany	46 million	1945–49	4	Multilateral	Multilateral administration	Yes
Dominican Republic	895,000	1916–24	8	Unilateral	U.S. direct administration	No
Cuba	2.8 million	1917–22	5	Unilateral	U.S. surrogate regime	No
Haiti	2 million	1915–34	19	Unilateral	U.S. surrogate regime	No
Nicaragua	620,000	1909–33	18	Unilateral	U.S. surrogate regime	No
Cuba	2 million	1906–1909	3	Unilateral	U.S. direct administration	No
Panama	450,000	1903–36	33	Unilateral	U.S. surrogate regime	No
Cuba	1.6 million	1898–1902	3	Unilateral	U.S. direct administration	No

[a] The United States won World War II as part of the Allied victory over Japan but assumed exclusive occupation authority in Japan after the war.

the departure of U.S. forces, democracy had been sustained in only four. We judge a regime to be democratic or authoritarian on the basis of a widely used index provided by the Polity IV dataset. In that ranking, a fully democratic regime gets a score of 10, whereas a fully authoritarian regime is assigned minus-10. In our analysis, regimes scoring three or below (for example, today's Iran receives a three) are considered non-democratic. If we apply this yardstick, the United States' overall success rate in democratic nation-building is about 26 percent (4 out of 15 cases, excluding Iraq and Afghanistan).

The failure to sustain a democratic regime in a target nation can produce disastrous consequences for its citizens. In Cuba, Haiti, and Nicaragua, for example, brutal dictatorships emerged from the wreckage of botched nation-building efforts. These societies remained mired in misrule and widespread poverty. In Cambodia, a genocidal regime gained power after the departure of U.S. troops, and perpetrated one of the worst crimes against humanity in history. The U.S. defeat in Vietnam ushered in a communist regime that forced millions to flee their native land. Of the 17 cases of U.S. nation-building, 13 were pursued unilaterally. Two (Afghanistan and Haiti) were authorized by the United Nations. In these two difficult undertakings, U.N. resolutions provided the United States not only with helpful allies, but also with international legitimacy. One case, the rebuilding of West Germany, was undertaken after the Allied victory in World War II, whereas the U.S. occupation of Japan was multilateral in form but unilateral on the ground. American unilateralism in nation-building has been made possible by the preponderance of U.S. power. Except when taking on powerful states, such as Germany and Japan, the United States has faced few external constraints in imposing its will on other societies.

However, since the end of the Cold War, the United States has displayed a greater degree of willingness to assemble multilateral support for humanitarian interventions and for rebuilding failed states. In the case of Haiti in 1994, President Clinton obtained authorization from the U.N. Security Council. The ensuing nation-building efforts in Haiti, although ultimately unsuccessful, were supervised by the United Nations. Another case is the ongoing nation-building project in Afghanistan. Even though American military intervention was decisive in toppling the Taliban regime, the Bush administration ceded to the United Nations the primary responsibility for rebuilding the country. In Bosnia and Kosovo, two cases of multilateral humanitarian intervention (not regime change), postconflict nation-building is also being carried out under the auspices of the United Nations.

To probe the underlying causes and dynamics that contribute to the failure of nation-building by the United States, we examine three important cases: Haiti, Panama, and Japan. Our review of the American experience in these cases focuses on the two dimensions of nation-building—sustaining political support at home on the one hand, and executing a careful plan in targeted nations abroad on the other.

Requisites of Successful Nation-Building

Sustaining Political Support at Home

Despite the unique social, economic, and political context of each U.S. nation-building exercise, certain types of challenges that American policymakers face are almost universally encountered. Domestic political opposition will almost always seek to constrain troop levels, hasten the termination of occupation, and limit appropriations of development assistance to target countries. Domestic opposition may initially seek to prevent intervention, as was the case of Haiti, or may initially support intervention, as in the case of Japan. In either case, necessary investments in troops and cash following intervention become politically contentious. Although geostrategic interests often motivate interventions, the occupation mandate may expand to include liberal democratic goals to consolidate domestic political support. Mark Peceny shows that in cases of U.S. military intervention abroad, presidents tend to initially act out of national security concerns, but subsequently change their approach as a result of congressional pressure for "pro-liberalization," including support for free elections and deposing dictators. Thus, the promotion of democracy is used to legitimate the use of military force.[3] Given the inevitability of domestic constraints on troops, time, and money, the ability of the United States to maintain its commitment to the nation-building cause—historically, a category in which the United States has been weak—is a key variable in the success or failure of such endeavors.

Getting the Priorities Right in Planning

The reality that democratization is rarely the primary motivating factor for intervention is reflected in the fact that prior to the arrival of American troops, military planning is always prioritized over reconstruction planning. Although thorough military planning is certainly a requirement for successful civil reconstruction, the latter is equally important for successful nation-building. Ironically, it may be true that the more effective the military planning is, the more challenging civil reconstruction becomes, as suggested by James Dobbins and his colleagues.[4] The inevitable fact that military planning takes precedence underlines the outstandingly complex nature of planning nation-building. In addition, interagency co-ordination and balance between pre-intervention preparation and post-intervention flexibility have not been strengths of the United States in its nation-building experiences.

Overcoming Local Political Resistance

The rise of politicians and constituencies opposed to American occu-pation in the target country is inevitable. In many cases, the legitimacy of local politicians depends on their ability to demonstrate a compelling de-gree of independence in opposing American policies. To be sure, there is a trade-off between the short-term benefits derived by politicians who resist United States–backed policies and the long-term benefits that such policies may offer to their societies. But many politicians are tempted to seize these short-term advantages, even at the cost of their countries' long-term pros-pects. To the extent that the introduction of a democratic process opens channels of participation for various groups, political opposition to the United States in target countries is unavoidable. In some cases, the United States may have to acquiesce to some local demands to bolster the legiti-macy of the local political system while maintaining enough leverage to manipulate target country politicians on important reconstruction issues. Historically, the United States has a mixed record in managing the un-avoidable challenges of local political resistance.

Haiti, 1994–2004: A Case of Complete Failure

On September 19, 1994, an American-led multinational military force (MNF) of 23,000 troops occupied Haiti to reinstate Jean-Bertrand Aristide as president. Ten years later, on February 29, 2004, the United States en-couraged Aristide to resign and flee a rebellion organized by ex-police and military officers.[5] In many regards, Haiti's reconstruction fits the textbook version of what nation-building ought to be. The deployment of over-whelming military force quelled any thought of resistance from enemies of the displaced President Aristide. Multinational and interagency coordi-nation of economic reconstruction disbursed massive amounts of devel-opment assistance, negotiated debt forgiveness, and achieved currency stabilization. Nevertheless, a decade after American forces landed in Haiti, few would dispute that the American-led international nation-building effort was a complete failure.

The U.S. experience in Haiti demonstrates the pitfalls of inadequate commitment and of failing to balance local legitimacy with the retention of coercive authority. The failure of the American-led MNF and the U.N.

Mission in Haiti (UNMIH) to prevent electoral irregularities and to demand a semblance of political order stemmed from a quick repatriation of the bulk of American troops and, subsequently, a lack of coercive power. Eventually, the Haitian ruling elites' intransigence and the resulting electoral malfeasance made it pointless for external powers to continue their nation-building efforts.

Inadequate Military Commitment

The American-led MNF invaded in September 1994, but by November 1994, MNF troops numbered about half of the original invading force. Authority was officially transferred from the MNF to the UNMIH only 6 months after the intervention. The UNMIH was composed of about 6,000 military personnel, including 2,400 American troops.[6] The strict timeline for withdrawal of American forces is largely attributable to the contentious debate regarding the Haitian intervention within the United States. The American public was divided on the mission. A *New York Times* December 1994 poll indicated that more than 50 percent of American respondents thought the United States should have stayed out of Haiti.[7] Opinions in Congress reflected these public sentiments, with the Republican majority staunchly in opposition and the Congressional Black Caucus strongly in favor of the intervention.

Had the administration mustered the political courage to stay the course despite Congressional opposition, stability in Haiti might not have deteriorated. But the Clinton administration's decision to transfer authority to the UNMIH after only six months of occupation reflected a lack of political will. The diminished level of American military commitment directly detracted from the ability of the United States to curb violence and electoral irregularities, and indirectly limited its political leverage among Haitian leaders.

The political cycle of coups, fraudulent elections, and violence doomed the creation of a viable democratic government in Haiti, where there is a "time-honored tactic of losers who seek to discredit the [political] process itself and delegitimize the winners rather than form a loyal opposition."[8] Even the first election following the reinstatement of Aristide as president proved controversial. Irregularities in the June 1995 legislative and local elections, including incidents of violence, prompted opponents of Aristide's Lavalas party to reject the election results, which showed a sweep by Lavalas. Within months of the election, opposition parties withdrew their candidates from the Lavalas-controlled government to protest the lack of resolution concerning the electoral dispute. Following the election, Lavalas itself became divided over the question of whether Aristide should remain president for another three years to make up for his time in exile. Eventually Aristide, at the urging of Washington and some members of his own party, ended his term and supported the candidacy of Rene Preval, who easily prevailed in the December 1995 presidential election.

However, Haiti's political process began to unravel quickly. The legislative elections in April 1997 were boycotted by opposition parties, and less than 5 percent of the population voted. The Organization of American States (OAS) denounced the electoral irregularities. Subsequently, more than a year of conflict between the legislature and Preval ensued, culminating in Preval's decision in January 1999 not to recognize the legislature and to install a new government by presidential decree. Legislative elections did not take place until May 2000, and the OAS and the United Nations both supported the opposition parties' accusations that the results were inaccurate. In September 2000, Preval announced that presidential elections would be held in November, but some of the opposition immediately announced a boycott. In November 2000, Aristide was elected to the presidency by a majority of the 30 to 60 percent (estimates by the Haitian government and the Caribbean Community and Common Market differed) of the population that voted. Protest and violence spurred by opposition parties and Aristide supporters ensued, leading to two alleged coup attempts in 2001. In February 2004, Guy Philippe's force of a few hundred ex-soldiers and police entered Port-au-Prince and successfully deposed President Aristide.

Extending the commitment of the American military could have improved the security environment in Haiti and facilitated the political transition. Authority was officially transferred from the United States–led MNF to the UNMIH within months of the intervention. The UNMIH, however, abided by more restrictive rules of engagement prescribed by the U.N. Charter. Unlike the MNF, the UNMIH permanently placed units in the countryside as well as in the major cities.[9] The coincidence of the transfer of authority to the UNMIH and the rise in civil unrest suggests that the exit of the bulk of American troops might have been responsible for the deteriorating level of security. Further violence and intimidation during the June 1995 elections, which caused opposition parties to boycott the electoral process, underscored the rising instability under the UNMIH's circumscribed mandate.

Although rebuilding a domestic security force was essential to stability, the MNF considered police work outside of its mandate, and thus played a largely secondary role in the creation of an Interim Police Security Force (IPSF), which evolved into the Haitian National Police. The force was composed of former military leaders with clean records, Haitians from abroad, and refugees who had been intercepted by the U.S. Coast Guard and temporarily located at the Guantanamo Bay military base. The candidates were selected by the Aristide government and the U.S. Department of State based on literacy tests and interviews. By December 1994, 2,900 graduates of the introductory training course had joined the IPSF. IPSF recruits were monitored by international police monitors under the direction of the former police commissioner of New York. In addition, the International Organization for Migration administered a reintegration program for ex-soldiers, and the Department of Justice's International Criminal Investigative Training Assistance Program trained Haitian judges and lawyers.[10]

Faltering Reconstruction Efforts

Haiti's economic reconstruction was a major objective of the occupation. At the time of the intervention, the country was suffering from the debilitating economic embargo imposed by the OAS and the United Nations, with per capita income falling from $390 to $240 over the 3 years of military rule, and the loss of tens of thousands of light manufacturing jobs rendering around 70 percent of the population unemployed.[11] In the face of such economic catastrophe, the Aristide government-in-exile presented the international community with an emergency economic plan in August 1994.

Prior to the American intervention, the U.S. Agency for International Development (USAID) analyzed the Haitian economic situation and coordinated international donor institutions in anticipation of a major aid effort. Weeks after the MNF landed in Haiti, the United States set up the Economic Recovery Steering Group for Haiti as a coordinating mechanism for the economic rebuilding effort. Additionally, the U.S. Treasury facilitated the forgiveness or refinancing of Haiti's $81 million debt, which provided the necessary conditions for the International Monetary Fund to release $260 million of aid suspended since the 1991 coup.[12] In January 1995, international donors meeting in Paris pledged an initial contribution of $1.2 billion, of which the United States provided approximately $235 million.[13] But the infusion of external funding had minimal impact on reconstruction.

Although Aristide's economic policy would nominally privatize many state-owned industries, liberalize trade, and tighten the budget, Aristide and his supporters were some of the greatest impediments to economic reform. The political power and economic rents that Aristide and his supporters enjoyed through the control of state-owned enterprises proved too compelling. Resisting heavy pressure from the international community, Aristide and his successor, Preval, undermined a reform package that could have attracted foreign investments and improved the efficiency of the Haitian economy.

Greater coordination of the economic reconstruction efforts would have improved the nation-building effort in Haiti. The Economic Steering Group for Haiti, which served as an interagency facilitator of the economic reconstruction, was not established until weeks after Aristide was reinstalled as president. According to its chairman, David Rothkopf, the group enjoyed little support from participating agencies and could not influence budget decisions.[14] As Rothkopf suggests, the American economic reconstruction effort would have benefited by vesting greater authority in the interagency group and by creating economic tools to make low-interest capital available to private enterprises looking to invest in Haiti.[15] In general, the U.S. government lacked appropriate means of financing and facilitating development of foreign investment and trade with Haiti. Rigid institutional regulations impeded rapid response to an economic situation with which U.S. government agencies were not accustomed to working. The Overseas Private Investment Corporation (OPIC) was restricted from financing and insuring projects in certain sectors of industry, for fear of violating regulations that prevented OPIC from accepting projects that might cause the export of American jobs. Despite the formation of a joint Business Development Council and of a Presidential Business Mission to encourage foreign investment in Haiti, regulations restricted the Export-Import Bank from participating in the reconstruction efforts because of Haiti's low credit rating.[16] Finally, the Haitian government's lack of capacity created a situation in which nongovernmental organizations (NGOs) were responsible for administering most aid funds. Coordinating NGO administration of projects and U.S. short-term policy interests proved simply too challenging to all concerned.

Panama: A Mixed Success Story

The United States invaded Panama on December 19, 1989, to overthrow the military dictatorship of Manuel Noriega.[17] The military operations were decisive and quick: within two months of the invasion, United States–based invasion forces had been withdrawn from Panama. The invasion was followed by "Operation Promote Liberty," which aimed at economic reconstruction and the restoration of democracy. Washington's nation-building effort in Panama this time was ultimately successful because, 14 years after the invasion, Panama remains a democracy. Yet Panama's successful transition to democracy does not immediately qualify it as a positive model.

Rather, studying the invasion reveals numerous pitfalls in the complex task of nation-building.

Although power was almost immediately transferred to a government that had been popularly elected previously by the Panamanian population, the real seat of authority rested with the U.S. government. On the eve of the invasion, Guillermo Endara, Ricardo Arias Calderon, and Guillermo Ford, winners of the May 1989 presidential election annulled by Noriega, were declared president and vice presidents, respectively, by the American authorities at a private swearing-in ceremony.[18] On December 27, 1989, Panama's electoral tribunal invalidated the Noriega regime's annulment of the May 1989 election and confirmed the victory of the "big three." The instatement of the Endara government nominally made Panama an independent country with a democratically elected government. The reality, however, was quite different.

The United States had underestimated the degree to which Panama was unequipped for self-government. It was also unprepared for the political vacuum created by Noriega's ouster.[19] The American embassy had to assist the new administration with everything, ranging from administrative capacity to reaching important governmental decisions.[20] American advisors initially occupied the same building as the provisional government, and later moved to a building next door, from which they continued to provide support and advice. The United States was intimately involved in rebuilding the Panamanian government's institutions.

Prioritization of Military Operations over Reconstruction Efforts

The United States' pre-occupation planners failed to articulate detailed end goals prior to embarking on the nation-building enterprise in Panama. The declared goal—establishing democracy—was a great tool for generating American public support for intervention, but the very vagueness of the term complicates the exercise. In Panama, President George H. W. Bush's administration failed to provide adequate details about how it actually intended to achieve its goal. Nowhere was the desired end-state of democracy clearly defined.[21] This ambiguity had disastrous consequences for pre-intervention reconstruction planning. President Endara observed that the United States "didn't have a specific plan to help us in establishing democracy."[22] The United States was unclear on the level of democracy to be established, the amount of time it would take, the major obstacles to be expected, and the strategies to be used to overcome them. American planners had not anticipated the extent of the power void left by the ouster of the Panamanian Defense Force, nor had they bothered to specify who should rule after the invasion.[23]

This failure to strategically define and operationalize democracy-building underscores a recurring tendency in American nation-building efforts to focus far more on military operations than on postconflict reconstruction in the pre-intervention planning processes. Prior to the invasion of Panama, the military section of the plan ("Operation Just Cause") was repeatedly fine-tuned and revised. Although Washington had drafted a plan for the civil reconstruction phase ("Operation Promote Liberty"), it was not updated or improved as regularly. Key military leaders responsible for the Panama intervention did not pay adequate attention to the planning for "Operation Promote Liberty." General Maxwell R. Thurman, commander for the U.S. Southern Command, noted that "the least of my problems at the time was Blind Logic [as the civil restoration plan was previously named]. . . . We put together the campaign plan for Just Cause and probably did not spend enough time on the restoration."[24]

Flawed Planning

Part of the reason postconflict reconstruction was so easily sidelined may be attributed to the bifurcation of the policy planning process. The military operation and the civil restoration strategies were treated as distinct plans independent of each other. The high level of compartmentalization of planning, whereby individuals working on different aspects of reconstruction and invasion were not permitted to collaborate, further prevented effective planning and cooperation.[25] The marginalization of the postconflict reconstruction was also reflected in interagency dynamics. The State Department, USAID, the Justice Department, and the American Embassy in Panama were not allowed adequate access to the pre-intervention planning and were, therefore, unable to make real contributions. Because the embassy was brought into the planning process at a late stage, its local knowledge and civilian expertise were not utilized. Reconstruction efforts in Panama "lacked integrated and interagency political, economic, social, informational, and military policies and strategies to support short-term conflict resolution and longer term stability and development."[26]

The resulting ineptitude of U.S. reconstruction and contingency planning was evident on at least three fronts. First, rampant looting caused approximately $750 million in damage within the first 10 days following the invasion, and ultimately totaled $1–2 billion in Panama City and other metropolitan areas.[27] Second, the new Panamanian government was a "hollow force" installed by American decree and was plagued by endemic corruption and the intransigence of military officers, many of whom remained loyal to the Noriega regime. Third, Panama's economy had virtually collapsed, with the treasury nearly empty and unemployment greater than 35 percent.[28] These conditions made the original plans irrelevant and necessitated poor ad hoc solutions. President George H. W. Bush had promised more than $1 billion in reconstruction aid. But the Senate, after long delays, approved only $420 million, and by 1991, only slightly more than $100 million had been delivered. The failure of the United States to commit promised economic resources offers a vivid example of the inevitable constraints of domestic opposition to or lack of enthusiasm for nation-building projects abroad.[29]

Perceived Illegitimacy

Inevitably, political circumstances within Panama facilitated the rise of an anti-occupation movement that demanded greater sovereignty. The failure of the United States to appease this anti-American sentiment forced President Endara to distance himself from the occupation forces and aggressively assert Panama's identity as a sovereign state. Encouraged by Latin American countries to adopt greater independence, the Endara administration refused to sign an American-proposed Mutual Legal Assistance Treaty (MLAT), which required key changes in banking regulations and the disclosure of bank records to American investigators. The inability of the United States to balance Panamanian politicians' needs for greater legitimacy and reconstruction policies, such as the MLAT, proved disastrous to the Endara government. On December 5, 1990, the Endara government had to rely on American military assistance to crush a rebellion led by Eduardo Herrera Hasan, the former commander of the Panamanian Public Force (the police force that the United States and the Endara government had established after disbanding Noriega's defense forces). The coup attempt reflected growing public discontent with Endara, who was increasingly perceived as an American lackey. The failure of the Public Force to heed Endara's calls to quell the rebellion revealed the impotence of the new government. Panamanian forces watched on the sidelines as five hundred American troops surrounded the Public Force headquarters seized by Herrera and regained control over headquarters.[30] The attempted coup exposed the frailty of the newly established democratic institutions and damaged Panamanian national pride.

In the wake of the attempted coup, the Endara regime moderated its talk of independence. By April 1991, it acceded to the MLAT, aggravating already aggrieved Panamanian nationalist sensibilities.[31] Subsequently, the Endara government began to accept American edicts blindly, and lost credibility with its own people. A year after the invasion, the Endara regime was widely regarded as lacking legitimacy.[32] Although the Endara government completed its full term in office, nationalist groups soon garnered popular support. In May 1994, Noriega's nationalist Democratic Revolutionary Party won the elections. Although American intervention in the coup attempt rescued the floundering democracy, the United States continued to press for politically contentious reconstruction reforms. Washington's insensitivity to the Endara administration's needs for legitimacy resulted in the ascent of less friendly political forces, albeit through democratic elections. In the end, in spite of the United States' inadequate plans for civil reconstruction, its inability to balance local political and reconstruction needs, and its failure to deliver on economic aid pledges, Panama clumsily fulfilled Washington's stated goal of democratization.

Japan: A Model of Success

Crafting a workable plan for postwar Japan got off to a rocky start. Postwar planning largely took place in Washington, and was divided along ideological lines. The planning can be traced as far back as the establishment of the Advisory Committee on Postwar Foreign Policy under the secretary of state in February 1942, immediately after the outbreak of the war with Japan.[33] Many of the State Department's old Japan hands, including the pre-war ambassador to Japan, Joseph Grew, saw the problem of Japanese governance as rooted in the country's imperial history and cultural identity. Consequently, in early 1945, American policymakers planned to induce democratic revolution in the defeated nation, even though some of the old Japan hands who still controlled postsurrender planning anticipated mild reforms.[34] In August, less than a month before the Japanese formally surrendered, Assistant Secretary of State Dean Acheson's symbolic replacement of Grew as undersecretary of state reflected the triumph of liberal democratic ideals over the conservative "Japan Crowd."[35] Subsequent planning documents reflected the greater degree of priority granted to democratization.

As reflected in these documents, the U.S. strategy prioritized the democratization of Japan through re-education, the dissolution of trusts called *zaibatsu*, land redistribution, and demilitarization.[36] Notably, economic reconstruction was only prescribed as a means of preventing economic crisis and chaos. This economic approach changed radically in response to unexpected geostrategic developments precipitated by the Cold War.[37] The plan to utilize the Japanese bureaucracy reflected the realization that the United States did not have the linguistic or technical capacity to replace an entire national bureaucracy. This last-minute planning change reflected the realism of pre-surrender planners. Additionally, the controversial policy of retaining Emperor Hirohito in spite of his complicity in war atrocities demonstrated flexibility on the part of the American planners. The Supreme Command of the Allied Powers (SCAP) skillfully exploited the emperor's symbolic authority throughout the occupation to gain Japanese public trust. Although SCAP was run like a military hierarchy, it was able to integrate military and civil personnel and objectives, thus setting a sharp contrast to the poor interagency cooperation that characterized the American interventions in Haiti and Panama.

Balancing Legitimate Democracy and Reconstruction Realities

The absence of politically motivated violence under American occupation is anomalous in the history of nation-building. The extraordinary casualties suffered by Japan, the formal unconditional surrender, and the plummeting standard of living certainly contributed to the passivity of the Japanese population.[38] The well-formulated pre-surrender plans also helped to maintain stability. However, the occupation authority's political acumen was a hidden asset. In rationing freedoms through the Japanese bureaucracy, SCAP managed to legitimize democratic institutions without relinquishing authority over Japan's social revolution. This "revolution from above" reflected both sensitivity to the Japanese political process and resistance to impediments to reconstruction. To build a new, liberal political order, the United States pursued a policy of complete demilitarization, only allowing for the establishment of the Police Reserve, which later evolved into the Self-Defense Forces. Demilitarization included the destruction of military equipment, the Imperial fleet, and some military-industrial complexes. Extralegal "patriotic societies" that functioned as gangs were outlawed, and the secret police were abolished. The demilitarization required vast numbers of troops, and the initial occupation force numbered about 250,000, with 52 local military-government teams stationed in the 46 prefectures.[39] Although troop deployment was lower per capita in Japan than in other nation-building efforts, the gross number of American personnel deployed clearly demonstrated the United States' commitment.[40] American, Australian, and British forces searched extensively for arms stockpiles, collecting and destroying everything from poison gas and explosives to revolvers and swords.[41] In addition to purging the country of the materials of war, SCAP pacified the country through the trial and purge of war criminals.

SCAP's approach to the prosecution of war criminals was legally and morally inconsistent, but nonetheless, successful in avoiding political turmoil and arousing resistance. Many of the conservative politicians and bureaucrats behind Japanese militancy were spared, and the emperor was protected. Of the roughly 200,000 individuals who were purged, approximately 80 percent were from the military.[42] But this moral inconsistency proved useful in co-opting Japanese politicians. The threat of purge may have been more useful than the actual purge itself. The Shidehara government allegedly accepted the new SCAP-authored constitution under the threat of prosecution.[43] Similar blackmail techniques were used to pacify elements of the Japanese military leadership that could have organized violent resistance to the occupation. Ironically, this authoritarian tendency on the part of SCAP contributed to the political stability necessary for alternative democratic measures.

Initial efforts to expand civil liberties brought leftist movements out from underground and facilitated the institutionalization of democracy. In October 1945, SCAP issued a civil-liberties directive legalizing political parties and assuring freedom of speech and assembly, although criticism of the occupation was not permitted. The first postwar election in April 1946 was also the first in which women were permitted to vote, a condition later enshrined in the new constitution. The diversity of the 2,770 candidates from 363 parties in that election reflected the extent to which democratic organization had been liberated.[44] However, neophyte leftist parties lacked finances and organization, and conservative Progressive and Liberal parties managed to win a majority of the Diet seats.[45] Again, ironically, SCAP's implementation of land redistribution created a solid electoral base for the conservative parties.

However, SCAP was not unconditionally in support of all things democratic. The occupation authority employed thousands of censors in the Civil Censorship Detachment who scrutinized tens of thousands of publications a month. Rights of free speech did not include the freedom to criticize the occupation. American criminals were not subject to the jurisdiction of Japanese courts. A radio broadcast monopoly was enforced until 1951. Although reforms redistributing land from large landlords to small farmers was highly successful (with nearly one-third of all land changing hands by the end of the occupation), the dismantling of the *zaibatsu* industrial conglomerates was not as widespread as initially intended. Most conspicuously, the new Japanese constitution, for all its democratic virtues, was virtually stuffed down the throat of the Japanese Diet.

The absence of violent political dissent disguised the deep social fissures of postwar Japan. The vast majority of Japanese supported the American occupation. Even when laborers organized strikes, they were largely targeted at the Japanese bureaucracy, not SCAP. Nevertheless, SCAP constantly disappointed some Japanese constituencies. The resignation of the prime minister's cabinet in protesting the freeing of leftist political dissidents exemplifies such a disappointment. Labor unrest following the American "reverse course" on labor policy is a similar example from the polar opposite constituency. Land reform, military purges, industrial decentralization, and other reform efforts marginalized some groups, and the gloss with which history paints such reforms should not misconstrue the reality that the Japanese political process was highly contentious.

For all the effort expended by SCAP in choreographing Japan's revolution from above, economic instability threatened to undercut social and political achievements. Economic reconstruction of Japan was explicitly not included in pre-occupation planning priorities. Consistent with the demilitarization plans, the United States initially intended to transfer Japan's surplus manufacturing to neighboring countries as reparation.[46] However, massive inflation, an expansive black market, and commodity shortages quickly made American policymakers understand the importance of Japan's economic stabilization. By June of 1948, the U.S. National Security Council suggested that the economic recovery of Japan be the prime objective of American policy in Japan. Between 1945 and 1949, American aid totaled $1.53 billion, approximately 60–70 percent of Japanese imports. By the end of 1948, however, the U.S. National Advisory Council on International Monetary Affairs (in charge of all foreign aid budgets following the Marshall Plan) cancelled aid to Japan for 1950, judging that without economic stability, aid would be wasted. Subsequently, President Truman appointed a banker, Joseph Dodge, as financial advisor to SCAP. Dodge advocated a number of economic austerity measures that proved politically unpopular in Japan, but he stayed course, fighting inflation by controlling wages and prices, cutting subsidies, and tightening credit. Setting an appropriately low exchange rate also provided one of the necessary conditions for promoting Japanese exports, which were deemed the lynchpin of the Japanese economic recovery.[47] The failure to incorporate aggressive economic policy in the reconstruction plan may have constituted the largest shortcoming of the pre-occupation plan. The versatility demonstrated by Washington and SCAP bureaucrats through their reformulation of economic policy reflected the flexibility and open-mindedness of the nation-building effort. Pre-occupation plans proved a solid foundation, but did not guarantee a flawless evolution of American policy. In the face of the emerging Cold War, such flexibility was invaluable.

Out of concern for losing Japan to the Soviet Union, the United States hastened plans for peace and security treaties with Japan. The Chinese intervention in the Korean War only bolstered arguments within Washington's policy community that Japan should rearm. Rearmament was a divisive issue in Japan for a number of reasons. Many Japanese feared the possibility of a return of militarism and regression of democracy. Others argued that Japan simply did not have the economic capacity to rearm. Finally, Article 9 of the constitution complicated the legality of rearmament.[48] The San Francisco Peace Treaty and the Japan-U.S. Security Treaty, both signed in 1951, officially returned sovereignty to Japan with Japan's promise to rearm in the future. In stark contrast to the United States' pre-occupation commitment to democratize and demilitarize Japan with little concern for the economy, the treaties committed the United States to Japan's security and economic prosperity. Although its character changed radically over the course of the occupation, the U.S. commitment to building Japanese nation proved durable.

Principles of Nation-Building

The Haiti, Panama, and Japan nation-building efforts arose under different U.S. administrations. They had different causes and took starkly distinct forms. The lessons of the specific successes and failures of each case coalesce around three general principles that should guide future nation-building efforts. First, the United States must sustain its commitments of troops, time, and money despite domestic political opposition. Second, the United States should balance the demands for greater legitimacy by political opposition in the target country with reconstruction needs. Third, the United States ought to develop civil reconstruction plans despite the priority given to military operations. These general principles further suggest specific policy recommendations that we discuss here.

Maintaining Commitment

Even in Japan, where the American commitment to reconstruction was the strongest, Congress did not relent from curtailing aid expenditures when it felt that the money was not spent effectively. Such an opposition is an inescapable reality in a democratic society. But the need for large commitments of troops, time, and money to successfully build nations is no less a reality. This tension shows that American administrations should only pursue nation-building if they have the will and the political skills to maintain Congressional support. It is also imperative that no administration should inflate the political expectations of its efforts, for example, by attaching extraneous but dubious importance to its military undertakings. Short commitments of U.S. troops and money may result in prolonged postconflict instability and, most importantly, constrain U.S. leverage over local politics and reconstruction policy. The short timeline for the MNF's withdrawal from Haiti required Washington to limit its disarmament and policing mandate. Subsequently, Haitian society retained the capacity for substantial violence. Paramilitaries reemerged at the hands of politicians who could not be kept in check by a foreign force determined to leave quickly. Additionally, the short duration of the U.S. military commitment enfeebled international efforts to jumpstart Haiti's much needed economic liberalization, as local politicians had little personal incentive to acquiesce to foreign demands. Conversely, in Panama, the Endara administration's reliance on American development assistance and, most importantly, military protection provided the United States with the leverage necessary to pass the MLAT despite massive local political opposition. Greater commitment translates into greater leverage and increased capacity to implement reconstruction policies.

Balancing Political Legitimacy and Reconstruction Effectiveness

The process of nation-building is necessarily political, and not merely a technical endeavor. Therefore, U.S. occupation authorities must strike a balance between the competing needs for technically effective measures of reconstruction and the legitimacy of the target country's leadership. Technical reconstruction and local political legitimacy frequently occupy opposite ends of a scale. Thus, sacrifices on one end may yield benefits on the other. The occupational authorities in Japan were masterful at the art of balancing local technical and political needs. This, unfortunately, was not the case in either Haiti or Panama. The balance between legitimacy and reconstruction may not accord well with the notion of full sovereignty for targeted nations. Implicit in this argument is the suggestion that the full sovereignty of target countries must be curtailed. In some cases, even civil liberties and local politicians' power will have to be limited. It also implies that original reconstruction policies, however important, may have to be sacrificed for political needs.

Planning Reconstruction

From the perspective of pre-occupation planning, the ability to see nation-building holistically as both a military and civil operation is imperative. The success in Japan and the near-disaster in Panama both demonstrate this point. Within months of the U.S. entry into World War II, President Franklin Roosevelt had already established the Advisory Committee on Postwar Foreign Policy, planting the seed of what eventually became a massive and successful planning effort. In Panama, occupation goals were nebulous, and pre-intervention planning was highly fragmented among diverse agencies. The government body most in touch with the local Panamanian conditions, the American Embassy in Panama, was restricted from the planning process. Subsequently, massive looting and general civil unrest set reconstruction efforts back billions of dollars. All of these observations suggest that policy planning needs to articulate specific goals and, at the same time, provide for flexible implementation and policy reformulation. In the Haitian case, failure to plan around the restrictive regulations governing OPIC and the Export-Import Bank frustrated economic reconstruction efforts. In contrast, plans for Japan specifically prioritized demilitarization and democratization over economic reconstruction. The sophisticated interagency mechanism that pre-occupation planning exercises had fostered in the Japanese case, nevertheless, facilitated the revision of the initial plans to limit communist organization, redevelop the economy, and rearm the Japanese.

Ultimately, however, the United States will have a greater probability of success if its broad geopolitical interests dovetail with those of *both* the elites and the people in the target nation. In this particular regard, three conditions must be met. First, the commitment of the outside power (i.e., the United States) must be sustained by a compelling strategic interest. In the case of Japan, American resolve was bolstered by the need to contain the Soviet Union during the Cold War. Second, this strategic interest should be broadly aligned with the national interests of the target country. In the case of Japan, American and Japanese national interests were basically aligned during the early stages of the Cold War. This was not, however, the case in either Haiti or Panama. Third, there should also be a consensus on such shared strategic interests within the society of the target nation. In the case of Japan, the majority of the public in Japan agreed with their leaders' policy of allying with the United States to resist the spread of communism. Popular acceptance of nation-building by outsiders becomes unsustainable if the local population perceives the occupying foreign power as advancing its own interests or the interests of domestic ruling elites at the expense of theirs.

Notes

1. Part of the material in this section draws from Minxin Pei and Sara Kasper, "Lessons from the Past: The American Record on Nation-Building," Carnegie Policy Brief no. 24, 2003.
2. The criteria used in this chapter are different from those adopted by James Dobbins, Keith Crane, Seth Jones, et al., *America's Role in Nation-Building: From Germany to Iraq* (Santa Monica, Calif.: RAND, 2003). The authors applied a more expansive definition of nation-building and consequently included Somalia and Bosnia in their case studies. In our judgment, Somalia and Bosnia were quintessential humanitarian missions, not nation-building efforts.
3. Mark Peceny, *Democracy at the Point of Bayonets* (University Park: Pennsylvania State University Press, 1999).
4. Dobbins et al., *America's Role in Nation-Building*.
5. Joseph Contreras, "The Ghosts of War," *Newsweek*, March 8, 2004, 30.

6. Marcos Mendiburu and Sarah Meek, *Managing Arms in Peace Processes: Haiti* (New York: United Nations, 1996), 15–16.
7. News Surveys, *New York Times,* December 9, 1994.
8. James R. Morrell, Rachel Neild, and Hugh Byrne, "Haiti and the Limits to Nation-Building," *Current History* 98 (March 1999): 132.
9. Mendiburu and Meek, *Managing Arms in Peace Processes: Haiti,* 30.
10. Ibid., 21–23.
11. Anthony T. Bryan, "Haiti: Kick Starting the Economy," *Current History* 94 (March 1995): 66; David J. Rothkopf, *The Price of Peace: Emergency Economic Intervention and U.S. Foreign Policy* (Washington, D.C.: Carnegie Endowment for International Peace, 1998), 14.
12. Bryan, "Haiti: Kick Starting the Economy," 68.
13. Rothkopf, *The Price of Peace,* 17–18.
14. Ibid., 30.
15. Ibid., 13.
16. Ibid., 32.
17. George H. W. Bush, "A Transcript of Bush's Address on the Decision to Use Force in Panama," *New York Times,* December 21, 1989, A19.
18. Andres Oppenheimer, "Panama's Troubled Resuscitation as a Nation-State," in Eva Loser, ed., *Conflict Resolution and Democratization in Panama: Implications for U.S. Policy* (Washington, D.C.: Center for International and Strategic Studies, 1992), 35–54.
19. Richard H. Schultz, Jr., *In the Aftermath of War: U.S. Support for Reconstruction and Nation-Building in Panama Following Just Cause* (Maxwell Air Force Base, Ala.: Air University Press, 1993), 16.
20. Oppenheimer, "Panama's Troubled Resuscitation as a Nation-State."
21. John T. Fischel, *The Fog of Peace: Planning and Executing the Restoration of Panama* (Carlisle, Pa.: Strategic Studies Institute, 1992), v.
22. Ibid., vii.
23. Schultz, *In the Aftermath of War,* 16.
24. Ibid.
25. Fischel, *The Fog of Peace,* vii.
26. Schultz, *In the Aftermath of War,* 28–29.
27. Steve Davis, "Panama's Economy in Disarray," *USA Today,* December 28, 1989; Eusebio Mujal-Leon and Christopher Bruneau, "Foreign Assistance in Reconstruction Efforts," in Loser, ed., *Conflict Resolution and Democratization in Panama,* 61.
28. Schultz, *In the Aftermath of War,* 28–29.
29. Mujal-Leon and Bruneau, "Foreign Assistance in Reconstruction Efforts," 61.
30. Oppenheimer, "Panama's Troubled Resuscitation as a Nation-State," 46–48.
31. Ibid., 46–52.

32. Irving Louis Horowitz, "Panama: National Shadow without Political Substance," in Loser, ed., *Conflict Resolution and Democratization in Panama,* 46–48.
33. Hugh Borton, *American Presurrender Planning for Postwar Japan* (New York: East Asian Institute of Columbia University, 1967), 5.
34. John W. Dower, *Embracing Defeat: Japan in the Wake of World War II* (New York: W. W. Norton, 1999), 219–20.
35. Ibid., 222.
36. Ibid., 73–77.
37. Ibid., 212.
38. Thomas Berger, "Political Order in Occupied Societies" (Boston: Boston University, 2004).
39. Russell Brines, *MacArthur's Japan* (New York: J. B. Lippincott, 1948), 80.
40. Dobbins et al., *America's Role in Nation-Building,* xvii.
41. Brines, *MacArthur's Japan,* 104.
42. Michael Schaller, *Altered States: The United States and Japan since the Occupation* (New York: Oxford University Press, 1997), 11.
43. Berger, "Political Order in Occupied Societies," 18.
44. Dower, *Embracing Defeat,* 259.
45. Schaller, *Altered States,* 11.
46. Jerome Cohen, *Japan's Economy in War and Reconstruction* (Minneapolis: University of Minnesota Press, 1949), 420.
47. Yoneyuki Sugita, *Pitfall or Panacea: The Irony of U.S. Power in Occupied Japan 1945–1952* (New York: Routledge, 2003), 65–75.
48. Article 9: "War as a sovereign right of the nation is abolished. The threat or use of force is forever renounced as a means for settling disputes with any other nation," cited in Sugita, *Pitfall or Panacea,* 17.

CHAPTER 4

Nation-Building

Lessons Learned and Unlearned

Michèle A. Flournoy

DURING THE 1990s, the United States, in partnership with others in the international community, undertook a number of interventions abroad that involved nation-building. The United States deployed military forces, devoted substantial resources, and spent considerable political capital in multilateral operations in Somalia, Haiti, Bosnia, and Kosovo. It also played a supporting role in operations ranging from Eastern Slavonia to East Timor. Although the reasons for and circumstances of each of these cases were unique, collectively they yielded a set of lessons that came to be broadly understood among senior officials in the Clinton administration. Many of these lessons were ultimately codified in Presidential Decision Directive (PDD) 56 on "Managing Complex Contingency Operations."[1]

Since then, however, ample evidence suggests that many of these lessons have been "unlearned"—that is, they have been ignored or rejected by the U.S. government in its approach to subsequent nation-building operations; most notably, postconflict operations in Afghanistan and Iraq.

Several reasons explain why this reversal has occurred. First, and perhaps foremost, the Bush administration came into office decrying U.S. involvement in nation-building, particularly the use of the U.S. military for such missions.[2] From the perspective of the new president and many in his cabinet, the principal lesson from the 1990s was, quite simply, to avoid nation-building altogether. Thus, the incoming Bush administration had little interest in any of the lessons learned by the Clinton administration regarding how best to undertake such missions.

More generally, new presidents and administrations tend to discount the advice and recommendations of their predecessors. Too often, the assumption going in is that the previous administration's policies are a legacy to be rejected or overcome, and that the outgoing team lacks wisdom to pass on to the incoming one. Consequently, one administration's lessons learned and best practices often end up the proverbial "baby thrown out with the bathwater" during presidential transitions.

The U.S. government lacks the necessary mechanisms to institutionalize lessons learned over time. With the notable exception of the U.S. military, which has an elaborate system for collecting and disseminating "after action reviews" of its operations, the U.S. government as a whole does not have organizations devoted to identifying, analyzing, and promulgating lessons learned from nation-building or any other type of complex operation. Consequently, the lessons of one overseas intervention tend to be lost in the next, unless there happens to be some continuity of personnel.

Finally, in some sectors of the U.S. government, cultural factors can further hinder the experience gained in one nation-building operation from being applied to the next. State Department culture, for example, tends to emphasize the uniqueness of each crisis situation, given the importance of local culture, history, language, and other factors. In this context, the validity of applying previous experiences in one part of the world to operations in another is fundamentally questioned. As one former State Department official put it when told that the Defense Department was taking its experience in Somalia into account in planning for operations in Haiti, "What could we possibly learn from Somalia that would be relevant to Haiti?"

This propensity to overlook or unlearn lessons would not be all that worrisome if the United States were not likely to engage in nation-building operations in the future. But if the history of the twentieth century is any indication, future U.S. presidents are likely to determine that it is in U.S. interests to conduct nation-building operations. Nation-building is, after all, a mission that the United States has undertaken repeatedly over the course of its history (see table 3.1 and the discussion in chapter 3). Moreover, given the nature of the post–Cold War, post-9/11 security environment and the now well-understood link between failed states and transnational terrorism, U.S. involvement in future nation-building operations seems a near certainty.

In this chapter, I review some of the most important lessons that many officials in the Clinton administration thought the United States learned from its nation-building experiences in the 1990s. I then assess the extent to which these lessons have been applied or ignored in subsequent operations, most notably Afghanistan and Iraq. I conclude by offering some recommendations on how the U.S. government could improve its capacity and performance in this realm.

Lessons of the 1990s

Most of the lessons learned from U.S. involvement in nation-building operations in the 1990s have their roots in Somalia, from which the United States ultimately withdrew without achieving its stated objectives after a tragic debacle. These experiences produced new presidential guidance on managing complex nation-building operations and substantially influenced how the Clinton administration planned and conducted subsequent operations. Of the many lessons learned, six of them stand out as particularly important.

First, a successful nation-building operation requires a comprehensive strategy, along with the mechanisms for integrating the efforts of various agencies and actors. Second, the command and control arrangements and the delineation of authority between civil and military forces must be clearly spelled out before the operation begins. Third, strong public support, both domestic and international, must be cultivated from the beginning, and must be sustained throughout the operation. Fourth, military forces must be adapted to the nature and scope of each mission, and a rapidly deployable civilian force is a critical component to successful nation-building. Fifth, once the operation is under way, senior decisionmakers must sustain policy oversight and continually reassess the mission to make sure that its execution remains consistent with its objectives and strategy. And finally, the successful transition of power or hand-off of responsibility must be meticulously planned and orchestrated.

Integrated Planning and Execution

Success in nation-building operations requires a multidimensional strategy and mechanisms for integrating the efforts of various agencies and actors. Nation-building operations are not purely or even predominantly military operations. Any strategy for success must integrate the political, military, economic, humanitarian, and other aspects of U.S. and international efforts. In practice, this integration requires establishing mechanisms to ensure unity of effort during both the planning and execution phases of an operation. This lesson led directly to PDD 56, which, among other things, directed the establishment of an interagency Executive Committee (ExCom) to coordinate U.S. government activities in a given operation. Composed of accountable presidential appointees at the assistant-secretary level from every agency with a role on the ground, the ExCom was charged with (1) developing an integrated political-military plan for presentation to the deputies committee and the principals committee; (2) rehearsing the plan prior to execution (as well as any major transition or hand-off of responsibility); and (3) monitoring execution to ensure unity of effort across the various U.S. government agencies. Although PDD 56 was never fully implemented, those aspects of the directive that were put into practice did contribute to greater interagency unity of effort in a number of operations.

Upon taking office, the Bush administration drafted its own presidential guidance on these issues, then known as "NSPD [National Security Presidential Directive] XX," which clearly recognized the importance of developing integrated strategies to deal with complex operations. It also built on and, in some areas, even extended many of the principles of PDD 56. But NSPD XX was never signed. More importantly, it was largely ignored when the Bush administration developed its post-9/11 strategy for Afghanistan and subsequent plans to overthrow Saddam Hussein's regime in Iraq. Postconflict operations in both cases suffered early on from the absence of a fully integrated approach.

This is a lesson that seemed to be learned in one administration and then unlearned in the next. The U.S. government still does not have the mechanisms in place to institutionalize a more integrated approach to planning and conducting these operations.

Delineation of Authority in the Field

The Clinton administration learned the hard way how important it is to be crystal clear in determining and communicating who will lead an operation and what the command and control arrangements will be. Recalling the United Nations operation in Somalia in 1993, tension arose between the de jure leadership role of the United Nations and the de facto role played by the United States, which had launched the initial United Task Force intervention to stop the famine in Somalia and still had substantial military forces on the ground after handing the operation off to the United Nations. The result was that there were multiple chains of command at work simultaneously—with disastrous results.

Since then, the United States has been much more careful to clarify what its role is—and is not—in the various U.N. and coalition operations it has been involved in. It has also taken pains to avoid, where possible, multiple chains of command for military forces on the ground. This aspect of the lesson appears to have been learned.

There remains some debate, however, about the question of who should be "in charge" of any given nation-building operation, and how to create unity of effort among a diverse array of agency representatives reporting through separate chains of command to their home agencies in Washington.[3] Most experts would agree that once major combat operations have ceased, leadership of the operation should pass from the senior military commander in the theater to a senior civilian representative on the ground, be it a representative of the U.N. secretary general (in the case of a U.N. operation), a U.S. ambassador or special representative of the president (in the case of a United States–led coalition operation), or a senior civilian from another lead nation (in a coalition operation led by a country other than the United States). Yet whoever the senior civilian "in charge" of the operation is, he or she is almost certain not to have directive authority over all of the civilian and military actors involved. Even with the authority to direct all civilian operations in the field, the senior civilian would remain outside the traditional U.S. military chain of command, which extends from the commander of the joint task force (CJTF) on the ground through the theater combatant commander to the secretary of defense. Although the Bush administration finessed the unity of command problem in Iraq by having both the civilian head of the Coalition Provisional Authority (Ambassador Paul Bremer) and the commander of Central Command (General John Abizaid) report to the secretary of defense, this arrangement was the exception rather than the rule; coordinating the civilian aspects of complex operations generally does not fall to the Defense Department.

Achieving success and reducing risk in nation-building operations requires a new approach to integrating U.S. civilian and military efforts in the field. For each operation, the president should appoint a senior civilian to serve as his special representative,[4] charged with the overall success of the interagency campaign. Together, the special representative and the CJTF would lead an interagency task force (IATF) to integrate U.S. interagency operations in the field. The IATF's principal purpose would be to enhance the unity of effort among all U.S. government actors involved— civilian and military—with the ultimate aim of improving the chances of success on the ground.[5]

The IATF would be led by the president's special representative, who would report to the president through the secretary of state; and the CJTF, who would report to the combatant commander, who in turn reports to the president through the secretary of defense. The president's special representative would be responsible for achieving the intervention's strategic objectives and accountable for the success of the overall campaign. The CJTF would be responsible for all military operations in the campaign. Throughout the intervention, the combatant commander would retain operational control over all U.S. military forces involved in the operation, leaving the customary military chain of command unbroken. The special representative and the CJTF would both be able to raise any serious disagreements to the National Security Council for resolution. Together they would be supported by a fully integrated civil-military staff organized along functional lines, with staffs for intelligence, planning, operations, logistics, administrative matters, and so on.[6] Coalition partners' civilian and military representatives could also be integrated into the task force.

Strong Public Support

Building and sustaining strong public support, both domestic and international, is critical to the success of a nation-building mission. It is imperative that U.S. officials explain to the American people the U.S. interests at stake in a given operation, the objectives sought, the strategy for achieving them, and the likely risks and costs associated with the intervention. The United States must also make its case to allies and partners and to their publics if it is to form a cohesive and effective coalition to conduct the operation.

Efforts to build public support for an operation must be undertaken not only before the operation begins, but also whenever significant changes on the ground or in overall strategy occur. Failing to do so can have significant ramifications. In Somalia, for example, by the time the battle of Mogadishu occurred in October 1994, most Americans no longer understood why the United States still had troops on the ground, let alone why they were being killed and dragged through the streets. Hadn't the United States gone to Somalia to stop a famine? Hadn't the United Nations since taken lead responsibility for the operation? The failure to sustain American public support for the operation after the hand-off to the United Nations contributed to the rapid U.S. withdrawal from the country after 18 U.S. soldiers were killed.

This lesson appears to have been well learned. For every operation since Somalia, the U.S. president has gone to the American people (usually via a televised address) and to the court of international public opinion (often via the United Nations) to make the case for the intervention. Although building strong domestic and international support can prove challenging or even elusive, as President Bush has learned with his Iraq experience, senior U.S. officials seem to have internalized the need to try.

Enhanced Military and Civilian Capabilities

Military forces must be tailored to and adequate for the mission. It should not be assumed that just because a force can prevail in major combat operations, it will be able to succeed in nation-building. Nation-building missions are complex civil-military operations that pose unique requirements for the U.S. military and require a different mix of capabilities. For example, specialized capabilities, such as civil affairs, special forces, psychological operations, engineers, linguists, and military police, often play invaluable roles in these operations and are generally needed in greater numbers in nation-building than in war fighting. Nation-building operations may also require specialized training for the units involved, as military personnel are asked to perform different tasks under conditions other than those for which they normally train. In addition, nation-building operations in the wake of a conflict sometimes require a larger force than the conduct of the war itself. Nation-building is generally a highly manpower-intensive endeavor, particularly early on, when indigenous security forces may be unwilling or unable to provide for public security.

This lesson appears to have been unlearned in Afghanistan and in Iraq. In both cases, the Bush administration demonstrated tremendous reluctance to provide the number and mix of troops required to execute these missions with a lower level of risk. As a result, coalition forces in Afghanistan had great difficulty creating a stable and secure environment beyond Kabul and a few other major cities, which increased the level of cost and risk associated with achieving key milestones in the country's nascent political process (e.g., registering voters, holding elections) and its economic development. Similarly, the Bush administration's failure to anticipate and plan for the postconflict security vacuum in Iraq—despite the appearance of similar vacuums in nearly every postconflict operation of the 1990s— left the U.S. military without the resources it needed to successfully create a secure and stable environment for reconstruction early on. In short, it simply is not possible to do nation-building "on the cheap." What appears to be "saved" in the initial allocation of U.S. resources is ultimately paid for—sometimes dearly—with greater risk to those in harm's way executing the mission.

An important corollary to this lesson is that the United States also needs rapidly deployable civilian capabilities for the full range of nation-building tasks. Despite the recent and projected demand for nation-building operations, the United States still lacks adequate numbers of deployable civilian teams capable of undertaking the full range of critical nation-building tasks, from reconstituting indigenous police forces, rebuilding justice systems, and reinvigorating civil administration to repairing civil infrastructure, jumpstarting economic development, and holding elections.[7] As a result, military forces often experience "mission creep" as they are required to perform nation-building tasks for which they do not have a comparative advantage and endure extended deployments as exit strategy timelines get pushed into the future.

Senators Richard Lugar and Joseph Biden introduced a bill in 2004 proposing the creation of a civilian rapid response corps and reserve, but it did not pass into law.[8] The legislation did serve as a catalyst, however, for the August 2004 creation of the new State Department Office of the Coordinator for Reconstruction and Stabilization, which envisions building cadres of rapidly deployable civilians but has yet to secure the necessary funding. Creating a civilian response corps as well as an on-call reserve of civilian experts is critical to improving performance and reducing costs in nation-building operations.

Sustained Policy Oversight

Once an operation is under way, senior decisionmakers must continually reassess the mission to ensure that its execution remains consistent with overall U.S. objectives and strategy. When conditions on the ground change significantly, senior officials must fully assess the impact of the change on U.S. strategy and the means required to carry it out. Shifts in policy guidance must be coordinated with coalition partners and communicated as clear decisions to personnel in the field. Whenever U.S. personnel are put in harm's way, the U.S. government must ensure that policy issues are brought to light and resolved in a timely manner and that the operation receives sustained policy oversight. There is no such thing as benign neglect when lives are on the line.

The secretary of defense and the chairman of the Joint Chiefs of Staff have a particular responsibility to ensure that any changes in policy are communicated down the chain of command as clearly and as rapidly as possible. Somalia is a vivid example of a case in which such communication did not occur. When the policy authorizing the manhunt for notorious Somali warlord Mohammed Farrah Aideed was being reevaluated in Washington and at U.N. headquarters in New York in September 1994, no change of orders was issued to the special operations forces who were conducting the manhunt on the ground. Raids continued into early October, when the battle of Mogadishu occurred.

For the most part, this tragic and costly lesson seems to have been learned since Somalia. But any time an administration is overseeing more than one complex operation at a time, as in the case of Iraq and Afghanistan, there is always a risk that one operation will eclipse the other, distracting decisionmakers from the still-critical task of closely monitoring developments in both arenas. Oversight structures must be put into place to ensure that such a lapse is not allowed to happen.

Well Planned and Resourced Transitions

Executing a smooth and seamless transition or hand-off can make or break an operation. Every United States–led nation-building operation ends in a hand-off, whether to an international body, such as the United Nations or the North Atlantic Treaty Organization, or to an indigenous authority, such as an interim government. A well-orchestrated transition can build momentum for success, whereas a poorly executed one can significantly undermine it.

A smooth and seamless transition has several requirements:

- A clear transition plan, developed early on and based on milestones that are driven by events on the ground rather than external factors or timelines;
- Carefully worded, agreed-upon language governing the transition (often but not always a U.N. Security Council resolution);
- Early designation of the follow-on authority (whether indigenous or international);
- Early deployment of an advance team or core staff from the follow-on authority to work alongside the existing authority; and
- Ample commitment of time and resources to help build the capacity of those who will receive the hand-off.

Clearly, this is a lesson that the Bush administration did not fully appreciate or apply in the months leading up to the June 2004 transition of power in Iraq. Although some of these elements were eventually put in place, most were absent, which has increased the level of risk associated with an already difficult and ambitious hand-off.

Recommendations

In light of these lessons, both learned and unlearned, the United States would be wise to undertake a number of steps to improve its capacity for and performance in nation-building operations.[9]

- *Establish a standard NSC-led approach to interagency planning and oversight of complex contingency operations.* This approach should build on the best practices of PDD 56 and NSPD XX and be codified in a new presidential directive.
- *Create planning offices in the NSC and key civilian agencies.* Planning capacity outside the Department of Defense is imperative to nation-

building mission success. The establishment of the State Department Office of the Coordinator for Reconstruction and Stabilization is a positive first step. Congress should grant other agencies that regularly participate in complex contingency operations, such as Treasury, Justice, and Commerce, the resources necessary to create staffs with operational planning expertise as well.

- *Create interagency planning teams for nation-building and other complex contingencies.* Chaired by NSC staff, the interagency planning team for a given operation would be responsible for developing a truly integrated interagency campaign plan, based on the president's planning guidance for the operation. Each team should be composed of regional and functional experts from all of the agencies involved, and would have "reach back" capabilities to draw on the broader expertise of these agencies.

- *Establish an IATF in the field for each operation to integrate the day-to-day efforts of all U.S. government agencies.* Each IATF would be led by a senior civilian appointed by the president to lead the overall campaign and the commander of the military's joint task force for the operation. Together, they would be supported by a fully integrated staff of civilian and military professionals organized along functional lines. The IATF structure should be flexible enough to include coalition partner representatives, and should be adapted to operational circumstances.

- *Fully fund the creation of rapidly deployable civilian cadres for nation-building and other complex contingencies.* The pilot project would begin with 250 full-time U.S. government personnel and 500 in reserve, and the program would expand as necessary. These personnel could be deployed to serve on the IATFs described above or in other operational activities. The program would also offer incentives, such as increased pay and benefits, to those willing to be designated as deployable personnel. In addition, it would provide more personnel and funding to the USAID Office of Transition Initiatives.

- *Create an interagency and coalition training center.* The president should ask Congress to authorize and fund an interagency center devoted to the collection, analysis, and dissemination of lessons learned from nation-building and other complex operations. Such a center would have several distinct yet related missions: collecting and analyzing strategic and operational lessons learned from across the U.S. government; serving as a clearinghouse to make these lessons available to U.S. agencies and coalition partners; and training U.S. and coalition personnel involved in the planning and conduct of such operations, making them aware of lessons learned and best practices from past experience.

Ideally, such a center would have co-sponsorship from both the Defense Department and the State Department to ensure that it could effectively serve both the military and civilian communities.

In learning the lessons of Somalia and its other nation-building endeavors of the 1990s, the United States has a mixed record. Changes of administration, differences of ideology and worldview, and the absence of any institutional keeper of acquired wisdom have all contributed to the loss or unlearning of critical lessons. As it is often said, those who ignore history are doomed to repeat it. One of the most important challenges, therefore, is to develop ways to institutionalize the insights gained from such complex operations as nation-building. The above recommendations offer a starting point for such an effort.

Ultimately, whether we learn the right lessons from our nation-building experiences is about far more than efficiency or even effectiveness. Failure to learn from past efforts has very real costs—in terms of U.S. security, resources expended to achieve our aims, and American lives lost or forever changed. The United States can and must do better.

Appendix: The Clinton Administration's Policy on Managing Complex Contingency Operations

Presidential Decision Directive 56
May 1997

Purpose

This white paper explains key elements of the Clinton administration's policy on managing complex contingency operations. This unclassified document is promulgated for use by government officials as a handy reference for interagency planning of future complex contingency operations. Also, it is intended for use in U.S. government professional education institutions, such as the National Defense University and the National Foreign Affairs Training Center, for coursework and exercises on interagency practices and procedures. Regarding this paper's utility as representation of the president's directive, it contains all the key elements of the original PDD that are needed for effective implementation by agency officials. Therefore, wide dissemination of this unclassified white paper is encouraged by all agencies of the U.S. government. Note that while this white paper explains the PDD, it does not override the official PDD.

Background

In the wake of the Cold War, attention has focused on a rising number of territorial disputes, armed ethnic conflicts, and civil wars that pose threats to regional and international peace and may be accompanied by natural or manmade disasters which precipitate massive human suffering. We have learned that effective responses to these situations may require multidimensional operations composed of such components as political/diplomatic, humanitarian, intelligence, economic development, and security: hence the term complex contingency operations.

The PDD defines "complex contingency operations" as peace operations such as the peace accord implementation operation conducted by NATO in Bosnia (1995–present) and the humanitarian intervention in northern Iraq called "Operation Provide Comfort" (1991); and foreign humanitarian assistance operations, such as "Operation Support Hope" in central Africa (1994) and "Operation Sea Angel" in Bangladesh (1991). Unless otherwise directed, this PDD does not apply to domestic disaster relief or to relatively routine or small-scale operations, or to military operations conducted in defense of U.S. citizens, territory, or property, including counterterrorism and hostage-rescue operations and international armed conflict.

In recent situations as diverse as Haiti, Somalia, northern Iraq, and the former Yugoslavia, the United States has engaged in complex contingency operations in coalition, either under the auspices of an international or regional organization or in ad hoc, temporary coalitions of like-minded states. While never relinquishing the capability to respond unilaterally, the PDD assumes that the U.S. will continue to conduct future operations in coalition whenever possible.

We must also be prepared to manage the humanitarian, economic, and political consequences of a technological crisis where chemical, biological, and/or radiological hazards may be present. The occurrence of any one of these dimensions could significantly increase the sensitivity and complexity of a U.S. response to a technological crisis.

In many complex emergencies, the appropriate U.S. government response will incur the involvement of only non-military assets. In some situations, we have learned that military forces can quickly affect the dynamics of the situation, and may create the conditions necessary to make significant progress in mitigating or resolving underlying conflict or dispute. However, we have also learned that many aspects of complex emergencies may not be best addressed through military measures. Furthermore, given the level of U.S. interests at stake in most of these situations, we recognize that U.S. forces should not be deployed in an operation indefinitely.

It is essential that the necessary resources be provided to ensure that we are prepared to respond in a robust, effective manner. To foster a durable peace or stability in these situations and to maximize the effect of judicious military deployments, the civilian components of an operation must be integrated closely with the military components.

While agencies of government have developed independent capacities to respond to complex emergencies, military and civilian agencies should operate in a synchronized manner through effective interagency management and the use of special mechanisms to coordinate agency efforts. Integrated planning and effective management of agency operations early on in an operation can avoid delays, reduce pressure on the military to expand its involvement in unplanned ways, and create unity of effort within an operation that is essential for success of the mission.

Intent of the PDD

The need for complex contingency operations is likely to recur in future years, demanding varying degrees of U.S. involvement. The PDD calls for all U.S. government agencies to institutionalize what we have learned from our recent experiences and to continue the process of improving the planning and management of complex contingency operations. The PDD is designed to ensure that the lessons learned—including proven planning processes and implementation mechanisms—will be incorporated into the interagency process on a regular basis. The PDD's intent is to establish these management practices to achieve unity of effort among U.S. government agencies and international organizations engaged in complex contingency operations. Dedicated mechanisms and integrated planning processes are needed. From our recent experiences, we have learned that these can help to:

- identify appropriate missions and tasks, if any, for U.S. government agencies in a U.S. government response;
- develop strategies for early resolution of crises, thereby minimizing the loss of life and establishing the basis for reconciliation and reconstruction;
- accelerate planning and implementation of the civilian aspects of the operation;
- intensify action on critical funding and personnel requirements early on;

- integrate all components of a U.S. response (e.g., civilian, military, police) at the policy level and facilitate the creation of coordination mechanisms at the operational level; and
- rapidly identify issues for senior policy makers and ensure expeditious implementation of decisions.

The PDD requires all agencies to review their legislative and budget authorities for supporting complex contingency operations and, where such authorities are inadequate to fund an agency's mission and operations in complex contingencies, propose legislative and budgetary solutions.

Executive Committee

The PDD calls upon the Deputies Committee to establish appropriate interagency working groups to assist in policy development, planning, and execution of complex contingency operations. Normally, the Deputies Committee will form an Executive Committee (ExCom) with appropriate membership to supervise the day-to-day management of U.S. participation in a complex contingency operation. The ExCom will bring together representatives of all agencies that might participate in the operation, including those not normally part of the NSC structure. When this is the case, both the Deputies Committee and the ExCom will normally be augmented by participating agency representatives. In addition, the chair of the ExCom will normally designate an agency to lead a legal and fiscal advisory subgroup, whose role is to consult with the ExCom to ensure that tasks assigned by the ExCom can be performed by the assigned agencies consistent with legal and fiscal authorities. This ExCom approach has proved useful in clarifying agency responsibilities, strengthening agency accountability, ensuring interagency coordination, and developing policy options for consideration by senior policy makers.

The guiding principle behind the ExCom approach to interagency management is the personal accountability of presidential appointees. Members of the ExCom effectively serve as functional managers for specific elements of the U.S. government response (e.g., refugees, demobilization, elections, economic assistance, police reform, public information). They implement the strategies agreed to by senior policy makers in the interagency and report to the ExCom and Deputies Committee on any problems or issues that need to be resolved.

In future complex contingency operations to which the United States contributes substantial resources, the PDD calls upon the Deputies Committee to establish organizational arrangements akin to those of the ExCom approach.

The Political-Military Implementation Plan

The PDD requires that a political-military implementation plan (or "pol-mil" plan) be developed as an integrated planning tool for coordinating U.S. government actions in a complex contingency operation. The pol-mil plan will include a comprehensive situation assessment, mission statement, agency objectives, and desired end state. It will outline an integrated concept of operations to synchronize agency efforts. The plan will identify the primary preparatory issues and tasks for conducting an operation (e.g., congressional consultations, diplomatic efforts, troop recruitment, legal authorities, funding requirements and sources, media coordination). It will also address major functional/mission area tasks (e.g., political mediation/reconciliation, military support, demobilization, humanitarian assistance, police reform, basic public services, economic restoration, human rights monitoring, social reconciliation, public information). (Annex A contains an illustrative outline of a pol-mil plan.)

With the use of the pol-mil plan, the interagency can implement effective management practices, namely, to centralize planning and decentralize execution during the operation. The desired unity of effort among the various agencies that is created through the use of the pol-mil plan contributes to the overall success of these complex operations.

When a complex contingency operation is contemplated in which the U.S. government will play a substantial role, the PDD calls upon the Deputies Committee to task the development of a pol-mil plan and assign specific responsibilities to the appropriate ExCom officials.

Each ExCom official will be required to develop their respective part of the plan, which will be fully coordinated among all relevant agencies. This development process will be transparent and analytical, resulting in issues being posed to senior policy makers for resolution. Based on the resulting decisions, the plan will be finalized and widely distributed among relevant agencies.

The PDD also requires that the pol-mil plan include demonstrable milestones and measures of success including detailed planning for the transition of the operation to activities which might be performed by a follow-on operation or by the host government. According to the PDD, the pol-mil plan should be updated as the mission progresses to reflect milestones that are (or are not) met and to incorporate changes in the situation on the ground.

Interagency Pol-Mil Plan Rehearsal

A critical aspect of the planning process will be the interagency rehearsal/review of the pol-mil plan. As outlined in the PDD, this activity involves a rehearsal of the plan's main elements, with the appropriate Ex-Com official presenting the elements for which he or she is responsible. By simultaneously rehearsing/reviewing all elements of the plan, differences over mission objectives, agency responsibilities, timing/synchronization, and resource allocation can be identified and resolved early, preferably before the operation begins. The interagency rehearsal/review also under-scores the accountability of each program manager in implementing their assigned area of responsibility. During execution, regular reviews of the plan ensure that milestones are met and that appropriate adjustments are made.

The PDD calls upon the Deputies Committee to conduct the inter-agency rehearsal/review of the pol-mil plan. Supporting agency plans are to be presented by ExCom officials before a complex contingency opera-tion is launched (or as early as possible once the operation begins), before a subsequent critical phase during the operation, as major changes in the mission occur, and prior to an operation's termination.

After-Action Review

After the conclusion of each operation in which this planning process is employed, the PDD directs the ExCom to charter an after-action review involving both those who participated in the operation and government experts who monitored its execution. This comprehensive assessment of interagency performance will include a review of interagency planning and coordination (both in Washington and in the field), legal and budg-etary difficulties encountered, problems in agency execution, as well as proposed solutions, in order to capture lessons learned and to ensure their dissemination to relevant agencies.

Training

The U.S. government requires the capacity to prepare agency officials for the responsibilities they will be expected to take on in planning and managing agency efforts in a complex contingency operation. Creating a cadre of professionals familiar with this integrated planning process will improve the U.S. government's ability to manage future operations.

In the interest of advancing the expertise of government officials, agen-cies are encouraged to disseminate the *Handbook for Interagency Manage-ment of Complex Contingency Operations* published by the National Defense University in January 2003.

With the support of the State and Defense Departments, the PDD re-quires the NSC to work with the appropriate U.S. government educational institutions—including the National Defense University, the National

Foreign Affairs Training Center, and the Army War College—to develop and conduct an interagency training program. This program, which should be held at least annually, will train mid-level managers (deputy assistant secretary level) in the development and implementation of pol-mil plans for complex contingency operations. Those participating should have an opportunity to interact with expert officials from previous operations to learn what has worked in the past. Also, the PDD calls upon appropriate U.S. government educational institutions to explore the appropriate way to incorporate the pol-mil planning process into their curricula.

Agency Review and Implementation

Finally, the PDD directs each agency to review the adequacy of their agency's structure, legal authorities, budget levels, personnel system, training, and crisis management procedures to insure that we, as a government, are learning from our experiences with complex contingency operations and institutionalizing the lessons learned.

Annex A: Illustrative Components of a Political-Military Plan for a Complex Contingency Operation

Situation Assessment. A comprehensive assessment of the situation to clarify essential information that, in the aggregate, provides a multidimensional picture of the crisis.

U.S. Interests. A statement of U.S. interests at stake in the crisis and the requirement to secure those interests.

Mission Statement. A clear statement of the U.S. government's strategic purpose for the operation and the pol-mil mission.

Objectives. The key civil-military objectives to be accomplished during the operation.

Desired Pol-Mil End State. The conditions the operation is intended to create before the operation transitions to a follow-on operation and/or terminates.

Concept of the Operation. A conceptual description of how the various instruments of U.S. government policy will be integrated to get the job done throughout all phases of the operation.

Lead Agency Responsibilities. An assignment of responsibilities for participating agencies.

Transition/Exit Strategy. A strategy that is linked to the realization of the end state described above, requiring the integrated efforts of diplomats, military leaders, and relief officials of the U.S. government and the international community.

Organizational Concept. A schematic of the various organizational structures of the operation, in Washington and in theater, including a description of the chain of authority and associated reporting channels.

Preparatory Tasks. A layout of specific tasks to be undertaken before the operation begins (e.g., congressional consultations, diplomatic efforts, troop recruitment, legal authorities, funding requirements and sources, media coordination).

Functional or Mission Area Tasks/Agency Plans. Key operational and support plans written by U.S. government agencies that pertain to critical parts of the operation (e.g., political mediation/reconciliation, military support, demobilization, humanitarian assistance, police reform, basic public services, economic restoration, human rights monitoring, social reconciliation, public information).

Notes

1. PDD 56 on "Managing Complex Contingency Operations" was signed in May 1997. See white paper on PDD 56 in the appendix to this chapter (also available at http://clinton2.nara.gov/WH/EOP/NSC/html/documents/NSCDoc2.html).
2. For a representative point of view, see Condoleezza Rice, "Campaign 2000: Promoting the National Interest," *Foreign Affairs* 79 (January/February 2000), available at www.foreignaffairs.org/20000101faessay5/condoleezza-rice/campaign-2000-promoting-the-national-interest.html.
3. This question is equally relevant and even more difficult in the context of an international operation in which multiple civilian and military actors from different countries and international organizations are involved. But given the focus in this chapter on U.S. lessons learned, here I deal primarily with the relationship between various U.S. civilian and military representatives in an operation.
4. The official could be the U.S. ambassador to a given country or another senior civilian of comparable stature. Note that in many cases, the United States may not have an ambassador in the target country at the time of the intervention.
5. This approach is based on an assessment of a range of models that the United States has used in recent operations, including the civil-military operations center (used in Somalia, Haiti, and Bosnia); the joint interagency task force (used in counter-drug operations); coordination between the U.S. embassy and the CJTF (as in Afghanistan); and coordination between the Coalition Provisional Authority and the CJTF (in Iraq).
6. The majority of IATF staff would be military personnel under the command of the CJTF and civilian personnel detailed from their home agencies to work for the senior civilian. Private contractors and nongovernmental organizations

(NGOs) might also be included. While providing the expertise and perspectives of their home agencies, civilian U.S. government personnel would be expected to take direction from the president's special representative and the CJTF. The interagency delegations that supported various U.S. arms control negotiators during the Cold War provide an interesting historical precedent for such a model. If a significant disagreement arises over a given decision or direction, the National Security Council (NSC) process remains the ultimate court of appeals—that is, a staff member can raise the issue via his or her home agency to be addressed by the ExCom in Washington.

7. Although the U.S. Agency for International Development has rapidly deployable teams for emergency humanitarian assistance and experts in long-term economic development, it has only a small, underfunded office devoted to the sorts of "transition initiatives" that often make the difference between success or failure in nation-building operations. State, Justice, and Treasury also lack rapidly deployable capabilities.

8. The Lugar-Biden initiative was formally known as the Stabilization and Reconstruction Civilian Management Act of 2004.

9. These recommendations are drawn from a broader set of proposals detailed in Clark A. Murdock, Michèle A. Flournoy, Kurt M. Campbell, and Pierre A. Chao, *Beyond Goldwater Nichols: Defense Reform for a New Strategic Era, Phase II Report* (Washington, D.C.: Center for Strategic and International Studies, July 2005).

Part II · Afghanistan

CHAPTER 5

Sovereignty and Legitimacy in Afghan Nation-Building

S. Frederick Starr

AFGHANISTAN PRESENTS fundamental issues of nation-building in the starkest light possible. The immensity of the task that America and its partners faced after bringing down the Taliban was staggering. Even before the Soviet invasion of 1979, the country had been miserably poor and governed with only a thin web of civic institutions. The Soviet invasion and occupation, civil war, and then Taliban rule left the country and its partially built structures of rule in utter shambles. It is no exaggeration to say that by the time the Taliban fell, the entire country had become, for the nation-builder, a tabula rasa.

Under such circumstances, it was easier to ask what did not need to be done than what did. With the "must do" list so long, there was an unavoidable need to choose among the various possible projects. In the end, virtually all the international forces involved in the project of nation-building in Afghanistan concluded that the one obvious and overriding focus should be the reestablishment and confirmation of the country's territorial integrity and sovereignty. Emergency relief was an equally compelling concern, but one that would have existed with or without nation-building. The reestablishment of Afghanistan's sovereignty presented itself as the foundation that had to be put in place before everything else that was considered desirable in the political, economic, and social spheres could be built. There were ample reasons, both practical and philosophical, that seemed to justify this decision.

On the practical side was the widespread concern at the time that Afghanistan might break apart into autonomous fiefdoms run by competing warlords. Related to this was the suspicion that Afghanistan was not really a country but a patchwork of ethnicities that a resourceful but weak monarchy had cobbled together through a system of deals, all of which had been broken by a generation of conflict.

On the theoretical side, European history seemed to justify this emphasis on sovereignty. In France in the seventeenth century and Germany and Italy in the nineteenth century, the great challenge and call to heroic action was to create sovereignty at the national level and use it as an instrument for strengthening nationwide identity. The experience of the United States seemed also to support the same focus—extend sovereignty and both national identity and legitimacy would follow in due course. Thus, by absorbing the geographical remnants of French and Spanish rule, the fledgling American union set in train a natural process that resulted in an expanded and vigorous new identity.

Initial Coalition Involvement in Afghanistan

During the period from 2001 to 2003, the United States and Europe, as well as the United Nations, approached Afghanistan on the basis of this verity. The recent Balkan crisis reinforced the same lesson—namely, that the coalition should focus first on the problem of sovereignty and then, with that identity firmly in place, address the issue of legitimacy. In practice, this strategy meant focusing on reaffirming Afghanistan's traditional territorial boundaries and on extending central rule throughout the territory thus defined. This was the first assignment, and the success of everything else desired for the country was thought to depend on its successful completion.

The centrality of sovereignty-building as the first step towards nation-building seemed so obvious on both the practical and theoretical levels that no one felt the need to defend it against possible alternative approaches. Indeed, it was scarcely acknowledged that any serious alternative strategy existed, let alone that it should be considered. On this point, the international community spoke with one voice.

But there was an alterative view, and it was one shared by many, if not most, Afghans. Politically active Afghans operated on the basis of a very different road map. They assumed that the territorial boundaries of their country had been defined once and for all by the eighteenth century.

Granted, British rule had left parts of the border with Pakistan still to be delineated, but this circumstance only reinforced the larger point. Afghanistan as a state had existed for two centuries within roughly its present boundaries. The location of its capital was fixed and not in dispute. Most Afghans assumed, furthermore, that Afghanistan would return to the status of a unitary state that had existed prior to the Soviet invasion. Nor did they doubt that such a unitary state should regain the power to levy taxes, raise an army, establish a judiciary, and carry out other functions at the national and regional levels.

Given these views, the mere reestablishment of sovereignty did not strike most Afghans as a major challenge. Unlike the international community, which saw secession as a constant threat, they did not consider secessionism likely or possible. What concerned Afghans from the outset, and what sharply separated their thinking from that of the coalition partners and the United Nations, was the legitimacy of the new government. By legitimacy, they meant the voluntary acceptance by the majority of the population in every area of the government's right and responsibility to rule at the national level and throughout the land, and the willingness of most people to pay taxes and serve in the army to enable the government to achieve that task. For Afghans, but not for the international experts who met at Bonn and convened in Washington and elsewhere, the big issue was not sovereignty but legitimacy.

This is not to say that the United Nations, the Americans, or other coalition members denied the importance of establishing the new government's legitimacy. But their approach differed fundamentally with that of many Afghans on two points. First, the international community believed that sovereignty and legitimacy should be addressed *seriatem*, and not simultaneously. Second, it believed that the main and essential measure needed to establish legitimacy was the holding of national elections. By contrast, most politically active Afghans held that Afghan sovereignty could not be reforged without addressing the problem of legitimacy. This meant assuring that the populace of the various regions and groups comprising Afghanistan had to perceive the new government as being worthy of their support, and that they be willing to accept its decrees, pay the taxes it levies, and respect the fairness of its police and judiciary. Only when these conditions were met would they sign on to the new sovereignty.

Most Afghans also disagreed about elections. Even though open elections had never been held in their country, Afghans of all persuasions agreed that they were now important. But their role was not so much to create legitimacy as to confirm it. The creation of legitimacy required that each group in the population be convinced that it would have a fair voice in the deliberations of the Kabul government, and that its members would have a reasonable number of places in the new administrative apparatuses being set up. Without such regional and ethnic balance, legitimacy would be nonexistent and elections useless.

The priority that the international community gave to issues of sovereignty as opposed to those of legitimacy was manifested in the conclusions of the United Nations' Bonn Conference, held in December 2001. The conferees defined the new government it put in place as an "Interim Authority," which would in time become a "Transitional Authority," which would in turn evolve in to the "Transitional Islamic State of Afghanistan" once a Loya Jirga, or national assembly, had ratified its existence. Only with elections would Afghanistan acquire a true government. But the Loya Jirga was up to 18 months in the future, with the elections coming another year after that, if at all. What degree of legitimacy would the government headed by Hamid Karzai enjoy until then?

Afghans who were otherwise sharply at odds with one another were generally prepared to answer this question on the basis of two practical tests. First, is the government providing, or likely to provide, their specific region and group what they see as "governmental" services? These services included securing borders, providing internal policing, freeing roads of bandits, rebuilding and tending the main irrigation channels, and providing basic medical help and education. Second, is the government, as the country's chief employer, distributing its jobs and the authority and resources that go with them in a fair and equitable manner—that is, one that benefits their specific region and group? Because they were convinced that the former test depended entirely on the latter, Afghans watched warily to see whether members of their particular group or region were fairly represented among the men and women being appointed by the new government.

For Afghan people of all persuasions, this evidence of fairness was the criterion on which they would base their support for, or opposition to, the new regime. Significantly, it was scarcely mentioned at Bonn. When it did come up for discussion, it was cavalierly put aside as something that would be dealt with over time, but not requiring any formal decrees by the conferees, let alone mechanisms to enforce them. Not surprisingly, over the following months and years, many, if not most, Afghans found the new government wanting on precisely this measure.

How the First Phase of Nation-Building Was Doomed Even before Bonn

A historian would be quite justified to begin the story of nation-building in post-Taliban Afghanistan with the Bonn Conference. In terms of sovereignty, this viewpoint is certainly warranted. Since the Taliban's fall, Afghanistan had existed as a geographical but not a political entity. Bonn brought to bear the authority of the United Nations to create a new sovereignty, and established what became the Karzai administration to rule it.

However, with respect to legitimacy, the Bonn meetings marked an unsuccessful end to a critical phase of nation-building rather than a beginning. This phase had begun when the Northern Alliance forces, having reached the outskirts of Kabul in their pursuit of the Taliban, defied pleas by the U.S. president and secretary of state and invested their troops in the capital, after first rebranding them as "police." Having enjoyed apparently unqualified support down to that moment, the move may have seemed to Alliance leaders a natural and inevitable step, notwithstanding Washington's command not to take it. Undoubtedly, they had been encouraged in this action by their chief backers before 9/11, Russia's President Putin and General Kvashnin, the same Russian officer who had risked outright war with the West by devising and orchestrating the ill-advised Russian rush on the airport at Kosovo on June 12, 1999.

Once in Kabul, the Tajiks and Uzbeks who made up the Alliance proceeded to fill governmental positions with their own cadres, to name new governors from among their supporters, and generally to behave as the sole governmental authority in the land. In short, they pursued a winner-take-all policy. As part of this tactic, they took total control of the three "power ministries," Defense, Interior, and Foreign Affairs, as well as the intelligence services, and were prepared to name their political head, the professor-mullah Burhanuddin Rabbani, as president.

Virtually all of the new ministers, governors, and staff members were Tajiks, mainly from the Panjshir valley. Absent from their ranks were members of the largest single group in the population, the Pashtuns of the east and south of the country, and the Shia Muslim Hazaras from the center. In their one compromise at Bonn, the Northern Alliance ministers jettisoned their elderly president in favor of the one Pashtun leader who commanded no troops of his own, Hamid Karzai.

The notables of the world community who gathered at Bonn saw their role as one of classic nation-building—that is, to create a new sovereignty on a tabula rasa. But for all practical purposes, this task had already been accomplished by General Mohammad Fahim, the Afghan minister of defense, and Dr. Abdullah Abdullah, the minister of foreign affairs.

Preoccupied with the issue of sovereignty, the international experts gathered in Bonn feared separatism above all, even though the one group that was most likely to toy with separatism—the Tajiks of the north—was already solidly established in power and flaunting that fact before the hapless delegates. Talk of federalism as a possible solution to the nonexistent problem of separatism was muted in Bonn, but was already abroad. Joschka Fischer, Germany's foreign minister, had advanced this idea, which fit so conveniently with the history of nation-building in post–World War II Germany. The conferees side-stepped this issue by putting off the question of the form of Afghanistan's future government to the Loya Jirga, a year hence.

In due course, the Bonn meeting tacitly ratified the fait accompli of Northern Alliance rule and domination of the new administration, even while vigorously denying that it had done so. Not everyone accepted this decision. Those aligned with the former king, Mohammed Zahir Shah, argued that by ratifying the Northern Alliance's power grab, the conference had planted a time bomb that would explode as soon as the Pashtuns and other excluded groups realized what had been done to them. But the king's group based its case on legitimacy, not sovereignty, and the conference had unequivocally declared that its task was to take the first step toward European-style nation-building by confirming sovereignty.

In fairness, it must be acknowledged that the conferees were aware of the imbalance they had created when they enshrined the Northern Alliance in Kabul. But they saw the Alliance's firmness and unity as a plus in the process of creating sovereignty, and convinced themselves that greater ethnic and regional diversity could be introduced into the Kabul administration over time. In so doing, they naively and gravely underestimated the Northern Alliance. The conferees congratulated themselves on their work and departed Bonn euphoric over a job of nation-building well done. In actuality, they had sacrificed the legitimacy of their new construct to what they wrongly conceived as the higher value of sovereignty.

Mixed Messages from the Loya Jirga

During the 18 months between the Bonn Conference and the Loya Jirga, the Northern Alliance team further consolidated its grip, posting loyalists in all the main ministries and governorships and filling the lower ranks with their acolytes. General, now Marshall, Fahim defied the specific decrees of the Bonn Conference and the will of the international community by keeping his private army in Kabul, and at the same time consolidating his and his family's control over markets, service contracts with the government, and key embassy positions abroad. Astonishingly, the extent and success of this single-minded and tenacious effort eluded the United Nations, the U.S. Central Intelligence Agency, and most other foreign experts on the country.

These legitimacy-destroying acts escaped notice because the international community remained focused on removing the perceived threats to Afghanistan's new sovereignty, and especially on rooting out al-Qaeda and destroying the remnants of Taliban forces still in the field. These were important tasks, to be sure, but the methods adopted for achieving them had the effect of further undermining the legitimacy of the Karzai administration.

Cooperation with local warlords in the south and southeast enhanced the coalition's effectiveness in the short run. But because it was not conditioned by demands that the warlords subordinate themselves to the new administration in Kabul, this cooperation strengthened centrifugal tendencies at the same time that Karzai, isolated within his own government, was crying out for help in reinforcing the centripetal forces. Gradually, the very warlords with whom the U.S. forces were collaborating were moving away from what they perceived as the unbalanced and unrepresentative government in Kabul.

Afghanistan, like all of Central Asia, is a land whose people rely on word of mouth and who do not need newspapers to know what is happening. As Pashtuns and other excluded groups came to realize that few of their kind had found places in the Kabul government, they came to view the Karzai administration as at best semi-legitimate. Simultaneously, large, geographically focused segments of the Afghan population grew alienated from Kabul. Their alienation found expression in covert support for local warlords, reluctance to cooperate with administrators sent to their areas by Kabul, and support for any local authority who refused to turn over tax revenues to the capital.

There is little reason to ascribe this alienation to Karzai's status and that of a few of his ministers as former émigrés. On the contrary, these people were in most cases respected for their knowledge and competence. The problem was that nearly all the lesser posts, both in Kabul and in the regions, were being handed over to Tajiks and especially Panjshiris.

Excluded and alienated groups fell back on local clientage systems and regionally based warlords. Thanks to local support, these leaders often came to enjoy a kind of ersatz legitimacy in the absence of true legitimacy at the national level. Thus, Karzai and his international backers unwittingly perpetuated and even strengthened conditions that kept 100,000 opposition fighters in the field.

This development was dubbed at the time a "Taliban revival." Such a characterization is accurate but incomplete. Many of those who raised the Taliban banner had indeed supported the Taliban prior to 9/11, if only because that government had stopped much of the internecine killing that had long bled the country. More often than not, however, they were people who would have cooperated with Kabul, if only minimally, had Kabul cooperated with them. Theirs was definitely not a separatist movement but an armed opposition fighting against what its members saw as illegitimate rule in the capital.

Thus, a year after the Bonn meetings, problems of legitimacy that had been swept under the carpet were beginning to threaten sovereignty itself. Amid this situation, the Loya Jirga met in June 2002. Misreading the causes of the opposition to Kabul, many international observers argued that the time had come to establish a federal system in Afghanistan. Thinking that the problem was over control at the local rather than the national level, they proposed to give each ethnic group its own territory.

The Afghans themselves decisively rejected this proposal and the gross misunderstanding of the needs of nation-building on which it was based. In the clearest possible manner, they demonstrated that the issue of sovereignty was not in question. Representatives of the Afghan nation showed surprising cohesion in the face of the pro-federalist campaign, and manifested this cohesion in the total absence of calls for secession or even the use of threats of secession as a negotiating ploy. In the end, they opted decisively for a unitary state.

Legitimacy, not sovereignty, was the main concern of that large majority of Afghans whose members had been excluded from the new government service. It is for this reason that a solid majority favored a serious overture to the former king, on the grounds that he, a Pashtun whose government had conducted business in Dari (Tajik), could reign (but not rule), as a symbol of national unity and inter-regional and inter-ethnic balance. The Americans, under pressure from Northern Alliance members of the Karzai government, derailed this plan, but without offering anything better to solve the problem.

The core issue for those concerned over legitimacy involved the state and who would control and staff it. Until that question had been addressed, nation-building would remain on hold or slip into reverse. Nor could this dilemma have been solved through elections. Elections were still a year away, and neither their viability nor their outcome was assured. Therefore, at the Loya Jirga, Afghans concerned about legitimacy did not look to elections to resolve the issue. Rather, they demanded balanced staffing in Kabul and the provinces, and effective delivery of normal services to their localities.

Even at this late date, few in the international community appreciated the extent to which the government's legitimacy was waning, or connected the mounting crisis of legitimacy with the fair distribution of places and the delivery of governmental services. Appalled by the misery in which most of the population lived, they focused instead on delivering urgently needed assistance through whatever channels were at hand. In practice, this meant using nongovernmental organizations (NGOs). In an impressive mobilization supported mainly by American tax dollars, hundreds of NGOs appeared on the scene and began dispensing services. Thanks to them, a humanitarian crisis was averted. Only later did it become clear that to some extent, the NGOs and the Kabul administration were on a collision course, and one that affected the legitimacy of the latter.

Meanwhile, coalition forces continued to concentrate on the destruction of al-Qaeda and the defeat of Taliban holdouts. American planners continued to believe that it would be possible for them to use the warlords in Phase I of nation-building and then transform them into loyal citizens of a new Afghanistan during a Phase II. Missing from this formulation was an appreciation of the fact that the writ of the central government extended only to those areas whence its key staff were drawn—that is, the northeast and north-central regions, and not the south, center, southeast, or northwest. The "birth defect" with which the Karzai administration left Bonn continued to define the limits of nation-building in Afghanistan after the Loya Jirga.

Post–Loya Jirga Erosion and the Problem of the NGOs

The success of the Loya Jirga should have ushered in a new phase of nation-building. The country had opted for a unitary government and presidential rule. U.S. and North Atlantic Treaty Organization forces were busy hunting the last remnants of al-Qaeda and Taliban diehards. Thousands of NGOs were engaged in basic economic and social development. Following a period of renewal, elections in 2004 would then place a capstone on the entire process of nation-building.

Much was indeed accomplished following the Loya Jirga. The United States had already worked with the Afghans to introduce a new currency, and solid fiscal policies had brought macroeconomic stabilization in their wake. The United States alone reconstructed 700 schools and delivered enough new textbooks for the entire country. NGOs removed a million mines, high-yield seeds brought increased agricultural production, and work began on rebuilding the country's trunk roads.

What did not change, however, was the one-sided control of the entire administration of state by men loyal to the Northern Alliance, and the overweening political and economic power of Marshall Fahim as minister of defense. Pashtuns, Hazaras, and members of other excluded groups and factions knew this from the accounts of friends and relatives who had visited the capital. They could see the effects of this continuing problem in their own provinces and towns. Many concluded that Karzai was either unwilling or unable to address this fundamental issue of balance.

In the absence of legitimacy, what should have been a period of consolidation and nation-building descended into a maze of contradictory
impulses, many of them negative. The national army gradually expanded,
but warlords' forces far outstripped it. Agricultural production rebounded,
but drug production grew far more vigorously. More taxes were collected
locally, but the amounts remitted to Kabul scarcely increased. New roads
were opened, but illicit roadblocks continued, even in nominally secure
areas. And the existence of armed units claiming to be Taliban continued
to advertise the fact that the Karzai administration enjoyed at best partial
legitimacy in the eyes of most Afghans. This process led to the erosion of
sovereignty.

By mid-2003, no fewer than two thousand national and international
NGOs were operating in Afghanistan, mainly in the fields of poverty reduction, education, and health. Most viewed the civil administration as
intrusive and bumbling. They therefore preferred to distance themselves
from the government at both the national and local levels. As the number
of NGO workers killed in the line of duty grew, the gap of understanding
between NGOs and the government became an alarming chasm.

The NGOs' case was clear: to do their job, they needed direct and un-
mediated contact with the local population, with as little governmental
interference as possible. They did not perceive local administrators as representing or serving the populations among whom they, the NGOs, worked.
The government's case was also clear, and had the most serious implications for the process of nation-building, and particularly for the key issue
of legitimacy and sovereignty. From the government's perspective, the
NGOs appeared to be undermining civil administration at the local level,
even in cases where local officials were trying to do their jobs. NGO staffs
made little attempt to hide their contempt for local bureaucrats, whom
they regarded, usually correctly, as corrupt. They also resented the central
government's attempt to monitor and regulate their work.

The government, seeing its legitimacy undermined, pleaded with the
international community for aid money to be channeled through it rather
than to the NGOs directly, on the grounds that such controls were a normal exercise of sovereignty. Ashraf Ghani, in his role as minister of finances,
was particularly forceful in making this argument in countless face-to-face
meetings with donor countries. Unfortunately, for all too long, the international community objected on the grounds of efficiency and of its
one-sided belief in the transformative role of "civil society"—even in the
absence of normal institutions of state and law—naively and irresponsibly
disregarding the larger concerns of nation-building that were at issue.

These processes turned many NGOs into what even the most competent and efficient members of Karzai's circle perceived as a de facto oppo-

sition force, which, over time, became self-fulfilling. But the reverse process also occurred, as many local administrators and police set themselves in opposition to NGOs. And why should they not have done so? From their perspective, the NGOs brought scores of overpaid young people into their communities, where they flaunted their high salaries and new motor vehicles. Worse, their well-funded activities highlighted the poverty and ineffectiveness of the civil administration and discredited its local representatives in the eyes of the local populace. No wonder that many frustrated local administrators and police made deals with their enemy's enemies—warlords and drug traffickers.

At a meeting in Kabul in April 2004, shortly after the Berlin donors'-conference, Ramazan Bashar Dost, Afghan minister of planning, declared that it would do more harm than good if aid money were given directly to NGOs rather than channeled through the government. In November 2004, he put it more bluntly: "I have yet to see a NGO that has spent 80% of its money for the benefit of the Afghans."[1] Strong words, but solidly grounded in reality. Donors were blind to the extent to which the work of NGOs undermined local administrators in the public's mind. Worse, they were blind to the Afghans' view that the delivery of services at the local level was one of the two prime tests of the government's legitimacy.

Donor countries were slow to acknowledge the need for a fundamental rethinking of the role of NGOs in the overall development process. Viewing NGOs as an end in themselves, they ignored the ways in which NGOs were undermining rather than supporting the process of institutional development. For their part, the NGOs showed a remarkable disinterest in the larger developmental process and its needs. In spite of laudable work by hundreds of them, NGOs all too often appeared arrogant to local sensitivities and disrespectful of legitimate authority, especially at the local level. Demanding accountability of others, they were all too frequently guilty of operating without normal transparency, and hence subject to what many local people and administrators took to be corrupt practices of their own.

This set of attitudes of donors and of the NGOs through which they chose to channel their funds had the most serious consequences. Even though most Afghans' sole contact with their government was through local officials and law enforcement officers, donors long refused to focus their developmental energies on local governors and police. The sustained negligence had the effect of undercutting legitimacy when it should have been reinforced, and hence of retarding nation-building as a whole.

To summarize, in the aftermath of the Loya Jirga, the international community failed to identify and address the core issue of legitimacy and the chief indicators by which Afghans evaluated their government—namely, the degree of regional and ethnic balance in staffing and the ability of government to deliver services locally. The failure invited warlords and other independent forces to reassert themselves, especially among those people least represented in Kabul and where local administration was weakest. Security began to erode overall. Once more, the international community focused its energy on controlling the effects of persistent imbalances in the government rather than on strongly backing Karzai in an effort to change the balances themselves. Calls were heard for massive increases in peacekeeping forces, and also for more rapid development of the Afghan National Army. These suggestions accorded well with the prevailing notion that sovereignty was weak and had to be shored up. To be sure, such steps would have to have been taken under any circumstances. But because they were carried out in the absence of similar attention to creating the needed balances in Kabul and building the state's effectiveness at the local level, these measures suggested that the coalition thought it could employ military means to solve problems that were, at bottom, political and administrative.

It was easy to blame this state of affairs on Karzai's weakness. But because his neglect of legitimacy issues had the Americans' imprimatur, the United States was held equally to blame. This circumstance played directly into the hands of those who were raising the old Taliban banner as a symbol of opposition to Karzai and the Americans. Consequently, over the year following the Loya Jirga, what should have been a period of consolidation and growing security showed signs of becoming a period of fragmentation and insecurity.

Signs of destabilization and imbalance were everywhere. Except for the presidency and a couple of competent émigré ministers, the government was controlled by Tajiks, other northerners, and their allies. Its writ was limited to Kabul and areas from which its key civil servants were drawn. Others, notably Pashtuns and Hazaras, still felt systematically excluded.

Locally based leaders and warlords withheld taxes, which weakened the government's ability to maintain order, establish land rights, and perform other necessary functions. Warlords even undermined the new Afghan National Army by implanting their own clientage groups in its midst. The result was not a full-blown crisis, but something worse—a steady erosion of support for the enterprise of nation-building in Afghanistan as it had been carried out since Bonn. If unchecked, this erosion could have led to the collapse of the entire enterprise.

Breakthrough for Legitimacy, 2003–2004

Between late autumn of 2001 and mid-2003, nation-building in Afghanistan was dangerously undermined by the assumption that issues of sovereignty and legitimacy could be addressed *seriatem* rather than together, and that the latter issue could be postponed until it could be dealt with in the one manner that was considered proper and acceptable—namely, the holding of elections. As a result, legitimacy was weak, if not nonexistent, and its absence systematically undermined efforts to firm up Afghan sovereignty.

To some extent, the above formulation ascribes a unity and coherence to the policies of the United Nations, the United States, and coalition partners that did not exist in reality. The various bodies consulted regularly, but each had its own favorite concerns and remedies.

Even within the U.S. government, differences of emphasis between the Pentagon, the State Department, the U.S. Agency for International Development (USAID), and the various other agencies involved were sufficiently broad as to cause objective observers to speak in terms of "U.S. policies" rather than of a single policy. The Pentagon's "Operation Enduring Freedom" focused exclusively on eliminating al-Qaeda and Taliban remnants, employing warlords where necessary to advance the mission. Other agencies operated as if this task had already been accomplished, and wanted only to cut the warlords down to size. The Pentagon's provincial reconstruction teams represented a bold effort to bridge this gap, but found critics among other U.S. representatives on the ground.

In this maze of uncoordinated goals and methods, two common threads stand out. First, virtually all U.S. and other international entities in Afghanistan continued to underestimate the urgent importance of achieving ethnic and regional balance in the government. Second, they continued to undervalue the need to build up local administrators and police on the basis of that balance. Thus, for all the inconsistencies that are probably inevitable in a vast operation with many independent players, the two factors that could have contributed most directly to enhancing legitimacy were both neglected. As a result, during the critical year following the Loya Jirga, the entire operation stood still or even slipped backward, threatening not only the legitimacy of the new Afghan government but also the very sovereignty that should have been its foundation stone. Down to mid-2003, the fundamental strategy of nation-building in Afghanistan was flawed, and none of the many palliatives that were applied following the Loya Jirga neutralized the consequences of the strategic errors that had been committed even before Bonn.

It is impossible to know how long this situation might have endured had not unexpected developments impinged. But during the last half of 2003 and 2004, with virtually no publicity, a radically different approach to nation-building in Afghanistan was formulated and adopted as policy across the entire U.S. government. This fundamental strategic shift was conceived initially by the Pentagon in the late spring and summer of 2003.

Very soon thereafter, the State Department and other U.S. agencies signed on, and by autumn, the new approach was adopted as common policy. Unlike the earlier policy, this one fully coordinated actions in the military, political, and economic spheres. Unlike the earlier strategy, too, this policy was to be implemented not from a series of ill-coordinated offices in different Washington agencies, but directly from the U.S. Embassy in Kabul, under the sole leadership of an individual in the combined position of the president's special envoy for Afghanistan and ambassador. The new approach called for:

- Working with the Karzai government to balance representation of personnel from all regions in the staffs of central ministries;
- Working with the Kabul government to remove and replaced unqualified or disloyal governors and local chiefs of police;
- Pressuring warlords to turn over tax receipts to the central government, promote cantonment of heavy weapons under the United Nations' disarmament program, and make deals with the Karzai government regarding their own futures;
- Supporting the Afghan government's demand that NGO activity henceforth be fully coordinated with Afghan officials at both the national and local levels, and that NGOs be held fully accountable to national laws and local officials; and
- Retraining and upgrading local civil servants and police through extensive new programs at the national and local levels, to enable them to interact lawfully, honestly, and productively with the local populace, businesses, and voluntary groups and organizations.

It can readily be seen that these various measures directly address the "birth defects" that were the Bonn Conference's legacy to the Karzai government—namely, gross ethnic, regional, and political imbalances in the new central administrations and the undercutting of the role and legitimacy of local administrators. Stated differently, they represent a strategic shift away from a narrowly defined notion of sovereignty focusing on military and security considerations to a broader emphasis on legitimacy as the Afghans themselves define it. As such, the new approach was nothing short of a strategic revolution, a fundamental redirection of U.S. policy on nation-building, conceived and implemented midstream.

Why did this strategic shift occur? The simplest and most accurate explanation is that it was due to leadership, initially within the Pentagon, but eventually in other departments as well. The change of direction occurred when individuals ranging up to the secretary of defense accepted that the old approach was leading nowhere.

It is equally accurate to say that the shift was driven by new information. During the spring of 2003, precise and comprehensive data was assembled on the ethnic, regional, and political makeup of the Kabul administration that the United States was supporting. Without the weight of this new evidence, it is highly unlikely that so basic a shift in direction ever would have been made.

The midstream change of direction in U.S. policy conforms to what Thomas Kuhn described as the structure of scientific revolutions.[2] The old approach fit most of the data then available, and inconvenient anomalies could be brushed aside, as occurred when nearly the same data on the composition of the central administration were collected and published in 2002. Gradually, however, the number of anomalies multiplied, calling into question the usefulness of the old paradigm (in this case, the emphasis on sovereignty alone, to the neglect of issues of legitimacy). Finally, an entirely new paradigm was introduced and a host of corollaries were derived from it, which constituted the new policy.

Once introduced, the new policy advanced steadily. Several new ministers not aligned with the Northern Alliance were named. In the case of the defense ministry, Fahim initially was not ousted, but three new non-Tajik deputies were named, one of them with firm control over the ministry's budget. Lower officials in many ministries were replaced. By basing all staffing changes on professional competence rather than ethnicity or region of origin, President Karzai was able to gain the support of many erstwhile critics. A May 2004 agreement that shifted Fahim completely out of the defense ministry and made him first vice premier represented a particularly important step, although one entailing considerable risk, should any misfortune befall President Karzai.

The new minister of internal affairs, Ali Jalali, moved quickly to remove fully half of the provincial governors and three-quarters of the local chiefs of police, replacing them with more competent people who enjoyed local legitimacy and who were ready to cooperate with Kabul. They in turn began the work of bringing more able and acceptable people into town and district administrative posts. Because most Afghans' contact with governmental authority is limited to officials at the local level, the importance of these measures cannot be overstated.

The chances of success of all these measures were, and still are, greatly limited by the Kabul government's inability to pay adequate salaries. This issue is clearly the Achilles' heel of nation-building in Afghanistan today. On the one hand, depressed salaries render it difficult to attract competent people to government service, which is bound over time to weaken the state vis-à-vis nonstate actors. On the other hand, it opens unpaid local administrators to corruption, which in Afghanistan, means narcotics trafficking. Unless civil service salaries can be raised, the otherwise laudable new policies will be neutralized.

Negotiations between President Karzai and local warlords produced significant deals, notably including the decision by Ismail Khan of Herat to abandon his local power base in favor of a ministerial portfolio in Kabul. Similar negotiations were successfully undertaken with leaders of several Taliban groups that were prepared to lay down their arms and join mainstream society. Each of these negotiations was unique, but they had the common purpose of enabling a former foe to find a face-saving and adequately remunerative position within the emerging state apparatus. Again, the ability of the Afghan government to collect taxes over the long run will determine whether it is able to continue to keep these former enemies safely on the payroll.

At the Tokyo meeting of donors in January 2002, Finance Minister Ghani had persuaded donor countries to back fully his demand that NGOs be properly registered with the government, that they coordinate their work closely with national priorities, and that they either develop productive and nonconflictual relations with local representatives of the state, or else leave the country. Furthermore, the upgrading and retraining of local civil servants had already begun, with Germany's training program for new police chiefs being typical of efforts in this area.

The World Bank and the European Bank for Reconstruction and Development also refocused their efforts on capacity-building in local administrations, as opposed to their earlier emphasis on NGOs and other autonomous social initiatives. For its part, the U.S. government advanced a proposal to establish a civil service academy in Kabul, and the European Union proposed a similar initiative.

All of these projects reflect the growing realization that nation-building must begin with effective and honest state institutions at all levels. Without them, it is pointless to think of the development of private business or even a productive relationship with NGOs. Above all, the development of committed and open-minded civil servants at central and local levels is a necessary precondition for elections that are free and fair, and for the functioning of the other institutions of civil society, including courts.

If elections are viewed as one of the key means of legitimizing a new government, then the importance of capable and honest administrators at local levels is a sine qua non of nation-building itself. The Afghanistan example proves that initiatives independent of the state can do little for nation-building unless they are coordinated, assisted, and protected by government administrators at both central and local levels. "Civil society" without state institutions leads nowhere, and can even undermine nation-building.

What Has Been Learned?

On the basis of this sketch of nation-building in Afghanistan in 2001–2005, the following conclusions would appear warranted:

- Building legitimacy for a new government cannot be postponed until a second stage of nation-building, but must begin at the earliest possible point and be pursued vigorously thereafter. Military actions involved with securing territorial sovereignty cannot be allowed to undermine this process.
- Those involved with nation-building have to accept the reality that legitimacy derives from whatever local people believe it derives from, and nothing else.
- Elections remain a powerful and essential means of legitimizing a new regime, but their credibility depends on the prior institution of nonelectoral measures that enhance legitimacy, including a local civil administration. It is unlikely that ineffective or corrupt administrators can mount elections that will be deemed credible and that will foster legitimacy.
- Whatever national or international gatherings may have installed a pro tempore head of state, the public will judge that leader and his administration unfavorably if he fails to follow policies of balance and inclusion in the staffing of key offices at all levels of government.
- Especially in traditional and nondemocratic societies, the effectiveness of representatives of state power at the most local levels are critical to the development of a sense of the government's legitimacy among the public at large.
- The full benefit of nongovernmental organizations to nation-building cannot be reaped without the prior existence of a legitimate national government and viable governmental institutions at the local level. NGOs can help train such personnel, but must avoid under any circumstances actions that tend to undermine them. Stated bluntly, as an absolute condition of their operation on the territory of the host country, NGOs must work with local governments and in coordination with legitimately established national objectives. Those failing or refusing to do so should be asked to leave.

In the end, the lesson of Afghanistan reminds us that, however minimal a state we may wish for, it must nonetheless be perceived as fair and competent if it is to function nationally. Similarly, until it can function effectively at the regional and local levels, it will be unable to provide the necessary framework in which private economic endeavor and voluntary initiatives can go forward, and in which fair elections can be held.

Afghans voted for a unified state and against federalism, let alone separatism. They have supported a strong executive. Neither could be achieved without first providing regional and ethnic balance in the staffing of core governmental offices in Kabul and elsewhere, and then providing the support and training necessary for local administrators to carry out their work without succumbing to corruption. Reasonable pay for civil administrators is an absolutely essential component of nation-building. Its absence will undermine and destroy even the best efforts to that end.

During the last half of 2003 and early 2004, the U.S. government introduced a radically new strategy to nation-building in Afghanistan. Unlike the policy it replaced, this one was coordinated among all key agencies and implemented on the spot rather than by proxy, with all local agency heads reporting to and through the U.S. ambassador in Kabul. The new approach focused on achieving balances within the government, strengthening essential governmental institutions at all levels, and neutralizing the centrifugal power of warlords and other illegal forces. These ends were pursued by working with rather than on the government in Kabul. Without this new approach, it is unlikely that Afghanistan would have been able to conduct presidential elections successfully. As of this writing, there is extensive evidence that the new approach is contributing directly and powerfully to nation-building in that long-suffering land.[3]

Notes

1. Afghan Recovery Report, no. 147 (London: Institute of War and Peace Reporting, November 11, 2004).
2. Thomas Kuhn, *The Structure of Scientific Revolutions* (Chicago: University of Chicago Press, 1962).
3. S. Frederick Starr, "U.S. Afghanistan Policy," policy paper (Washington, D.C.: Central Asia–Caucasus Institute, October 2004).

CHAPTER 6

Rebuilding Afghanistan

Impediments, Lessons, and Prospects

Marvin G. Weinbaum

NEARLY A QUARTER-CENTURY of armed conflict left the Afghan state broken, its national institutions virtually nonexistent, and its economy in ruins. Traditional authority was undermined and many of the society's norms seemed transformed. At the end of 2001, the country had effectively become a ward of the international community, with the United States taking the lead in defending the new regime from its enemies. Progress was soon registered in establishing an interim leadership, a transitional government framework, and democratic goals. By mid-2005, Afghanistan had a relatively liberal constitution, a president chosen in a credible national election, and plans for a popularly chosen parliament later in the year. But the rebuilding of an Afghan state continues to be a slow and difficult project, dependent on a number of developments, most of all a more secure environment, a continued international commitment of assistance, and the ability of Afghans to mitigate their endemic ethnic and kinship divisions.

Afghanistan is historically a weak state; the scope and depth of central government authority has been limited, as have efforts to deliver the basic security needs of its citizens. With its rentier economy, Afghanistan has for 50 years been heavily reliant on bilateral and multilateral foreign aid for its modest development goals. The country's leaders undertook little effort to bridge social cleavages. The communist period beginning in 1978 imposed an alien ideology on Afghanistan and engendered continuous armed resistance from within and without. Propped up by the Soviet military, a communist regime struggled in vain for legitimacy. With the ascent of a victorious but contentious mujahidin to power in 1992, law and order deteriorated further, and economic recovery was shelved. The Taliban leaders who replaced the mujahidin over nearly all Afghanistan between 1994 and 2001 had little capacity or interest in running a modern state or economy.

I begin this chapter by positing several requisites for Afghanistan to make a postconflict recovery. I then identify the most salient obstacles to progress, and briefly assess the achievements and setbacks to date in the country's political and economic reconstruction. There follows a discussion of the orientations and goals that have marked U.S. policies for Afghanistan and of how harsh realities have forced structural and attitudinal changes in the reconstruction effort. I then suggest a series of lessons that can be educed from the Afghan experience, some with broader application in the rebuilding of other states and economies. The chapter concludes with observations on future prospects and possible pitfalls for Afghanistan, and draws some possibly instructive comparisons with Iraq.

Requisites

The first and prime requisite in rebuilding Afghanistan is the provision of functioning state institutions. Institutional performance determines whether Afghans acquire confidence that their state, economy, and society can become inclusive, just, and prosperous. A rebuilt administration in Afghanistan calls for a bureaucracy with a reasonable capacity to plan, budget, and recruit personnel, as well as enforce policy. The recovery of judicial institutions and a workable legal framework are necessary to restore an orderly society, protect individual rights, and also attract private economic investment. A national bank and stable currency are indispensable to a regulated economy. With few other sources of revenue, a rebuilding state must improve its means for collecting taxes and tariffs. To realize a democratic polity, Afghanistan requires credible elections, a broadly representative parliament, multiple political parties, and institutional means to check the executive. A credible national army, expected to buttress central authority, is usually cited, along with an expanded and more effective police force, as necessary to ensure greater security in Afghan society.

A second requisite is an invigorated economy. Revived commerce spurs demands for the rule of law and security, and strengthens civil society. Revenues extracted from business activities are required not only for

government programs and services but also to eventually lessen dependence on external sources of economic assistance. A stimulated economy
provides the income necessary for the disarmament, demobilization, and
reintegration of private militias across the country, whose continued presence retards the establishment of national authority and threatens reconstruction programs. A revived agricultural sector calls for improvements in
the country's physical infrastructure and for the availability of inputs and
microcredit; its success is critical to overcoming the illicit economy from
opium-poppy growing that challenges state authority and is corrosive to
Afghan society. Importantly, a reviving economy fosters the popularity of
the Kabul government, ultimately also enhancing its legitimacy.

The third requisite for creating a stable, modern Afghan state and economy is generous, sustained foreign assistance. Only with this aid can basic
humanitarian needs be addressed, development goals advanced, and security enhanced. Financial support and technical assistance can be used to
build confidence in the central government, as well as empower civil society and ensure wider public involvement. Aid can also make a direct contribution to improving justice, human rights, and administration. Until an
indigenous capacity can be created, a direct foreign military presence is
indispensable for peacekeeping and political stability. Willingness by donor
countries and international agencies to invest in multiyear material and
moral support is necessary for aid givers to remain credible and effective.

The fourth is the resolution, or at least management, of outstanding,
divisive political and constitutional issues. Politically laden ethnic divisions
and a related center-periphery struggle over access to coveted resources
are familiar to Afghanistan. The former pits the country's largest ethnic
community, the Pashtuns, against smaller groups that have long been
politically subordinated, most importantly, the country's Tajiks, Uzbeks,
and Hazaras. Each maintains geographic strongholds under suzerainty of
regional power holders and subcommanders. The Kabul government con-
fronts private regional militias, the larger of them led by figures known as
warlords. Many warlords seek enough autonomy from the center to protect their sources of revenue, most of which comes from drugs and con-
sumer goods transiting the country and its borders. Strategies for reconstructing the state and economy and introducing democracy must be
sensitive to these ethnic and regional allegiances and the realities of power.
Another contentious issue, so far finessed, involves whether future law-
makers need only avoid violating the tenets of Islam or must subject their
actions to the approval of religious authority.

The fifth requirement is the reviving and strengthening of constructive national myths. These myths and the beliefs they convey are necessary
for social cohesion and raising national consciousness. Some consensus on

values is essential for adherence to laws and the exercise of political and societal trust and tolerance. Myths derived from recent and distant historical memories, including common images of Afghanistan at peace under the monarchy, the heroic jihad against the Soviets, and stifling Taliban repression, contribute to bridging differences between modernizers and traditionalists. They can also help resolve identity issues over who is an Afghan and what it means to be a citizen of an Islamic state. Given enough time, a constitution can create impelling national symbols that help bridge differences between ethnic factions, the forces of centralization and decentralization, and contending views of the role of religion in politics.

Finally, state-building may falter without reasonably capable, legitimate, and visionary leaders. Leadership is essential to providing purpose and direction for an Afghanistan emerging from its long national trauma. To the extent that the leaders succeed in transcending parochial differences and major societal cleavages, they are better able to forge compromise among entrenched, competing national interests. Establishing legitimacy is critical after decades of rule in which legitimacy was either taken for granted or its symbols callously dismissed. With the challenges of recovery seeming so overwhelming, citizens may also look for larger-than-life figures to deliver the country from its myriad problems. A freely elected national leadership is usually thought to be best able to lay out a vision that energizes reconstruction and unifies the country. However, elections by themselves can also raise unrealistic expectations of accomplishment.

Impediments

At present, the impediments to nation-state building in Afghanistan are many and formidable. Most are interconnected and mutually reinforcing, and any one of them could seriously set back economic and political development, national cohesion, and democratization. There is also evidence of progress in overcoming some of these impediments.

Inadequate Security

Rapacious local militias and bandits and aggressive antiregime militants remain a fact of life. Aside from Kabul and a few other urban centers, the level of security environment in Afghanistan is modest and has deteriorated in several southern and eastern provinces. Warlords and their subordinate commanders, operating through force and intimidation over local populations, often create deep resentments, although some also deliver services and enforce order. At times, these power brokers engage their private militias in turf battles. Public alienation from local commanders and disappointment with the central government over reconstruction efforts set the stage for inroads by insurgent forces. Where basic security remains weak, the delivery of humanitarian aid and the activities of Afghan and international aid workers becomes difficult, if not impossible.

Prospects that a Kabul government may some day provide for the security of its people rest on building an Afghan National Army. Plans for a projected 70,000 troops slated for nationwide deployment got off to a slow start through 2003, owing to serious recruitment and retention problems. Training accelerated during 2004, and by mid-2005, approximately 22,000 soldiers were beginning to assume some responsibilities for domestic security. A national police force is supposed to number 50,000 by the end of 2005, but although most have been enrolled in a prescribed, short training course, the poorly paid police inspire little confidence. Absent reliable Afghan security forces, a North Atlantic Treaty Organization–led International Security Assistance Force for Afghanistan (ISAF) of 10,500 troops is assigned to policing and public services, mostly in the Kabul area, but increasingly operating from provincial capitals. This is in addition to an American-dominated coalition force of 20,000, dedicated mainly to the pursuit of remnants of the Taliban and other antiregime insurgents. An agreement was reached in early 2005 to complete by mid-2006 a merger of United States–led counterinsurgency and ISAF peacekeeping missions under a unified NATO command.

Both the ISAF and the coalition forces were augmented during 2004. The introduction in 2003 and rapid expansion through 2004 of provincial reconstruction teams (PRTs) explains much of this growth. PRTs were conceived to help coordinate and fund small infrastructural projects and provide limited local security, while also helping to extend the writ of the central government throughout Afghanistan. The U.S. teams of roughly 80 individuals include members of special forces units, army civil affairs officers and engineers, and representatives from the U.S. State Department, the U.S. Agency for International Development (USAID), and the U.S. Department of Agriculture, as well the Afghan Ministry of Interior. Starting with five American teams concentrated in the south and east, by 2004, the United Kingdom, Germany, New Zealand, and the Netherlands had formed PRT teams in northern, western, and central areas, along with a combined U.K.-Norwegian-Finnish unit. Canada, Spain, Italy, and Lithuania, among other NATO countries were also in the process of fielding their own teams. By mid-2005, there were 22 PRTs, 13 of them American, with at least one team planned eventually for most of the country's 34 provinces. With the expanded NATO rule, other countries have agreed to locate PRTs in southern and eastern provinces, thereby sharing with the United States future counterinsurgency responsibilities.

The success of individual PRTs varies widely. Units in the Pashtun tribal areas face serious security issues and have had little time for reconstruction activities. Some have been criticized as poorly equipped to supervise building schools and medical facilities or engage in other development activities. The best PRTs make a contribution in creating ties with community groups and helping to settle or at least mitigate local disputes. They have tried as well to justify their mission by providing a more secure environment for nongovernmental organizations (NGOs). Nonetheless, many foreign NGOs in particular have opposed the concept, arguing that PRTs by their very nature blur humanitarian and development objectives with military ones, and thus place local aid workers in jeopardy. Even with their drawbacks—they are not a substitute for mobile peacekeeping forces—PRTs represent a tangible expression of a multinational commitment to Afghanistan's recovery.

Limited Economic Recovery

Economic growth has been uneven and remains fragile. There are, to be sure, some notable accomplishments during the tenure of Hamid Karzai as head of the country's interim and transitional governments and as its popularly elected president in October 2004. The economy grew by an average of 15 percent over 2003–4, according to the International Monetary Fund. The government has won wide approval for its conservative fiscal and financial policies and determination to pursue policy reforms. It has maintained a stable exchange rate and brought down inflation. In September 2002, the central bank successfully introduced a new, revalued currency. An aggressive finance minister brought about a remarkable degree of macroeconomic stabilization and took charge of planning and monitoring the reconstruction agenda. The government has also enacted a liberal investment law and introduced an open trade regime.

The impressive growth rate and other achievements are, however, an uneven measure of progress nationally, and mostly reflect how moribund the economy had been. Although foreign spending has stimulated commercial activity in the capital and several other cities, most of the country has experienced little of this economic improvement. The anticipated creation of public sector jobs through investment in rebuilding the country's infrastructure has not been realized. Even with the incentives to encourage domestic enterprise and attract foreign capital, substantial foreign private investment seems remote. Little is expected until security improves, laws are enforced, and greater profitability is demonstrated. The reliable supply of power and water will be necessary before industrial projects are likely to materialize. Overall, income-generating employment and increased agricultural output are critical to winning the confidence and cooperation of the population and directing the agriculture sector away from opium-poppy production.

Insufficient Resources

With few natural resources, a largely devastated agricultural economy, and little domestic investment or extractive financial capacity, Afghanistan is heavily dependent on international largesse for its recovery. Few observers question that the country has the capacity to absorb more resources, and that resource scarcity countrywide slows the pace of reconstruction. Although Afghans fiercely resist perceived exploitation and domination, they have always welcomed foreigners who bring humanitarian and development assistance. The Kabul government, the World Bank, and the Asian Development Bank have estimated that to meet development goals will require more than $28 billion in foreign grants and loans through 2011.

Compared to postconflict countries elsewhere, overall aid flows to Afghanistan are strikingly low. Failure by most countries to deliver more quickly or fully on commitments is usually explained by poor security countrywide and the lagging implementation of planned projects. Coordination among donors has also been a problem, leading to duplication and competition in some development sectors. Several international agencies and donor countries failed to meet commitments (totaling pledges of $4.5 billion) of financial aid made in Tokyo in January 2002. Moreover, the bulk of the funds received were absorbed by humanitarian relief efforts rather than by development projects.

The prospect of a loss of momentum in aid disbursements led 50 countries to gather in Berlin in April 2004 to recommit the international community to long-term support for Afghanistan. This meeting promised $8.2 billion in non-military aid over the 2004–7 period, including the $4.4 billion already pledged for 2004–5, of which the United States agreed to cover about half. But this commitment falls short of what Afghan officials claim is necessary to become just a "normal" low-income country. Even at the promised level of future funding, it remains to be seen whether commitments will be met. There is no guarantee against donor fatigue, should the implementation of programs suffer further from problems of security or emerging political instability.

Enduring Ethnic Cleavages

Ethnic divisions, reinforced by linguistic, sectarian, and geographic differences, have caused major fissures within the Afghan political elite that have, in turn, retarded state-building. The country, although deeply religious on a personal level, is not predisposed to radical Islam as an ideology. What appear among Afghans to be ideologically based differences are almost always a cover for kinship, personal, and, above all, ethnic rivalries. The minority ethnic communities are determined not to allow the Pashtuns to regain their traditional political dominance. The refugee experience—roughly half of the five million people who for 20 years lived in Pakistan and Iran have returned—and domestic dislocations have contributed to politicizing these ethnic minorities.

Programs of reconstruction have to deal with the ongoing struggle among these groups as they compete not only for political power, but also for economic advantage, including the demands of different groups for a fair share of government positions and the distribution of development monies. Pashtuns initially complained bitterly that Tajiks from the Panjshir Valley had taken over key government ministries with the Taliban's ouster and that they had been shortchanged in the dispersal of reconstruction funds. Ethnic tensions eased somewhat in 2004 and 2005, however, with the appointment of larger numbers of Pashtuns to important government posts. President Karzai's removal of several leading Tajik and Uzbek commanders from his cabinet was instrumental to a more balanced bureaucracy and perhaps signals waning warlordism. Although lingering grievances could threaten the rebuilding of the state, Afghanistan may be fortunate in that current demands by ethnic groups appear largely negotiable. In the absence of rich oil resources, fears of ethnic cleansing, or sectarian threats, the stakes for Afghan groups are relatively low—especially compared with the stakes in Iraq.

Poor Human Resource Base

Never well endowed with a skilled and educated population, a full generation of armed conflict mainly fostered the training of Afghans for fighting and brought the exodus of many of the country's better educated and experienced people. Particularly during the 1990s, education in Afghanistan was largely nonexistent, and women were denied entry to the workplace. A lack of trained and motivated personnel is apparent in the country's bureaucracy. District administrators and even governors are often unqualified, and the low salaries in the public sector deter capable individuals from taking jobs in the ministries. Personnel problems in the law enforcement and justice systems are especially deleterious to reconstruction.

Because it is too expensive to import many skilled foreigners, the attraction of qualified people from the Afghan diaspora would seem an obvious way to fill critical roles for government and the economy. Some wealthier Afghans living abroad could also provide fresh investment. But returnees have been of uneven skill quality, and many of those with capital to bring to the private sector are waiting for greater stability and assurances of a quick return on their investment. Moreover, those returning from the diaspora frequently draw the resentment of individuals who remained behind to fight the communists and the Taliban. In general, long-term development is thought better served by expanding the indigenous human resource pool.

Poor Governance in an Increasingly Narco-Mafia State

Overcoming corruption and nepotism is one of the major hurdles facing nation-state builders. Both problems are endemic to Afghanistan, and have intensified with the injection of foreign assistance capital. Transparency and public accountability are almost entirely absent in Afghan government activities, leading to distrust of and within the county's bloated bureaucracy. Not incidentally, most government employees are poorly and irregularly paid. Without reforms, it may be difficult to make an otherwise commendable constitution work. Concern over limited administrative capacity and corruption leads international agencies and donor countries, ordinarily state-focused, to channel aid programs largely through NGOs and U.N. agencies. Poor coordination among these groups—and among them, the Afghan government, and the private sector—remains a serious impediment to the recovery.

Narcotics traffickers, many of them regional militia commanders, form networks with corrupt government officials. At every level, there are complicit government officials who receive a cut from the handsome profits in growing and transporting opium. The lion's share of the proceeds from opium—of which Afghanistan supplies more than 80 percent of world output—has served to prop up warlords, enabling them to finance their fiefdoms and private armies. Acting as political spoilers, they collaborate against those institutions impeding their activities, even to the point of distorting reconstruction efforts and undermining respect for government authority.

The Karzai government faces two choices, both unpalatable. To allow poppy growing and trafficking to go unchallenged threatens the fabric of Afghan society and also provides income for those seeking to defy the central government, including increasingly antiregime insurgents. It could lead to Afghanistan's domination by criminal elements linked to international cartels, in the fashion of Colombia, with private armies specifically built to protect trafficking. Karzai is also anxious to please his international benefactors, notably in Washington, who call for a more rigorous eradication program. Yet a serious, indiscriminate campaign to destroy poppy production is almost certain to alienate large numbers of farmers of modest means and deeply affect an economy in which more than half of the GDP comes from the business of drugs. Serious efforts could also lead to a show-down with regional power brokers, whom central authorities would still rather co-opt than confront. At least for the time being, the government's policy is to vigorously assert its determination to eliminate drugs from Afghanistan's economy, but to move cautiously in choosing the means to do so, lest it provoke a popular backlash and invite political instability.

Influence of Regional Powers

Afghanistan's future is, to a great extent, bound up with the relations that states in the region have with one another, as well as with domestic political developments in each of the countries. All of Afghanistan's neigh-bors have at one time or another interfered in the country's domestic pol-itics through support of clientele groups, deliberately trying to disunite Afghans. The country has also been a frequent theater for Indo-Pakistani enmity as those two states strove for strategic advantage. Additionally, interprovincial tensions in Pakistan have at times fueled ethnic resentments across the border.

Since the Taliban's fall, however, Pakistan and Iran, together with the former Soviet republics and Russia, have concluded that their interests are better served by Afghanistan's political stability and economic recovery. Pakistan has pledged development assistance. Pressed hard by the United States, Islamabad has also periodically mounted military operations de-signed to remove anti-Kabul militants who find sanctuary in Pakistan's border regions. Iran has offered $560 million in reconstruction assistance over 5 years, including a project to extend its electric grid across the bor-der and complete construction of a road to Afghanistan's western city of Herat. Tehran also anticipates extending a rail line into Afghanistan. Al-though none of Afghanistan's neighbors have actively worked to under-mine the Karzai government, all continue to hedge their bets and remain patrons to those groups and individuals in the country with whom they have traditionally been associated. Should Afghanistan, for whatever rea-son, begin to fragment, the resulting power vacuum would lead regional powers to again flagrantly intervene on behalf of their clients and stake claims to political and economic spheres of influence for themselves.

Managing Reconstruction: A Case Study

The U.S. and international presence in Afghanistan has usually been described as having made a "light footprint." Although this approach's defining policies are often criticized for having shortchanged economic development and security requirements, the implications for state-building are mainly positive. American participation in Afghanistan's governance stands in sharp contrast to the 14-month-long direct U.S. rule in Iraq and the level of involvement and control by the international community in Kosovo and East Timor. The light footprint's signature is most evident in the early transfer of power to an Afghan government and in according this government enough discretionary authority to establish reasonable credibility. Afghans were given responsibility for selecting their own transitional president and for forming and staffing ministries. Although the light approach has, at times, overestimated what the Afghans can do for themselves, foreigners have not tried to dictate financial planning and development priorities or become drawn into day-to-day governance. Of particular note, the United States and others have sought to avoid becoming deeply involved in disarming Afghan militias, dealing with warlords, or eradicating the opium poppy. The Karzai government took prime responsibility for writing a new constitution and has conducted an independent foreign policy with its neighbors.

The Kabul government has, to be sure, profited greatly from international advice and assistance for its programs. Foreign government personnel and contractors work closely with Afghan officials and their staffs. American intervention and a cooperative attitude by regional powers were critical in pressing Afghan leaders to compromise on factional differences at the Bonn conference in December 2001 that laid out a political framework and a timetable for a democratic polity. Outsiders also actively facilitated the emergency Loya Jirga in June 2002 and the constitutional Loya Jirga in December 2003–January 2004, both of which grew out of the Bonn agreement. Yet on each occasion, critical decisions have rested with Afghans.

Even with its relatively low profile, U.S. policy in post-Taliban Afghanistan has not escaped criticism. No small part of this criticism is traceable to inconsistent goals and problems of coordination, reflecting competing interests and actors involved with national reconstruction. A gap has existed between decisions reached in Washington and the capacity or willingness of Americans in Kabul to implement them. There have been differences among agencies located both in Washington and Afghanistan. Divergent perspectives often separate NGO and American officials, leading to disagreements over resource and operational priorities. And there sometimes exist contrasting views by U.S. and Afghan officials over the level and channeling of funds.

But the most telling structural differences have stemmed from an unbalanced partnership between the military and civilian or diplomatic bureaucracies, and their largely disparate approaches to carrying out the U.S.

mission in Afghanistan. In contention have been strategic policy choices, especially those concerning the determination by the U.S. military to carry out unimpeded its antiterrorism operations in Afghanistan. After having removed the Taliban regime and dispersed al-Qaeda cadres, the Pentagon's planners had no desire to see the United States become involved in the country's recovery efforts beyond humanitarian assistance. The relatively low funding requested for the postconflict period reflected this approach. Nor was the military anxious to become involved in long-term peace-keeping or in allowing its international partners in Afghanistan to assume the job of providing public security on a broad basis. Stating concerns that a larger, more widely deployed ISAF could interfere with or complicate military plans, Washington rejected a promise in the Bonn agreement to place multinational forces in several major cities.

For the U.S. military, Afghanistan was to be just the first (although critical) step in the emerging global war against terrorists and their supporters. With Iraq already in the planning, the military hoped to turn security over to the Afghans as soon as possible and to get the international community to take on much of the responsibility for the country's rehabilitation and reconstruction. The donor pledge conferences in Tokyo and Berlin were intended to demonstrate broad international backing for rebuilding Afghanistan, showing that other countries would be ready to assume a large portion of the financial burden. Nonmilitary assistance was parceled out among several nations that agreed to take the lead—police training to the Germans, narcotics control to the British, the judicial system to the Italians, and militia disarmament to the Japanese. As soon as they could be trained and deployed, a volunteer Afghan army and national police would provide for the country's basic security.

With the U.S. military's goals paramount, other departments and agencies had to compete for attention to their interests in drug enforcement, political reforms, and human rights, especially women's rights and religious freedom. The Defense Department's postconflict designs were particularly at variance from views of the State Department, which envisioned taking a leading part in orchestrating Afghanistan's recovery. The State Department's USAID was seen as especially equipped for assisting the reconstruction. Diplomats lobbied for increased funding, especially to shore up the fledgling interim government, and were concerned that many in the Afghan leadership believed that the United States would lose interest in the country once it had realized its military objectives. Then–U.S. Ambassador Robert Finn saw many of his diplomatic prerogatives usurped while he lacked the resources in personnel and facilities to meet the demands on the embassy from Washington. His differences with the Pentagon were sufficiently deep to require that they be resolved at the highest government levels. Instead, the White House chose to treat the interdepartmental conflict as merely a failure of bureaucratic coordination. By default, the Defense Department priorities continued to prevail, although Defense would, in time, have to make adjustments to meet unforeseen security challenges and to account for inadequate performances by those designated to take on responsibilities.

The focal point for political reconstruction through the first 18 months lay in the White House's National Security Council (NSC), and specifically with Zalmay Khalilzad, its Afghan-born member, who carried the title of presidential special envoy for Afghanistan. Particularly adept at mediating among Afghan personalities and factions, Khalilzad, formerly in the Department of Defense, frequently clashed with the Washington-based interagency coordinating committee for Afghanistan's reconstruction and its State Department–appointed head.

By mid-2003, lagging progress in reconstruction contributed to the decision to adopt a new management strategy for Afghanistan. The plan was given a fast track to presidential approval, bypassing full examination from various agencies and serious consideration of its appropriateness for the country. Implemented in September 2003, it bore some resemblance to the Bremer Plan for Iraq, concentrating responsibility in a single individual in the field who, working closely with the military, would report directly to the White House. Khalilzad—who also retained his position as special envoy—was named ambassador and was similarly able to bypass the State Department. The Afghan authority structure differed from the plan in Iraq in that the new ambassador, effectively Paul Bremer's counterpart, would not be expected to exercise proconsul-like powers. Khalilzad's personal influence with leading government officials was also more collaborative and informal.

Under the revised structure, a bureaucracy called the Afghan Reconstruction Group (ARG) was formed separately from the embassy to handle a wide range of activities. Its nine senior advisors, selected by the Defense Department, were expected to work directly under the ambassador. (Funding difficulties prevented Khalilzad from getting the 20 or so advisors that he requested.) ARG assumed the leading role in planning for rebuilding the army and police, disarmament, demobilization, and resettlement, as well as for decisions on major infrastructural programs. It also took responsibility for a rule of law program and elections, as well as for advising the Afghan government in the fields of health, higher education, agriculture, and mines and industry—most functional areas that would normally reside with embassy officials. Meanwhile, such agencies as USAID and the Bureau of International Narcotics and Law Enforcement, although remaining directly attached to the embassy, were badly understaffed and marginalized.

In the case of USAID, its effectiveness was further reduced by its own bureaucratic restrictions, notably the need to have specific Washington authorization for project expenditures of more than $25,000.

Although the senior ARG advisors who came to Afghanistan were experienced in the security or development sectors, few were acquainted with the country and its special challenges. Several of them had originally been slated for assignment to Iraq. Like officials in the embassy, they have found themselves physically isolated for security reasons, unable to determine personally what is happening outside their compound. As a result, the ARG is at times accused of making assessments and making decisions on the basis of incomplete or bad information and having too little appreciation for how policies are implemented.

In Washington, an Afghan Interagency Operating Group (AIOG) was formed to complement the ARG, to coordinate among the several agencies involved with reconstruction. As a sop to the State Department, coordination among the government departments and agencies in Washington was placed under its aegis. The absence of earlier personality-related differences with the NSC has, however, enabled the AIOG to operate smoothly, although it cannot be assured that its decisions are actually implemented in Afghanistan.

To some extent under the now-departed Ambassador Khalizad, the American footprint deepened. Through his frequent public appearances and his reputation for assertiveness, the U.S. ambassador assumed a high profile. At the same time, the less-than-stellar progress in those development sectors formally assigned to the Germans, British, Japanese, and Italians has prompted the United States, mostly through private contractors, to expand its areas of responsibility. Thus the preparation of a national police force has become an essentially American project, and the U.S. military has begun greater logistical assistance, although not direct participation, in poppy eradication and apprehension of drug traffickers. The increased willingness of the United States, through its ambassador, to become more closely associated with reconstruction and reforms has its drawbacks, however. It leaves Americans liable to be held accountable for the inevitable program setbacks and to accusations of diminishing Karzai's stature and authority. It remains to be seen whether under a new ambassador, the Afghan president will be inclined to act more independently.

A further concern is that in the strengthened resolve by the military to quash terrorist groups seeking to destabilize the Karzai regime, large numbers of tribal Pashtuns may be alienated from the United States and the Karzai government. The introduction during 2004 of ultrasecret "black" special operations forces, mostly transferred from Iraq, have complicated the tasks of the PRTs in the southwest and the few remaining relief and development organizations. These troops are often accused of indiscriminately employing aggressive and culturally insensitive tactics. A local population already skeptical about the benefits of cooperation with American forces sees the resemblance of their operations to those used in the area by the Soviet military during the 1980s. By spring 2005, Karzai was demanding greater say for his government in counterinsurgency operations.

Lessons Learned

Several lessons have (or should have) been learned from the experiences of rebuilding a state and an economy since 2001. Although there was much to be gained from observing the management of other recent post-conflict projects, none have served as good models for Afghanistan. Overall, those countries assisting Afghanistan, and principally the United States, underestimated the difficulty, scope, and costs of rebuilding the country. Many missteps and misconceptions have been rectified, but not all have been fully addressed. Among the lessons learned are the following.

Military operations against antiregime elements cannot be allowed to dictate the pace and commitment to reconstruction. Multilateral peacekeeping receives only a small fraction of the resources spent on military operations—which for the United States totals over $900 million a month. The role of international forces was constrained while the U.S. military pursued its objectives of eliminating terrorist and antiregime elements. When in late 2003, the U.S. military recognized its error in minimizing the contributions of international forces to bringing a greater sense of security to Afghanistan, most countries were reluctant to commit substantially larger numbers of troops and were uncertain about deploying them more broadly. Without international forces, the United States entered into alliances with regional Afghan commanders, using their militias as proxy forces against al-Qaeda and Taliban elements. It took some time for the United States to realize that its troops were often being used to settle parochial disputes and that it inadvertently was strengthening warlords intent on resisting central government authority. Only belatedly did the United States come to value the expansion of international forces outside of Kabul through the PRT concept as a means to further construction and security projects.

Security and reconstruction are two sides of the same coin. Mutually reinforcing, progress on one front is necessary for progress on the other. For too long, reconstruction was seen as contingent on demonstrable improvements in security. In general, there is increased appreciation of the synergistic effect among the several factors contributing to progress in

Afghanistan and an understanding that the failure to realize any one of the requisites can jeopardize gains in the others. There is a near consensus in the aid-giving community that once humanitarian needs have been addressed, progress in development and governance offers the most effective way to stave off political instability and terrorism.

Recovery of the state, the economy, and the society in Afghanistan must be a sustained international project. Although there was never any doubt that a multifaceted international role would be indispensable for the rebuilding process, appreciation of the need to involve a broad spectrum of countries both in peacekeeping and development activities emerged more slowly. The international community has also come to recognize that mere pledges of financial assistance do not ensure that individual donor countries have the political will and staying power to see Afghanistan through the toughest phases of its rebuilding process. Many Afghans remain convinced that the United States will abandon them once its military objectives have been realized—most of all, the capture of high-ranking al-Qaeda leaders.

A light-assistance footprint in state-building promises greater legitimacy for Afghan rule and acceptance of a foreign presence. The international role in rebuilding the economy and securing order is frequently derided as inadequate, but Afghans have welcomed being given the opportunity to control their political institutions. From the outset, it was understood that Afghans should be allowed to assume the prime responsibility for governing themselves and to assume accountability for their actions. Foreign assistance would be available for strengthening the central government and building administrative capacity. But the United States and others, although at times facilitating compromises among various political actors, have learned to avoid becoming embroiled in resolving Afghan policy differences or taking sides in factional disputes.

A highly centralized political system may not be appropriate for rebuilding the state and economy. Although donors prefer to funnel aid through a central authority and are anxious to strengthen the Kabul government, they have had to deal with the traditional resistance to centralized dominance and Kabul's own limited administrative capacity. As a result, donors have used more local channels for delivery of most of their humanitarian and development assistance, typically through NGOs and international agencies. Historically, the Afghan state has been most successful when central authority has the coercive force necessary to intervene countrywide (militarily or otherwise) in furtherance of its vital interests and the wisdom to use that force (or influence) only selectively and sparingly. This formula has long constituted the means by which formal government institutions could function alongside more informal, decentralized authority. In the current debate, most donors concede the need to help extend the limited authority of the central government, allowing it to capture a greater share of development spending as a means to build capacity.

Ambiguity in the Afghan context can be good. Historically, Afghans' ability to live with imperfectly defined lines of authority often acted to mitigate conflict. Rather than to trying to formalize or rationalize jurisdictions and assign clear administrative responsibilities, permitting some ambiguity may be preferable. The boundaries of authority between regional power brokers and Kabul-appointed governors are likely to be established through bargaining that follows no clear precedents. Informal, flexible arrangements are familiarly associated with the judicial system. The responsibilities of the formal and customary court systems may be best left vague, and the effective reach of the civil courts limited to the urban areas. Blurring lines of jurisdiction should allow for adjustment to the local context and avoid areas of potential judicial and social conflict. This should not, however, depreciate the need and urgency of strengthening the country's legal framework and judicial institutions, especially the training of judges and prosecutors.

Accountability may be left open in a rebuilding Afghanistan. Increasingly, there are demands domestically and from the international community that individuals responsible for the country's suffering ought to be brought to justice. However, postconflict realities have made reconciliation and reabsorption a preferable transitional government policy. The ease with which Afghans have switched sides ideologically has especially complicated holding people individually accountable for their past behavior. Amnesty has effectively been granted to all but higher-ranking Taliban figures. Fearing political controversy, government authorities have also shown no interest in punishing those mujahidin leaders who were responsible for the destruction of Kabul during the 1992–96 civil war and who committed particularly egregious human rights violations over that period. Concern for avoiding political polarization has meant that former communists have not had to face government tribunals and retribution. And in much the same vein, although it is necessary to proclaim and enforce certain universal values, including women's rights, the cultural setting is likely to mediate the extent to which such ideals can be achieved in the short or medium term.

Looking to the Future

What sets Afghanistan apart from so many other projects in nation-state building undertaken by the international community is that the overwhelming number of Afghans, in seeming contrast to Iraqis, approve of the sustained involvement of foreigners in their country. It is not that Afghans are less nationalistic, but rather that there is wide recognition that the country has neither the material nor human resources necessary to reconstruct the state and economy. Although Afghans fiercely resist invaders and foreigners who seek to dominate or exploit them, they have historically been able to distinguish such foreigners from those who are willing to help Afghanistan. Afghans today are less anxious about their sovereignty being compromised by foreigners than about their problems being addressed. Until 1979, Afghanistan's leaders were particularly adept at playing off the United States and the Soviet Union to attract development grants and loans. Currently, beyond assuring generous, sustained aid, the greatest gift that the international community can bestow is to buy Afghanistan time to allow assisted political and economic institutions to root.

The building of an Afghan state and economy is likely to be transformational as well as restorative. Devastated systems can, for all of their challenges, also create opportunities. Caution has to be exercised where traditional culture might be affected, and change is likely to be incremental, but a number of previous impediments to development have been weakened if not removed. Much of the country's traditional leadership has been swept away, and many in the new generation of leaders draw on experiences gained from years of exile in more economically advanced and often democratic countries. The Soviet occupation and the exhaustion brought on by the protracted war have eliminated the once-murderous left-right ideological struggle, even as ethnic cleavages intensified. Afghanistan's political and social institutions, under greater international scrutiny, probably stand a better chance of reform than at any time previously.

A liberal state is usually felt to be best suited to fostering a sustainable political system and economic growth in Afghanistan. Individual freedoms, a vibrant civil society, and an open economy are prescribed and several familiar benchmarks indicating progress have been laid out. The United States and other Western countries tend to put a high premium on holding elections to provide greater legitimacy for those in authority. Under the best of circumstances, elections can be a means of coalition-building and reconciliation. Great significance is also given to agreement on a constitution that parcels out powers and enshrines rights. Laws that create a market-friendly business climate and protect investors usually get high marks.

But many of these measures can, in fact, convey a false picture of progress and even set back the recovery process. Elections that are poorly planned or rushed can be discredited and prove to be destabilizing. By their nature, contentious elections can create stresses that the political system may not be prepared to handle. The legitimacy of elections depends on rules and norms that may be slow to take hold. Elections can also leave the opposition unreconciled to defeat where there are doubts about democratic continuity. Constitution writing may force to the political foreground deeply divisive issues not ripe for resolution. In addition, rapid economic expansion that increases inflationary pressures and does not address distributive inequities may increase popular alienation from the Kabul government and its international advisors.

Remarkably, especially with the achievement of several prescribed constitutional milestones, Afghanistan has so far managed to sidestep some potential pitfalls. The presidential election in October 2004 defied many predictions that balloting places could not be secured and that too few citizens would participate. Indeed, Karzai's impressive victory enhanced his sense of mission and legitimacy and strengthened his hand against the warlords. Still other challenges loom, however—above all, getting an elected, possibly fractious national parliament to function alongside the executive and keeping the country's higher judiciary from interpreting the constitution to impose restrictive Islamic legal doctrines.

For all the hurdles facing Afghanistan's nation builders, the country has two significant advantages over Iraq. Despite bitter ethnic and regional rivalries, virtually no sentiment exists for separation or autonomy on ethnic or other grounds. (Past calls for a new Pashtun state, called Pashtunistan, envisioned it being carved out of northwest Pakistan.) Afghans overwhelmingly favor the country's territorial integrity over joining ethnic cousins across the Pakistani, Iranian, Turkoman, Uzbek, or Tajik borders. Perhaps more importantly, unlike Iraq, Afghanistan has in Hamid Karzai a broadly acceptable national leader. Karzai, although a tribal Pashtun, has largely managed to transcend his ethnic identity.

All the same, the United States and others have perhaps unavoidably invested too heavily in Karzai, and are overly dependent on several of his key ministers for implementing the reconstruction agenda. Karzai's daily meetings with Ambassador Khalilzad and his reliance on a private American contractor for his personal security have been no secret. Karzai, of course, values Washington's unwavering support for him and his government. He seeks for Afghanistan to be included in the Bush administration's broader Middle East democratic initiative as a means of giving greater surety to an American long-term commitment. Karzai's designation as the individual best able to foster compromise in a moderate, progressive Islamic state assures continued international recognition. This backing may also be important in retaining the cooperation of regionally powerful figures and staving off the challenges of prominent political opponents in Kabul. But in appearing too eager to please the United States and others, Karzai tests Afghan pride and courts the loss of credibility with his own citizens. He must be especially careful before agreeing to a long-term strategic partnership that involves granting military bases.

There also remains the question of whether the commitment to Afghanistan has suffered as Washington has become absorbed with the more complicated and far more expensive mission in Iraq. This argument assumes that greater resolve and resources might have been provided in the absence of an Iraq war. In fact, the contrary may be the case. Initially, the fighting in Iraq may have been a distraction from the hunt for al-Qaeda militants. But the difficulty during 2003 and 2004 in meeting goals set for Iraq apparently refocused attention on and instilled a greater sense of urgency to the U.S. effort in Afghanistan as conceivably a more productive enterprise for demonstrating progress politically and economically. Judging from the elections conducted to date, Afghanistan may serve as a better venue for realizing a progressive, democratizing Islamic state than the more problematic Iraq. Afghanistan may no longer be the principal battleground in the war on terrorism, although it still offers the largest political prize with the possibility of apprehending al-Qaeda's top leadership. Finally, a number of NATO countries resisting participation with the United States–led coalition in Iraq but anxious to substantiate their commitment to fighting terrorism have raised their contributions to Afghanistan's security and to the rebuilding of its economic and political institutions.

CHAPTER 7

The Lessons of Nation-Building in Afghanistan

Larry P. Goodson

AFTER NEARLY A QUARTER-CENTURY of modern warfare in a very un-developed country, Afghanistan on the eve of September 11, 2001, was about as poor as any place on the planet, with little surviving infrastructure, hardly any government, not much of an economy, and a population scarred by conflict and upheaval. For Afghanistan to undergo nation-building, state failure would have to be reversed and virtually every aspect of Afghan society would need reconstruction—from rebuilding tangibles, such as roads, electrical grids, schools, and clinics, to reconfiguring less tangible but no less important institutions, such as reestablishing the rule of law, replacing warlords with tribal elders, and reclaiming a national spirit from ethnic divisiveness.[1] The daunting reality was that every economic and political element in Afghanistan would have to be rebuilt.

Earlier versions of this chapter appeared as "Building Democracy after Conflict: Bullets, Ballots, and Poppies in Afghanistan," *Journal of Democracy* 16 (January 2005): 24–38; and as "Afghanistan in 2004: Electoral Progress and an Opium Boom," *Asian Survey* 45 (January/ February 2005): 88–97. The views expressed in this chapter are those of the author and do not necessarily reflect the official policy or position of the Department of the Army, the Department of Defense, or the U.S. government.

The good news, however, was that the long international ennui with Afghanistan was finally over, as 9/11 revealed to the United States (and less so to the rest of the world) that state failure in Afghanistan could no longer be allowed to continue. Bolstered by rare international solidarity, the United States and United Nations could use the consensus and good will to attack the problem with laserlike intensity. A band of long-suffering nongovernmental organizations (NGOs) that had worked in Afghanistan during the lean years of the 1990s provided institutional capacity and memory, and recent nation-building operations and postcommunist transitions across the globe (e.g., Bosnia, East Timor, Haiti, Kosovo, most of Eastern Europe, the former Soviet Union) provided a wealth of experience upon which to draw. Moreover, the toppling of the Taliban regime and subsequent reconstruction efforts have enjoyed widespread international support, have proved relatively easy to manage in terms of military and economic resources, and have been wildly popular among most Afghans. Moreover, these efforts generally appear to be headed in a positive direction. But success is far from certain. Serious challenges remain that if inadequately met, could cause the whole project of Afghan nation-building to founder.

Many of the reasons for expecting eventual success can be traced to the presence of an overall framework to guide Afghanistan's ongoing journey from failed statehood under the brutal misrule of extreme Islamists and their terrorist allies to a moderate and functional democratic government. The Bonn Accords of December 2001 constitute this framework.[2] The accords brought together concerned parties from inside and outside Afghanistan who joined in setting up mid-range state-building targets and intermediate deadlines that, when met, have given impetus to further steps on the path of transition. The failure to develop a similar plan of graduated political transition in Iraq for more than a year after the American-led Operation Iraqi Freedom has delayed the nation-building project there.

As the nation-building experiment in Afghanistan approaches its fourth year, progress remains very mixed. Until recently, the lessons to be learned have been mostly negative, but important policy adjustments along the way—especially those made by the United States in 2003 and 2004—reveal a picture that is more positive. Although serious challenges remain, tremendous successes have been achieved across the whole spectrum of nation-building efforts, from security and humanitarian relief to physical and economic reconstruction and state building. Both the successes and the failures merit careful analysis.

A general first lesson may well be the most important: politics and a lack of preparation and understanding of both Afghanistan and the broader challenge facing the United States drove the initial strategy, causing U.S. mistakes that would shape Afghanistan on the ground and constrain later choices. Deep flaws in U.S. strategy occurred due to institutional incapacity within the U.S. government for nation-building, and the George W. Bush administration's initial reluctance to make nation-building in Afghanistan a priority. (As a presidential candidate, Bush had actively campaigned against nation-building.) As in virtually all recent nation-building cases, for postconflict Afghanistan to undergo successful nation-building, several significant challenges would need to be met. These were provision of security, relief of displaced populations, rehabilitation of the economy and accompanying reconstruction of infrastructure, and state-building. In all these areas, U.S. strategy was flawed at first.

Political and strategic constraints were often artificial and based on faulty assumptions. Among the most important of these constraints was the antipathy of Bush and some of his senior advisers toward nation-building as an appropriate activity for American troops. Moreover, a segment of senior administration national security officials viewed Iraq as a more lucrative target of opportunity presented by the 9/11 attacks.[3] These ambivalent attitudes were exacerbated by a misreading of history that caused some senior advisers to fear Afghanistan as a graveyard of armies rather than see it a place so destitute that its war-ravaged population would welcome the intervention of international forces.[4]

In addition, there were very few Afghan specialists within the U.S. government, as the American disengagement from the region following the Soviet withdrawal from Afghanistan in 1989 prompted most government specialists from the 1980s to turn to other subjects. Years of warfare in Afghanistan had made conducting field studies there virtually impossible, resulting in a generation of U.S. scholars of the Middle East and South Asia who were without expertise on Afghanistan.[5] Thus only a limited number of specialists were available for consultation following 9/11. The fears and lack of understanding were played upon by the Defense Department. As part of an ongoing internal battle concerning the doctrine of military "transformation," and perhaps also in their haste to develop a rapid response, Defense Department officials put in place an operational plan that emphasized leveraging special operations forces and forward-air controllers to utilize overwhelming air power and the indigenous forces of the anti-Taliban Northern Alliance—all of which allowed limited American exposure on the ground. When coupled with the inadequate capacity for nation-building on the civilian side of the U.S. government, the light American military footprint left the United States with little ability to engage in the kind of rapid, substantial, and sustained nation-building that was necessary from the very start in Afghanistan. This situation was exacerbated by an ongoing struggle within the Bush administration among the various national security departments and agencies and the principals who represented their bureaucratic interests before the president. The Department of Defense emerged preeminent in the days following 9/11, and it has remained the dominant player in Afghan policy ever since.

This picture of flawed assumptions and mistaken calculations represented at its most fundamental level a transposition of tactical and strategic goals. Rather than recognizing that strategic success in Afghanistan would be best achieved by successful nation-building and constructing operational and tactical plans to best achieve that goal, the United States pursued more narrowly defined goals aimed at destroying al-Qaeda and capturing or killing its senior leadership (most notably Osama bin Laden), as well as toppling the Taliban and capturing or killing its leadership. Nation-building efforts (e.g., putting in place a government to replace the Taliban, reconstructing infrastructure) were clearly addenda to the military campaign, reflecting the traditional Pentagon approach of war as occurring in phases (with the Phase 3 of major combat operations giving way to the Phase 4 of postcombat operations).

Further compounding the confusion over what strategic goals should be and how best to construct an operational plan to achieve those goals, the United States learned in Afghanistan that initial mistakes often complicate later operations, as I show below. Additionally, it became clear that nation-building required coordination in different areas. Security might have primacy, but success also had to be achieved on reconstruction and state-building as well—failure to move forward in any one area could unravel progress in other areas. For ease of analysis, I now consider in turn each pillar of America's nation-building strategy in Afghanistan.

Security

Both Afghanistan and Iraq (and, indeed, earlier nation-building experiences) suggest that the first priority of nation-builders must be to establish or maintain security for the civilian population (not just operational security or force protection for the troops) and to build on that security to push the postconflict society toward the rule of law. In this regard, the American "light footprint" would prove extremely problematic, producing a situation in which security could not be guaranteed by the American-led coalition, thus allowing a panoply of other actors to affect the security equation. A mantra of nation-builders is "security first," but in Afghanistan, too few troops on the ground pursuing a mission that was too narrowly defined (winning the global war on terror rather than fostering successful nation-building) allowed various warlords; opium and heroin smugglers;

retro- and neo-Taliban, al-Qaeda, and other Islamist militants; and concomitant corruption to return, survive, or arise to bedevil Afghanistan.

The plan was to limit American exposure in Afghanistan to minimize both U.S. casualties and the abrasive effect on local sensibilities of an occupying presence. Thus the American-led coalition was initially focused only on the pursuit of antiregime forces. Recognizing that a "security gap" would exist, the Pentagon planned to fill that gap in the short run not with international peacekeepers (the 5,000-strong International Security Assistance Force [ISAF], had its mandate limited to Kabul until late 2003) but with the militias of the Northern Alliance commanders, thus facilitating the reemergence and retrenchment of various warlords, some quite unsavory.[6] With the ISAF confined to Kabul, most Operation Enduring Freedom (OEF) forces limited to two main bases (at Bagram and Kandahar), and only a handful of special forces soldiers operating outside the wire, various bad actors found opportunity to engage in criminal acts that threatened the security of the country. Although these miscreants are often described as falling into distinctive categories (e.g., as drug smugglers, Islamic radicals, former Taliban), in truth they often overlapped such boundaries, creating a confusing mosaic of security threats in Afghanistan. Pro-regime militias were frequently the source of instability, either by way of rapacious behavior against local civilians, or through "green on green" encounters with other militias. Drug smuggling and other criminal behaviors were engaged in not only by Taliban and al-Qaeda remnants but also by government ministers and their supporters.

The longer-term plan was to develop an Afghan capacity within the central government to fill the security gap through a program of security-sector reform (SSR). The SSR edifice features five major pillars, each of which has been the responsibility of a different donor nation. The United States has taken on the formation and training of a 70,000-man Afghan National Army (ANA), whereas Germany has, until recently, had the lead in developing several police forces. Italy has been responsible for reforming the justice ministry; Britain has spearheaded anti-narcotics efforts; Japan has led the effort to neutralize private militias through the disarmament, demobilization, and reintegration (DDR) program. These projects started slowly, suffered from poor coordination with the other pillar-building efforts, and lost momentum at various times over issues ranging from inadequate salary to loyalty to local commanders rather than to the state. Ambitious initial targets had to be adjusted downward repeatedly, raising doubts about whether the "lead donor nation" model really works.

The development of the ANA has seen the most progress, as early delays and difficulties were overcome and steady progress occurred. Although only some 23,000 troops had been trained by the end of 2004, the requisite infrastructure was built and the training regimen improved as the program slowly acquired momentum. Various deployments of the forces throughout Afghanistan during 2004 demonstrated its growing capability.

The Japanese-led DDR program aimed to convert the private and ethnic militias of various Afghan factional leaders into peaceful, law-abiding civilians. Known as the Afghanistan New Beginnings Program, DDR has been far behind schedule, only kicking off in October 2003, due in large measure to the reluctance of senior factional commanders (including former Vice President and Defense Minister Fahim Khan) to submit to the process. The overly ambitious goal of full DDR of all Afghan militia fighters prior to the October 2004 elections was not met, but the pace of DDR picked up in the latter half of 2004. DDR was helped along by the humbling of several senior warlords, most notably Fahim Khan (dropped as vice president from Karzai's electoral ticket) and Ismail Khan (sacked as governor of Herat). DDR picked up significant momentum with Karzai's pronouncement in June 2004 that the warlords were the primary security threat in Afghanistan and that the revised target is for full DDR to be completed by June 2005. (More than 30,000 militia troops have been demobilized thus far.)

Not all SSR pillars witnessed such progress. The German-led police training was especially slow, causing the United States to pick up some police training programs starting in 2003. Police receive far less training than the ANA, return to their provinces and towns without embedded trainers (unlike the ANA forces), and are paid far less than the ANA soldiers, creating conditions for endemic police corruption. The last two SSR pillars have seen the least success. Italian-led reform of the judicial sector has been virtually nonexistent, undercut by limited funds, international inattention, and Afghan uncertainty about the role of Islamic law in the future legal system. Most significantly, the counternarcotics effort led by the United Kingdom has failed. Opium and heroin production threatens to turn Afghanistan into a narco-terrorist state. In 2004, 4,200 tons of opium was produced—87 percent of the world's total. There has been a huge increase in land under poppy cultivation, with 10 percent of the Afghan population engaged in growing opium on 131,000 hectares (a 67% increase over 2003). Drought reduced crop yield and a market glut has dropped prices, but the export value of the raw opium shipped out of the country in 2004 was $2.8 billion—in a country whose total licit GDP in 2003 was only $4.6 billion.[7] The narcotics trade, in other words, is now 60 percent the size of the legal Afghan economy. This illicit economic sector is producing huge distortions to the Afghan economy and, as in Colombia, creating dramatic threats to security throughout the country and region.

By mid-2003, the absence of a robust international peacekeeping presence had allowed security to become uncertain enough to threaten other dimensions of the nation-building process, especially state-building. The United States responded with a series of strategic adjustments, beginning with doubling forces from about 10,000 to more than 22,000 by mid-2004. These reinforcements added muscle to a summer offensive that suppressed Taliban activity leading up to the October 2004 Afghan presidential election. In late 2003, newly-arrived OEF commander Lieutenant General David Barno demonstrated the shift in thinking that had occurred in U.S. strategy toward Afghanistan by embracing a pilot program for peacekeepers there. A handful of provincial reconstruction teams (PRTs) had been created in 2003, but Barno made them the backbone of his strategy in Afghanistan, ramping up from four to 16 PRTs in about 6 months, as part of an effort to stabilize the countryside and facilitate reconstruction.[8] These mixed military-civilian teams of about 80 people work from bases in provincial capitals to stabilize surrounding areas with a combination of military patrols and hands-on reconstruction help. The PRTs include civil affairs specialists and have commander's funds to spend. The teams aim to create "islands of stability," within which NGOs can operate, even if some NGOs find the PRTs' blurring of traditional civil-military distinctions to be worrisome.[9]

The performance and impact of PRTs have been mixed. Some have struggled with inadequate staffing, especially from U.S. civilian agencies. A poor grasp of local political dynamics and circumstances has also been a problem. More mature PRTs that enjoy good relations with local officials have developed aid programs that have improved local conditions and strengthened positive views of coalition troops and the new Afghan government. Along with the growth in PRTs came other efforts to enhance the civil affairs and reconstruction aspects of U.S. military operations and to coordinate these more closely with the work of U.S. diplomats.

Work on persuading other countries to assume more significant roles continued despite rifts over the American-led invasion of Iraq and the subsequent demands for nation-building that came out of it. The North Atlantic Treaty Organization (NATO) took over the ISAF in August 2003, ending a pattern of finding a new lead for the ISAF every 6 months. Two months later, the U.N. Security Council expanded the ISAF's mission to include securing relatively quiet northeastern and north-central Afghanistan. Five PRTs are now under NATO command, and NATO nations are to take over all the PRTs in the north and west and, it is hoped, eventually take over for OEF throughout the country. At its Istanbul Conference in June 2004, NATO agreed to increase its forces in Afghanistan to 10,000 by the October 2004 presidential election, but thus far, NATO has struggled to find soldiers and equipment to meet its new Afghan commitments.[10]

Security threats may have diminished in Afghanistan during late 2004 and into 2005, but they still exist. The Taliban, al-Qaeda, and other anti-regime actors continue to mount attacks, especially in the southern and eastern areas bordering Pakistan, but the age of the warlords appeared to be ending in 2004. Warlords and militias had grown as security threats during 2003, empowered by cooperation with U.S. forces, illicit sources of income, their government positions, and in some cases, refusal to participate in DDR. With so much money at stake, many engaged in criminal acts that reduced security throughout the country. Ostensibly pro-regime warlords were paid by the Americans and used as an anti-Taliban bulwark, although their militias were frequently the source of instability. This instability primarily took the forms of predatory behavior against local civilians and factional fighting with other militias, such as the violence between Ismail Khan and Amanullah Khan in Herat and Farah provinces, or the repeated clashes in the north between the forces of Abdul Rashid Dostum and Atta Muhammad. Warlords and their militias also engaged in drug smuggling and other criminal behavior, as did Taliban and al-Qaeda remnants and government ministers and their supporters.

Although there is a widely held perception in Kabul that the warlords are nothing but paper tigers, many warlords have gained strength since 2001 and are unlikely to give up power altogether. Moreover, they continue to maintain de facto control over large portions of the country outside Kabul. Virtually all these warlords utilized their power to enrich themselves and their followers, gaining control over well more than half the cash economy—not only the opium and heroin trade, but also customs monies, illegal real estate transactions, mineral wealth, timber, and road tolls.[11] Many knowledgeable observers expect warlords to use their local power to further entrench themselves by way of the September 2005 parliamentary elections.

Several specific lessons on security can be derived from the Afghan experience thus far. *SSR pillars need timelines that reinforce rather than undercut one another.* Such reinforcement has not taken place in Afghanistan, in no small part because so many different donor nations and NGOs have held various pieces of the puzzle. For example, when early efforts to develop the ANA stumbled over its low level of professionalism and rate of retention, pay was hiked and Western military trainers were embedded in Afghan units. Failure to take similar steps in the case of the police has left that service worse paid, far less professional, and much more prone to corruption than is the army.

Although the "lead donor nation" model promotes political "buy-in" by sometimes-reluctant allied nations, it often leads to poor coordination and slow progress across nation-building pillars. In Afghanistan, the deficiencies of the "lead donor nation" model became clear enough that the United States either arranged specifically for improved coordination (usually through the Afghan government) or simply took the de facto lead when other countries failed to move quickly or successfully enough, as in police training and counternarcotics programs.

Any approach that requires working with warlords and local militias needs to plan for how this may make them stronger and harder to dislodge later, when the state-building process requires it. Although the major Afghan warlords were diminished in 2004 and 2005, lesser warlords remained powerful in localities throughout the country. The jury is still out on whether warlords will disappear altogether.

Military strategies (including force structure and rules of engagement) need to be crafted not only with an eye toward initial war-fighting, but also with a view to security and peacekeeping or nation-building operations that follow the end of major combat. Afghanistan suffered from having the lowest number of peacekeeping troops per capita of any recent postconflict situation—a state of affairs that would be far more problematic were antiregime forces more robust.[12]

Reconstruction

Early difficulties on the security front were exacerbated by slow progress on reconstruction, which is almost as important as security in Afghanistan. After conflict or regime change, societies usually require some degree of reconstruction or institutional transformation, but the destruction in Afghanistan in late 2001 was far beyond what is usually encountered in such disrupted societies. Nearly a quarter-century of warfare had reduced virtually all physical infrastructure in the country to rubble, created the largest refugee population in the world from 1981 to 1997, and destroyed or transformed most important social, economic, and political institutions. Thus for Afghanistan, reconstruction required the highest possible priority, as any successful rebuilding of the country would need a platform of reconstruction as a foundation. Unfortunately, more than 2 years were lost to inadequate initial commitment (as exhibited by inadequate funding), an inchoate organization for institutional reconstruction, and a necessary focus on relief and the resettlement of repatriating refugees rather than on reconstruction for the future. The low initial starting point, coupled with the unexpectedly rapid repatriation of more than two million refugees, resulted in a slower start-up than expected and a channeling of most initial funding to refugee relief and resettlement rather than to reconstruction.

Afghanistan is a case study in the sobering realities of international aid and crisis response. The most important of these realities is that no one agency or country is truly capable of coordinating the response. Needs assessments must be conducted, donors found, and NGOs funded to deliver projects, all without much effective central coordination or oversight. In the absence of a serious and functional Afghan government from October 2001 to the fall of 2002, the Afghans could provide little initial guidance to the reconstruction process. Ultimately, Afghan reconstruction has had multiple and often competing architects, including the Afghan government (eventually), the lead donor countries and multilateral organizations, the U.N. Assistance Mission in Afghanistan, the other 16 U.N. agencies operating in the field, the U.S. Agency for International Development (USAID), and some three thousand NGOs. This large number of participants has made the reconstruction process a complex mixture of projects, agencies, and priorities, with metrics that can demonstrate conclusively its overall success, or equally conclusively, its stunning failure.

On the positive side, sound macroeconomic policies and the very low starting point have made it possible for Afghanistan to enjoy rapid economic growth of "nearly 50 percent cumulatively over the last two years (not including drugs), with double-digit economic growth expected to continue in 2004."[13] The drivers of this growth are largely recovery-related and temporary, however, necessitating a continuing search for sustainable growth alternatives. Most (80–90%) of the Afghan labor force is employed in the informal economy, much of which will have to be formalized for Afghanistan's recovery to continue. Constraints to developing sustainable development alternatives in a formal economy are substantial, including continuing insecurity, corruption, burdensome regulations, and a broken infrastructure (especially the road network and power grids).[14] Also significant was the completion of the Kabul-to-Kandahar portion of the national highway, known as the "Ring Road." Rebuilding the Afghan roads had top priority, as the Afghan government constructed its long-term economic strategy around Afghanistan's position as the hub of trade from Central to South Asia. Finally, thousands of microprojects in education, health, agriculture, and other sectors were completed.

On the negative side, microeconomic and social indicators, although improving, still show Afghanistan to be a desperately poor country. The majority of Afghans live below the poverty line, with few individuals having access to safe drinking water (23%), adequate sanitation (12%), or electricity (6%). Agricultural production has increased, but a return of the drought of the late 1990s keeps the risk of famine high. Infant mortality at 115 per 1,000 live births and the highest rate of maternal mortality in the world contribute to the low life expectancy of 44 years. And, although more than three million children have returned to school since the fall of the Taliban, illiteracy remains high at 71 percent.[15] Moreover, the equivalent of almost 60 percent of Afghanistan's GDP now comes from growing opium poppies and smuggling heroin, most major infrastructure awaits rebuilding, and per capita spending on reconstruction is the lowest seen in any postconflict situation since the end of the Cold War.

The most pressing economic need is to move Afghanistan away from opium and heroin production, but the bumper crops of the past three growing seasons are by-products of the economic uncertainty that has led to huge increases in land under poppy cultivation and growing networks of farmers, processors, and smugglers. President Hamid Karzai announced in December 2004 a goal of complete eradication of the opium-heroin trade within 2 years, but so much of the economy is now tied to this industry and so many senior officials and their families are involved that such an ambitious goal will be difficult to achieve. The major approaches are poppy eradication, which threatens the fragile microeconomics of the Afghan rural sector; crop substitution, which is unattractive because of the high price per unit of production received for opium; and destruction of processing laboratories and interdiction of smugglers, which are difficult to accomplish due to the high-level protection provided by senior government officials. At its current growth rate, the illicit Afghan economy will soon equal the licit economy, on which the former already has a profoundly distorting effect. Preventing the cartelization of the drug industry that will promote Afghanistan's rapid descent into becoming a narco-terrorist state is now the most significant immediate reconstruction challenge facing the country.

Major international funding for Afghanistan's reconstruction has been raised through two large donor conferences. In January 2002, a Tokyo meeting held in the wake of a needs assessment produced by the World Bank, the U.N. Development Program (UNDP), and the Asian Development Bank secured pledges of $5.2 billion over 5 years, just over half of the $10.2 billion provided as the base amount required according to the needs assessment. Various constraints (including increasing insecurity, drought conditions, and refugee repatriation) have made reconstruction more costly, but the bigger problem is that needs have been greater than pledges, pledges greater than committed or disbursed funds, and those funds have been far greater than projects begun or completed. As of mid-2003, only $192 million worth of projects had been completed, less than 1 percent of the need.[16] Here again, though, a shift in the U.S. approach has been important. The November 2003 congressional supplemental appropriation of $87 billion aimed primarily at Iraq added an extra $1.6 billion for Afghanistan and spurred a renewed commitment to Afghanistan. This momentum was carried forward at the April 2004 Berlin Donors' Conference, where $8.2 billion was pledged over 3 years (including $4.4 billion from the United States). The first year's pledges alone amounted to $4.5 billion. Although this sum seems impressive, the Afghan government assessed reconstruction needs at $27.5 billion, more than twice the amount pledged in Tokyo and Berlin combined, suggesting that pledges continue to fall short of needs.

The lessons of reconstruction are multiple. *The cumbersome process of needs-assessments, international conferences to secure aid pledges from barely willing donor countries, and project-driven assistance routed through NGOs is neither efficient nor effective.* The Iraq experience, however, shows that aid from a single source can also be difficult to translate quickly into improved economic conditions in the postconflict society. (Of course, Iraq's growing insurgency provides a significant constraint on reconstruction work.) Still, Afghanistan's needs are so enormous and the rhetorical commitment of Western leaders to its rebuilding so loud that it is hard to understand why the United States has not treated infrastructure reconstruction and institutional capacity development with the same level of prioritization as combat operations. Even in 2005, nearly 4 years after American reengagement with Afghanistan, the mission there is conducted on a shoestring, including the military operations and the soldiers who conduct them. And 2005 may mark the high-water mark for international engagement in Afghanistan.

Linking reconstruction to security in Afghanistan has not been successful. DDR provides a telling example. What is really needed is RDD, where the reintegration of militiamen precedes and paves the way for their eventual demobilization and disarmament. Road-building contracts could have been let to companies that would agree to employ, through warlords, local fighters under their control as laborers on the roadbed, gradually tying both warlords and their soldiers to the reconstruction of the country.

The institutional capacity to rebuild a war-torn country rapidly does not seem to exist. The current model, in which vast bureaucracies such as the UNDP or USAID act as contract agents for thousands of high-overhead international NGOs and their expensive staffs, allows literally tens or even hundreds of thousands of projects to be implemented, but at the cost of long lead times, frequent duplications of effort, and staggering waste. A more streamlined method of at least picking the "low-hanging fruit" of a few big reconstruction projects, whose beneficial effects would have resonated widely throughout Afghan society, would have been enormously helpful in 2002. Nation-building may not always be able to wait on the ponderous pace and scattershot approach of the international-aid complex. It is necessary to develop a more streamlined capacity for rapid reconstruction, so that when necessary, nation-building can be expedited.

State-Building

The difficulties attached to the political development of Afghanistan, or what might be called state-building, have been more subtle than those encountered in the security and reconstruction sectors. The framework for state-building in Afghanistan has been the Bonn Accords, established at a meeting of anti-Taliban Afghan groups brokered by the United States and the United Nations in December 2001. The Bonn Accords laid out a process of graduated transition to full sovereignty by first establishing an Interim Afghan Authority headed by Pashtun tribal leader Hamid Karzai, who held office from January to June 2002. A grand council known as the emergency Loya Jirga met in June 2002 to choose a Transitional Administration (also headed by Karzai). The Transitional Administration was to rule until proper elections could take place under the new constitution, which was set to be deliberated upon and adopted within 18 months of the emergency Loya Jirga. A constitutional Loya Jirga duly met in December 2003 and January 2004 to draft and ratify a new Afghan constitution.

The final step in the Bonn timetable was for free and fair elections to occur within 2 years of the emergency Loya Jirga (that is, by June 2004). For primarily technical and political reasons, these elections fell behind schedule. The delay appears to have been no great loss and may even be a sign of resiliency, given that the initial timetable was quite arbitrary. Balloting to choose the president and a pair of vice presidents took place in early October 2004, and Hamid Karzai became the first freely elected president of Afghanistan.

The more complex legislative elections were postponed until September 2005, when Afghans will choose a popularly elected *Wolesi Jirga* (house of the people, or council of the people) as well as an upper chamber, or *Meshrano Jirga* (council of elders), some of whose members are to be selected by provincial and district councils, with others appointed by the president. This process aimed at giving Afghans a chance to gradually develop the political institutions and capacity for competent self-governance from initial conditions of complete state failure.

Although this graduated approach to creating a functioning Afghan government may have been the optimal way to structure the transition, it has the drawback of setting aside federalism (a natural fit for ethnically and regionally diverse Afghanistan) in favor of a problematic concept called "broad-based government." This idea grew out of U.N. efforts, dating back to the 1990s, to end the civil war by creating a strongly centralized national-unity government in Kabul, with seats for all the contending factions. The scheme was designed to assuage concerns that a single ethnic group—that is, the traditionally dominant Pashtuns, from whose ranks most of the Taliban also came—would grow too strong and abuse the other groups.

Afghanistan's complex welter of family and tribal-oriented political alignments did not adjust well to this system, however, and the problem was exacerbated by American patronage of various anti-Taliban warlords and commanders, who naturally preferred to gather power at the local level and were distrustful of Kabul and the Karzai government. Many among the Pashtuns, a group that accounts for two-fifths of all Afghans and that gave the Taliban its demographic base, felt that "broad-based government" was code for rule by non-Pashtun figures from the old anti-Taliban armed coalition, the Northern Alliance. Simmering resentment of Kabul among Pashtuns made it hard for Karzai's government to reconcile even the softer Taliban supporters to the new order. Pashtuns, with the encouragement of their coethnic Karzai, began to reassert themselves in the process at the constitutional Loya Jirga, thereby arousing predictable suspicions among Tajiks, Uzbeks, Hazaras, and other minority groups. This process would continue throughout 2004 and culminate during the October presidential balloting. Ethnic, linguistic, and sectarian divisions have been deepened by the long civil war and constantly threaten to overwhelm a broad-based government system.

The Bonn Accords laid out a process of graduated transition to full sovereignty, but the intermediate steps—establishing the Interim Afghan Authority, then the emergency and constitutional Loya Jirgas—all kicked the can down the road. Hard political decisions were made necessary by the return of the warlords and the decision to balance power in a broad-based but centralized government rather than locally through a federal arrangement, but those factors allowed international interlocutors and their Afghan proxies to postpone those hard political decisions until the October 2004 presidential elections and the September 2005 National Assembly elections. Karzai's playing of the Pashtun card at the constitutional Loya Jirga and the reaction of the northern minorities demonstrate how hard the state-building process will be, especially given the absence of institutional capacity, which exacerbates Afghanistan's overreliance on personality politics. Thus the success of the presidential elections of 2005, both procedurally and in terms of results (i.e., the election of a moderate, pro-Western candidate), was quite encouraging.

On October 9, 2004, some 4,900 polling centers (with 22,000 polling stations) in all 34 Afghan provinces—plus an additional 2,800 polling stations in Iran and Pakistan to serve the Afghan refugee population—handled more than 8 million Afghan voters (8,128,940, to be exact—a 70% turnout rate) in the first-ever presidential election in Afghanistan.[17] Despite significant security concerns motivated by Taliban threats to disrupt the elections, multiple attacks on election workers and voters in the weeks prior to the elections, complaints of fraud and unfair advantage for President Karzai (as well as of his being favored by the United States), and some election day glitches (most notably the failure of the indelible ink intended to prevent voters from casting ballots more than once), the elections were, overall, a remarkable success.

Transitional president Karzai won 55.4 percent of the vote—thus avoiding a run-off, as the Afghan Constitution provides for a two-round system when the top two vote-getters compete again 2 weeks after the initial election if no one receives over 50 percent of the vote in the first round—in a field of 18 candidates, defeating his former minister of education, Younus Qanooni, who had 16.3 percent of the vote. The election did break down along ethnic lines fairly significantly. Karzai, a Pashtun, polled well across the country and among the refugee population, but he did best among his fellow Pashtuns, and the other major candidates performed best in their respective ethnic strongholds. The Tajik Qanooni led the balloting in seven provinces, primarily in the northeastern Tajik part of the country. Third-place Haji Mohammad Mohaqiq, a Hazara, led the balloting in two Hazara-dominated provinces; the Uzbek warlord Abdul Rashid Dostum finished fourth and led in four provinces, especially in the north-central Uzbek part of the country.

Despite anger among these sometime allies of the former Northern Alliance when Karzai decided in July (under significant international pressure) to drop Interim Vice President Mohammad Fahim Khan as his running mate (prompting a last-minute decision by Qanooni to run against Karzai), longstanding rivalries from the Afghan civil war prevented the northern and central minorities from uniting behind one candidate. Had the Tajiks, Hazaras, Uzbeks, Turkmen, and recalcitrant Pashtun royalists been able to unite and attract the support of ousted Herat governor Ismail Khan, the election might have been much closer, maybe even moving into a run-off. As it was, Karzai's margin of victory was less impressive than earlier predictions of upwards of 70 percent had suggested it would be.

The presidential elections fostered an important development—the creation and utilization of political parties. Indeed, given that the outcome of the election was a foregone conclusion, the decision of so many other candidates to run suggested that they had other reasons for doing so. Some, like female candidate Masooda Jalal or the poet Latif Pedram, ran as an expression of the change that Afghanistan has undergone. Others ran or announced interest in running only to increase their leverage in post-electoral bargaining. One leading candidate told me openly how he had tried to strike a deal with Karzai for a ticket slot or a cabinet post, plus certain benefits to the candidate's home region. Others were more discreet but behaved in similar fashion.[18] Some individuals carried through with their campaigns, whereas others, such as former President Burhanuddin Rabbani, were convinced to remain on the sidelines. (Rabbani was quite pleased that Karzai dropped Fahim as vice president in favor of Rabbani's son-in-law, Ahmed Zia Massoud.)[19] Although most candidates (including Karzai) ran as independents, at least one major candidate, Qanooni, seemed to be using the election as an opportunity to develop a political party in preparation for the parliamentary elections in 2005. Although Qanooni was most popular in Tajik areas, he openly appealed to the legacy of the Soviet war in the 1980s and the "heroic mujahidin" who had fought in that war in an effort to broaden his appeal across ethnic lines. His party, Nuhzat-i-Milli Afghanistan (National Movement of Afghanistan), is one of more than 50 that have registered for the 2005 elections.[20]

These parties run the gamut from former mujahidin-run organizations and ethnic vehicles to former communist organizations. A September 2003 law on political parties places some limits on party formation: no party may have a militia, for example, or espouse goals "counter to Islam." Yet a taller hurdle may be the reluctance of Karzai and other senior government officials to see parties form, for fear that they will deepen ethnic and sectarian divisions. The failure to develop parties during the 1960s undercut Afghanistan's earlier experience with political liberalization. The rules now in place for the upcoming *Wolesi Jirga* elections call for a single, non-transferable vote (SNTV) system rather than a list-based proportional representation system. Some expect that the use of an SNTV system could sharply limit the role that parties can play in the upcoming elections. During the October election, however, Qanooni, Mohaqiq, and Dostum each benefited from party-based efforts to rally his respective ethnic supporters, which suggests that parties may well play a larger role in the parliamentary elections of 2005.[21]

Important lessons from the state-building effort in Afghanistan exist, but may be difficult to apply elsewhere. *There is an inherent trade-off in the heavy versus light footprint decision in state-building in terms of the choice between capacity-building and sovereignty.* That is, if existing institutional capacity is lacking (as is the case in Afghanistan following the nongovernance of the Taliban era), then the size of the international footprint and the level of international involvement will have significant implications for the governance of the country. If early sovereignty (or quasi-sovereignty) is a priority and capacity is lacking, a light U.N. or U.S. footprint will delay and possibly even cripple capacity development and force a continued reliance on a large NGO presence.

The question of how to manage the hand-off of real sovereignty to an indigenous national government is linked to the capacity/sovereignty/footprint trade-off. In Afghanistan, this task has occurred gradually through the Bonn Accords mechanisms, but it has not been entirely successful, as the Karzai government, the American-led coalition, the ISAF, various regional and local warlords, and antiregime elements all have some degree of power in varying places and over various issues around the country. The tolerance for ambiguity in Afghanistan has helped this at-times clumsy hand-off to work.

Security, reconstruction, state-building, and all other important elements of nation-building must be coordinated to reinforce one another. Otherwise, it is too easy for one pillar to achieve preeminence while slower progress on other pillars undercuts overall success. Sometimes this can be a problem of what retired U.S. General Tommy Franks calls "catastrophic success": The dramatically quick military triumph over the Taliban won with minimal U.S. ground forces, for instance, left Afghanistan without a government before state-building and reconstruction options could be developed. Later, the continued focus on security came at the expense of the other pillars of nation-building. The light footprint and the desire to "let the Afghans do it" just complicated matters, opening the door for numerous autonomous actors in various sectors. A more organized effort with a heavier footprint going in is probably preferable, although that still leaves the issue of the hand-off to a new sovereign government, as is apparent in Iraq.

Future Challenges of Nation-Building in Afghanistan

Even though the successes of Afghanistan's nation-building to date have been gratifying, important challenges remain for the Afghan government and for the international community that has been so instrumental in erecting and sustaining it. Four significant problems derive from unfinished business in the main pillars of nation-building over the past 3 years. These challenges are (1) the persistence of an antiregime, anti-Western insurgency; (2) the continuing presence of local and regional private armed forces, even when they are not actively fighting regime or international forces; (3) the disquieting growth of the opium-heroin economy; and (4) the looming and complex parliamentary elections. Increasing insecurity during

2003 and 2004 marks the reality that relentless antiregime elements still exist in Afghanistan. The overwhelming firepower of U.S. forces, particularly from the air, means that these antiregime elements find themselves unable to mount large-scale attacks. Yet they can still launch small-scale assaults that make use of improvised explosives or hit-and-run tactics. Although their Islamist rhetoric and social policies hold a certain appeal for many Afghans, their violent tactics do not. Moreover, the antiregime forces have made it so hard for reconstruction aid to reach parts of the south and east that any antiregime critique of the government for not doing enough in those areas has little persuasive force. The resilience of the antiregime movement is not founded solely on intimidation, however, but also has roots in preexisting Pashtun alienation from the Tajik-heavy Interim Authority government; in the concerns of some that lawlessness and corruption, largely eliminated under the Taliban, will flourish again; and in the ideological anti-Americanism that remains pervasive throughout the Pashtun belt along the mountainous Afghan-Pakistani border.

Despite progress on various SSR pillars that should help eliminate private militias, factional forces remain. These forces are a legacy of Afghanistan's long years of war, which began as a national resistance struggle against Soviet invasion and morphed over time into a multiethnic civil war. The legal economy is still sufficiently feeble—and the opium-heroin economy sufficiently lucrative—to keep many of the factional fighters from full commitment to legitimate civilian employment, even if they have formally gone through the DDR process and no longer are considered officially part of a private militia. Warlords and regional commanders themselves are turning to leadership roles in business and politics, which is promising, although some have found the transition to organized crime to be logical, easy, and profitable.

Organized crime in Afghanistan now encompasses multiple activities, but its foundation rests on the growing of opium poppies, the production of heroin from them, and the smuggling of that heroin out of the country to regional and global markets. In the 3 years since the Taliban fell, no front has lagged as badly as that of counternarcotics. Opium production has risen steadily since the mid-1980s, whether measured in terms of hectares under cultivation or metric tons of raw opium processed. Since 1990, production has never dropped below an estimated 2,000 metric tons per year, with a peak of 4,600 tons in 1999. The one exception to this trend was 2001, the last year of Taliban rule, when the Taliban regime cracked down on poppy planting and opium processing. During the post-Taliban period, economic uncertainty and weak policing have led to a rapid resurgence of opium production. Estimates of the opium crop's size have climbed from 3,200 tons in 2002 to 3,600 tons in 2003 and a near-record 4,200 tons in 2004—a figure that represents 87 percent of the world total for the year. Even more ominously, there has been a huge upsurge in land under poppy cultivation. A tenth of the Afghan population—more than two million people—now appears to be engaged in growing opium on 131,000 hectares. The rapid growth of this illicit economy (including an urban-construction boom at least partly fueled by drug money) is extremely alarming and could derail the progress made in other nation-building sectors.

A final challenge is the complex task of holding parliamentary elections, now scheduled for September 2005, which will determine the makeup of the Afghan legislature. The constitution passed in January 2004 provides for a legislature with two chambers, the aforementioned *Wolesi Jirga* and *Meshrano Jirga*. The procedures for constituting these bodies are laid out in the constitution and the electoral law that followed it by 2 months. The *Wolesi Jirga* is to have 249 members, all of whom are to be elected according to the SNTV system, with 215 chosen at the provincial level in proportion to the various provincial populations and 34 elected to fill nationwide "compensatory" seats. The *Wolesi Jirga* is required to have the equivalent of two female representatives per province, or 68 women, leaving 181 seats for open contestation by both men and women.

Choosing the 102 members of the *Meshrano Jirga* will be even more complicated. Three different processes are to be used. A third of the seats will be filled when each provincial council selects one of its members to serve a 4-year term in the national upper house. In a similar manner, the several district councils of each province are to elect from among their cumulative memberships a single person to go to Kabul for a 3-year term, adding 34 more legislators. Neither the provincial nor the district councils exist yet. They too will have to be elected and seated before two-thirds of the national upper house can be filled. Finally, President Karzai will appoint the remaining 34 members to 5-year terms, taking care to provide representation for underrepresented groups, such as the traditional nomadic population (Kochis) and the disabled. The constitution further mandates that half of Karzai's appointees (a sixth of the membership) must be women.

Many challenges make these elections problematic. District boundaries and provincial seat apportionments must be decided. Both in turn must rely on accurate population figures that are currently unavailable. Security concerns remain sufficiently urgent to prompt ongoing U.S. military operations aimed at disrupting the planning and preparations of antiregime elements prior to the parliamentary elections. The ethnic polarization exhibited in the presidential election is likely to be substantially greater in the parliamentary elections, as will be the influence of the militias and their leaders, especially if the DDR process slows. Finally, the management of these elections will be much more challenging than conducting the presidential election, as there will be thousands of candidates vying for multiple seats in five separate ballotings. Moreover, the level of voter awareness will be low, and the time for civic education is running short.[22] Finally, the delay of these elections until September 2005 has left President Karzai the only major elected official in Afghanistan, forcing him to keep ruling through his cabinet, powers of appointment, and decrees.

Lessons of Nation-Building from Afghanistan

Afghanistan was bound to be a tough case, and the halfhearted approaches to nation-building that the United States tried through mid-2003 did little to suggest success. Yet the Afghans have proven hopeful and resilient, and the United States has shown an ability to learn from its mistakes and make strategic fixes (although it is increasingly tiresome to watch successive administrations relearn the same lessons). Two major developments merit mention. First, there is now a viable security and reconstruction strategy for Afghanistan, as well as a growing awareness of the subtler difficulties inherent in the state-building strategy. On security, the Pentagon's willingness to abandon its aversion to peacekeeping has both allowed the ISAF to expand its mandate and made it possible for the U.S. military to alter its tactics. Killing or capturing Osama bin Laden and other top al-Qaeda and Taliban figures remains a priority for special-operations military units and U.S. intelligence agencies, but there is now also a large military effort aiming to support Afghanistan's broader transition to democracy and functional statehood under law. The rapid growth of the PRTs, the systematic support that they receive from mobile combat units, and the strengthened commitment to disarming and demobilizing militias all bespeak the promising and much-needed shift that has taken place since the summer of 2003. The change to the reconstruction strategy was mostly motivated by a growing recognition in Washington that more had to be done—the much-maligned failure of the Bush administration to provide funding for Afghanistan in the FY 2004 budget appeared both inexplicable and unconscionable when Afghan security began to slip during the summer of 2003, especially when juxtaposed with the level of commitment to nation-building in Iraq. Thus, in late 2003, the United States finally stepped up with big money ($2.4 billion and the appointment of Dr. Zalmay Khalilzad, President Bush's personal envoy, as the new ambassador), followed by significant pledges at the April 2004 Berlin Conference ($4.4 billion out of the $8.2 billion pledged).

Second, a new model of nation-building is being developed on the ground in Afghanistan, characterized by very close civil-military and interagency cooperation. The co-location of the U.S. Embassy and U.S. military command (the Combined Forces Command–Afghanistan [CFC-A]), along with the U.S. intelligence-gathering capacity, is symbolized by the side-by-side embassy offices occupied by Ambassador Zalmay Khalilzad (who became the U.S. ambassador to Iraq in the summer of 2005) and Lieutenant General Barno (replaced by Lieutenant General Karl Eikenberry in May 2005). This cooperation is also exemplified in the Interagency Planning Group, a U.S. Embassy-based operation run by U.S. military officers and aimed at bringing together data on all the nation-building programs to give Karzai, Khalilzad, and other senior leaders a broad view of how all the elements of the program are working. At the tactical level, the PRTs, although primarily military, have important civilian components and nation-building missions.

Despite these encouraging developments in the field, U.S. nation-building efforts in Afghanistan have been consistently undercut by institutional inertia originating in Washington. In Afghanistan, these problems have manifested in various ways. For example, the CFC-A commander has responsibility for military operations and presence in four countries (Afghanistan, Pakistan, parts of Tajikistan, and parts of Uzbekistan make up the combined joint operating area), but the commander has to coordinate with embassy country teams in each place. Other problems include staffing inadequacies, prompted by the multitude of different rules governing deployments to Afghanistan by different organizations operating there (both military and civilian); tremendous coordination requirements between different organizations, leading to numerous meetings; and the failure to develop or acquire a stable of Afghan specialists. This last problem leads to the question of a missing political strategy, for despite the apparent successes in state-building under the Bonn Accords, it is in this area that the United States will find its greatest challenges. Yet how can an effective political strategy be developed in the absence of country expertise?

In Washington, the institutional impediments to nation-building are far more significant and far-reaching, so much so that it is fair to ask whether the Bush administration is serious about nation-building. The evidence in Afghanistan (and also Iraq) suggests that the answer is no, but serious nation-building will be critical to strategic victory in the war on terror. Nation-building involves numerous activities that are not properly located anywhere in the U.S. government. Some nation-building jobs include building or rebuilding infrastructure, providing security in transitional situations, developing governance institutions, and providing basic services and welfare functions until permanent governments are sufficiently mature to take on those tasks. In part due to its historical experience with nation-building operations (Kosovo, Bosnia, Somalia, Haiti, and even post-World War II Japan and Germany all come to mind), the U.S. Army has developed some of the capabilities necessary to perform these tasks, at least in a rudimentary fashion. Until recently, no other branch of the armed services or the civilian component of the federal government could claim as much. However, the army has never been very excited about nation-building operations and has never made developing an appropriate force structure, doctrine, or training for such operations a priority. For example, virtually all civil affairs units and some 60 percent of the military police and engineers are Army Reserve or National Guard units. Not only does this preponderance of reserve units disrupt local communities and families when such units are deployed, but it also means less training is done in regular units in the kinds of skills needed in postconflict situations. Military training typically occurs at the unit level and is aimed at performing unit tasks. Although active component battalions might train in maneuvers to destroy or capture enemy positions, there is little coordinated training between such units and the primarily Reserve and National Guard components that might follow them into a captured town to establish an occupation government, rebuild its infrastructure, and establish basic security there.

Furthermore, the non-army elements of nation-building are even less developed. In 1997, President Clinton issued Presidential Decision Directive (PDD) 56, which was supposed to establish an interagency planning and training process for handling "complex contingency operations" (i.e., nation-building situations). But as noted in Michèle Flournoy's chapter in this volume, PDD 56 was rejected by the Bush administration and not replaced with any other framework for successful management of postconflict situations, so that the Afghan nation-building effort was an ad hoc operation. In July 2004, the State Department created a new Office of the Coordinator for Reconstruction and Stabilization, marking the first serious effort to institutionalize a nation-building capacity among the civilian agencies of the government since 9/11. Situating such an important task within an existing and overburdened department compounds the problem, however, as only a massive overhaul of the Cold War–era national security structure could provide the integrated and synergistic twenty-first-century organization needed to do the job properly. The United States has done this before: the current national security configuration reflects the effort to arrange the federal government to best face the challenges of the post–World War II era, through the National Security Act of 1947 that created the National Security Council, Central Intelligence Agency, and the Department of Defense (out of the preexisting War and Navy departments). More recently, the events of 9/11 caused the creation of the Department of Homeland Security, bringing together numerous preexisting agencies under one bureaucratic roof. The lessons of Afghanistan and Iraq should trigger senior U.S. officials to rethink how the government is set up to safeguard or restore the security of other "homelands," whose stability and at least modestly decent governance are of vital interest to the United States, to prevent them from becoming havens and avenues for terrorists who want to launch catastrophic attacks on the American homeland.

The final lesson from Afghanistan's nation-building may well be the most important: successful nation-building requires sustained, determined engagement by the international community, and often, leadership by the United States. The gradually increasing pace of progress across all nation-building pillars in Afghanistan is both legitimate and encouraging, but much can still go wrong there. The growing opium-fueled nexus between insurgency and terrorism is a ticking time bomb. Too many local warlords are showing too little inclination to find new careers. The specter of ethnic polarization haunts the upcoming elections and the efforts to develop a government out of that process. Afghan capacity, whether human, material, or institutional, is the key to making this nation-building project work. To ensure the development of such capacity and to secure the hard-won gains that have taken the international community more than 3 years —and the Afghan people nearly three decades—to acquire, demands continued engagement and attentive commitment. A foundation for the rebuilding of Afghanistan has been laid. Now it is time to finish the job.

Notes

1. Larry P. Goodson, *Afghanistan's Endless War: State Failure, Regional Politics, and the Rise of the Taliban* (Seattle: University of Washington Press, 2001), especially chapter 4, provides a good description of the situation prevailing just prior to Operation Enduring Freedom.

2. For more on the Bonn Accords and other matters relating to the nation-building effort in Afghanistan, see Larry Goodson, "Afghanistan's Long Road to Reconstruction," *Journal of Democracy* 14 (January 2003): 82–99; Barnett R. Rubin, "Crafting a Constitution for Afghanistan," *Journal of Democracy* 15 (July 2004): 5–19.

3. Bob Woodward, *Plan of Attack* (New York: Simon and Schuster, 2004).

4. Tommy Franks and Malcolm McConnell, *American Soldier* (New York: Regan Books, 2004); Sean Naylor, *Not a Good Day to Die: The Untold Story of Operation Anaconda* (New York: Berkley, 2005).

5. Likewise with Iraq, where the lack of diplomatic relations and sanctions limited the opportunity for American scholars to engage in field research there during the 1990s and later.
6. Figures available at www.nato.int. See also Michael Bhatia, Kevin Lanigan, and Philip Wilkinson, "Minimal Investments, Minimal Results: The Failure of Security Policy in Afghanistan," Afghanistan Research and Evaluation Unit Briefing Paper (Kabul: Afghanistan Research and Evaluation Unit, June 2004), 11.
7. All figures are from U.N. Office on Drugs and Crime, "Afghanistan Opium Survey 2004," November 2004, available at www.unodc.org/pdf/afg/afghanistan_opium_survey_2004.pdf.
8. As of this writing, there are 19 PRTs in Afghanistan, with several more scheduled to start up during 2006.
9. John Otis, "Afghanistan: The Other War—Military Says It's Winning Afghan Hearts, Minds, but Some Groups Say That Aid Work Isn't Troops' Turf," *Houston Chronicle,* September 5, 2004, 23. See also "Provincial Reconstruction Teams and the Security Situation in Afghanistan," Agency Coordinating Body for Afghan Relief Policy Brief, July 24, 2003, available at www.careinternational.org.uk/priorities/policy_documents/afghanistan/acbar_policy_brief_july_2003.doc.
10. Figures available at www.nato.int. See also Bhatia et al., "Minimal Investments, Minimal Results."
11. I derived this estimate from multiple interviews that I conducted with Afghan officials, personnel from the U.N. Assistance Mission in Afghanistan, and knowledgeable foreign observers in Kabul during research trips in April and July 2004.
12. See Bhatia et al., "Minimal Investments, Minimal Results."
13. World Bank, "Afghanistan: State Building, Sustaining Growth, and Reducing Poverty—A Country Economic Report," September 9, 2004, available at www-wds.worldbank.org/servlet/WDS_IBank_Servlet?pcont=details&eid=000160016_20040915113121.
14. World Bank, "Securing Afghanistan's Future: Accomplishments and the Strategic Path Forward" (Washington, D.C.: World Bank, March 17, 2004).
15. Ibid.
16. Barnett Rubin, Humayun Hamidzada, and Abby Stoddard, "Through the Fog of Peacebuilding: Evaluating the Reconstruction of Afghanistan," policy brief (New York: Center on International Cooperation, 2003), 1.
17. Data on the election results is available at the Joint Electoral Management Board Web site, www.elections-afghanistan.org.af/Election%20Results%20Website/english/english.htm.
18. Confidential author interview in July 2004 in Kabul.
19. Author interview in July 2004 in Kabul.

20. The list of registered political parties is available at www.elections-afghanistan .org.af.
21. See the recent report of the International Crisis Group, "Afghanistan: From Presidential to Parliamentary Elections," International Crisis Group Asia Report no. 88 (Washington, D.C.: International Crisis Group, November 23, 2004).
22. Ibid.

Part III · Iraq

CHAPTER 8

What Went Wrong and Right in Iraq

Larry Diamond

WITH THE TRANSFER OF POWER to a new Iraqi Interim Government on June 28, 2004, the political phase of the American occupation of Iraq came to an end. The transfer marked an urgently needed and, in some ways, hopeful development for Iraq. Although Iraqis were initially skeptical, they did recover their sovereignty, and if the subsequent period of interim rule did not achieve a great deal, it did at least end on schedule, with surprisingly successful national elections on January 30, 2005. Those elections for a transitional national assembly (as well as for provincial assemblies and a Kurdistan regional assembly) drew exceptionally high participation in the Shiite south (over 70% turnout) and in the Kurdish north of the country (well over 80% turnout). Although the campaign was marked by widespread violence, fear, and intimidation, a boycott by prominent Sunni political forces, and turnout as low as 2% in Anbar Province, the elections marked an even more significant development for Iraq—giving the country its first government with any claim to electoral legitimacy in half a century.

However, the handover of power, and even the subsequent elections, did not erase or initially much ease the most pressing problems confronting that beleaguered country: endemic terrorist, political, and criminal violence, a shattered state, and a decimated society and economy. To some extent, it was inevitable that postwar Iraq would face formidable challenges. But by the time the American occupation administration—the Coalition Provisional Authority (CPA)—came to an end in June 2004, Iraq had fallen far short of the political stability and reconstruction progress that the Bush administration had promised. As a result of a long chain of miscalculations, America's military and political occupation left Iraq in far worse shape than it need have, diminishing its prospects for political stability and democracy, and claiming many more Iraqi, American, and other foreign lives than would have been the case with a better strategy.

The American occupation of Iraq—for all the British and other international participation, it was in its leadership and design an American occupation—never came to grips with the massive security deficit in Iraq, and more fundamentally, with the nature of the social and political reality that the United States was bound to confront in postwar Iraq. Many of the Bush administration's original miscalculations had diffuse, profound, and lasting consequences.

First and foremost, the Bush administration was never willing to commit anything near the force necessary to secure a viable postwar order in Iraq. Military experts had warned that the task would require, as Army Chief of Staff Eric Shinseki told Congress in February 2003, "hundreds of thousands" of troops. If the United States had deployed in Iraq a force with the same ratio to population as in Bosnia, it would have numbered half a million troops; never did the total coalition troop commitment in Iraq reach much more than a third of that level. Secretary of Defense Donald Rumsfeld and his senior Pentagon civilian deputies rejected every call for a much larger force commitment, and made it very clear—despite their disingenuous promises to give our military mission in Iraq "everything they ask for"—that such requests would not be welcome. No officer missed the lesson of General Shinseki, who the Pentagon rewarded for his public candor by announcing his replacement a year early, making him a lame-duck leader before his term expired. Thus was opened a festering wound in U.S. civil-military relations, in which American military officers (and soldiers) in Iraq widely complained in private that they lacked the troops and equipment to succeed, but knew that a much greater commitment was not politically feasible. Top commanders thus kept emphasizing the need for "political solutions," while top political officials in the CPA complained about the need for greater military action to secure the country.

Something like 300,000 troops might have been enough to largely secure Iraq after the war. But security also required different kinds of troops, with different rules of engagement. The coalition should have deployed vastly more military police and other troops trained for urban patrols, crowd control, civil reconstruction, and peace maintenance and enforcement. Tens of thousands of troops and sophisticated monitoring equipment should have been deployed along the borders with Syria and Iran to intercept the subversive flows of foreign terrorists, Iranian intelligence agents, money, and arms.

But Washington failed to take such steps, for the same reason it decided to occupy Iraq with a relatively light force—the hubris, ideology, and highly centralized decisionmaking process that drove the ill-considered decision to go to war in the first place.

Contemptuous of State Department regional experts who were seen as too "soft" to remake Iraq, Pentagon planners shoved aside the elaborate State Department planning in the Future of Iraq project, which anticipated many of the problems that quickly emerged after the invasion. Instead of preparing for the worst, Pentagon officials assumed that Iraqis would broadly and joyously welcome American and international troops as liberators. With Saddam's military and security apparatus destroyed, the thinking went, Washington could capitalize on widespread feelings of gratitude and good will to hand the country over to Iraqi expatriates like Ahmed Chalabi, who would quickly rally the country to its democratic rebirth. Not only would this not require "hundreds of thousands" of U.S. troops, but within a year, only a few tens of thousands would be needed.

These naïve assumptions quickly collapsed in the immediate aftermath of the war, as American troops stood by helplessly, outnumbered and wholly unprepared, while much of the remaining physical, economic, and institutional infrastructure of the country was systematically looted and sabotaged. The initial strategic miscalculation was compounded by the stubborn refusal of the Bush administration to send in more troops once it became apparent that the looting was not a one-time breakdown of social order—that, in fact, an elaborately organized, armed, and financed resistance to the American occupation had emerged. Repeatedly, the administration deluded itself into believing that the defeat of this insurgency was just around the corner—as soon as the long hot summer of 2003 ended, or reconstruction dollars and jobs got flowing, or the political transition process got under way, or Saddam Hussein was captured, or once power was transferred to the Iraqi Interim Government. As in Vietnam, there was always an illusion of an imminent turning point, an unwillingness to grasp the depth of popular disaffection, and an inability to construct a political process that put forward effective and legitimate political leaders from within the country.

Under its administrator, Ambassador L. Paul Bremer III, the CPA worked hard and innovatively to try to craft a political process for transition to a legitimate, viable, and democratic system of government in Iraq, as well as to rebuild the Iraqi state, economy, and society. As I saw during my brief tenure as a senior adviser on governance during the first 3 months of 2004, the U.S. administration achieved a number of successes. But one cannot review the political record without underscoring the pervasive security deficit, which undermined everything else the coalition sought to achieve.

The Crippling Security Deficit

Any effort to rebuild a shattered, war-torn state depends on four foundations:

- Political reconstruction of a legitimate and capable state;
- Economic reconstruction of the country's physical infrastructure, as well as of the rules and institutions that enable a market economy;
- Social reconstruction by means of the renewal (or in some cases, creation) of a civil society and political culture that foster voluntary cooperation for development and the limitation of state power; and
- Security, in the provision of a relatively safe and orderly environment.

These four elements interact in intimate ways. Without legitimate, rule-based, and effective government, economic and physical reconstruction will lag, and investors will not risk the capital needed to produce jobs and new wealth. Without demonstrable progress on the economic front, government cannot develop real and sustainable legitimacy, and its effectiveness will therefore quickly wane. Without the development of social capital—in the form of horizontal bonds of trust and cooperation in a (re)emerging civil society—economic development will not proceed with sufficient vigor and diffusion, and the new system of government will not be properly scrutinized on the one hand or supported on the other. Finally, without security, none of the other foundations can develop.

In a postconflict situation in which the state has collapsed, security trumps everything else. It is not simply one leg of a table; it is the central pedestal that bears the bulk of the table's weight. Without some minimum level of security, people cannot engage in trade and commerce, organize to rebuild and revive their communities, or participate meaningfully in politics. Without security, a country has nothing but disorder, distrust, desperation, and despair—an utterly Hobbesian situation in which fear pervades and raw force dominates. This is why a violence-ridden society will turn to almost any political force or formula that is capable of providing order, even if it is oppressive. It is a big reason why the CPA was able to spend only a fraction of the $18.6 billion for Iraqi reconstruction approved by the U.S. Congress in the fall of 2003. And it is why a country must first have a state before it can have a democratic state. The primary requirement for a state is that it hold a monopoly over the means of violence. By that measure, the Iraqi interim authority to which the United States transferred power on June 28 may have been a government, but it did not really command a state.

Even with the inadequate force levels deployed, much more could have been done to build security and contain the disorder in postwar Iraq. Unfortunately, not only was the mission seriously underresourced, it also lacked the necessary understanding and organization. Thus the effort to train and deploy a new Iraqi police force withered from haste, inefficiency, poor planning, and sheer incompetence. Newly minted Iraqi police officers were rushed onto the job with too little training, inadequate vetting, and shameful inadequacies of equipment. If they had uniforms (of sorts), they lacked cars, radios, and body armor. Typically, they were outgunned by the criminals, terrorists, and saboteurs they faced. As vital symbols of the authority of the new Iraqi state, the police quickly became soft targets for terrorist attacks, and coalition forces did too little, too late, to protect them.

Iraqi politicians, civic leaders, and government officials, as well as coalition civilian officials and their Iraqi aides, paid a heavy price for the lack of security. More than 100 Iraqi government officials were killed during the occupation, including several high-ranking ministry officials and an occupant of the Governing Council's rotating presidency (Ezzedine Salim). Although a few CPA officials were killed, many others were attacked, and numerous civilian contractors were killed, kidnapped, or narrowly escaped such criminal attacks. The mounting insecurity drove the political occupation into a physical and psychological bunker. With the CPA already separated from Iraqis by the formidable security barriers of the 3-square-mile Green Zone around its Republican Palace headquarters, and by similar barriers at the coalition's regional and provincial headquarters, travel became more difficult with every passing month. By the early spring of 2004, it simply was not safe for foreign officials and contractors to move about Iraq without an armored car and a well-armed security escort. And even these precautions against the increasingly common ambushes and drive-by shootings did not protect them against well-placed and powerful roadside bombs. Throughout the occupation, there were far too few helicopters and armored cars, and too little suitable body armor, and the Pentagon was very slow, very late, and very inefficient in filling the gaps. Many contractors died because of these gaps, causing companies to pull back from desperately needed infrastructure projects and coalition officials to curtail—and, as the insurgency became more ferocious in the spring of 2004, virtually to halt—travel. As a result, the CPA did not have an adequate grasp of how the reconstruction was proceeding and how Iraqis viewed it.

The isolation was deepened by a language gap, which was then accentuated by the security gap. The insurgents were not only ruthless but also shrewd in their choice of targets. Any Iraqis collaborating with the occupation (including any lining up for jobs) were targets, but Iraqi translators were particular targets, because the coalition's dependence on them was well known. A number of Iraqi translators working for the CPA in Baghdad (and for the U.S. Embassy that succeeded it) were assassinated; others quit after threats of assassination. Although the coalition could do nothing to protect them, many others bravely continued, but in a state of fear and demoralization.

Even with the Bush administration's refusal to mobilize and deploy the force necessary to fill the security vacuum, there was much that the coalition could have done to relieve it, with more and better equipment and a tougher strategic determination to face down the rising threats to order in Iraq. But on the latter front as well, the administration was ineffectual. Never was this more vividly apparent than with the threat of Muqtada al-Sadr, a radical Shiite junior cleric who sought to fan and exploit anti-American, nationalist, and Islamic fundamentalist sentiments in a bid for power. Although he lacked the religious knowledge and authority of his father (who was assassinated in 1999) or of more senior and respected Shiite clerics, Sadr managed to mobilize a following among disaffected, unemployed, and poorly educated young men in the cities. As Sadr built his reactionary political movement and his al-Mahdi army, with support from hardliners in Iran, the coalition needed to develop a counterstrategy. Some Shiite leaders urged inclusion—co-opting Sadr explicitly into the political game. Many moderate Shiites and CPA officials, both in the Republican Palace and in the regional and provincial offices, urged legal and military action against Sadr's growing menace.

In fact, the coalition had been poised to act for months. In August, the Iraqi Central Criminal Court issued arrest warrants for Sadr and 11 of his top henchmen for the April 2003 murder of the most important moderate Shiite cleric, Ayatollah Majid al-Khoei, who had just returned from abroad and could have helped to rally Shiite support for the transition. The CPA kept the arrest warrants sealed, as an implicit warning to Sadr if he crossed some unspecified line of outrage. But over the subsequent months, Sadr kept pushing, and the coalition—which is to say the U.S. political and military leadership in Baghdad and Washington—kept waiting, warning, wavering, hesitating, and debating. If a transition to any kind of decent, lawful political order were to be feasible, Sadr's organization had to be put out of business. Coalition figures knew this. Repeatedly, plans were prepared to take down Sadr, but they were never executed.

There was certainly no shortage of warning signs, provocations, and justifications. In October, coalition forces intercepted thousands of heavily armed Sadr followers as they were headed in buses down to Karbala to seize control of the central city and its holy shrines. On March 12, Sadr's forces wiped the Gypsy village of Qawliyya off the face of the earth, sending most of its one thousand residents fleeing in terror. That same month, Sadr's organization publicly called for the assassination of the most influential pro-American cleric in the Shiite heartland, Sayyid Farqad al-Qizwini, and a number of his associates in a United States–supported pro-democracy movement. Between October and March, Sadr's army and organization grew alarmingly in size, muscle, and daring. In a Taliban-style bid for social power and Islamic purity, they seized public buildings, beat up moderate professors and deans, took over classrooms, forced women to wear the hijab, set up illegal shari'a courts, and imposed their own brutal penalties. Meanwhile, new al-Mahdi army recruits were openly training for warfare, terror, and mayhem. In the south-central region, which included Hilla and the holy cities of Najaf and Karbala, the Multinational Force (MNF) led by Spain and Poland assumed a largely passive posture, refusing to recognize that the al-Mahdi army and other religious and political militias threatened peace and order. Other party and religious militias in the area also became increasingly menacing to their more democratic opponents, but the MNF looked the other way.

When the coalition finally acted against Sadr and his organization, it was impromptu and incomprehensibly chaotic. On March 28, Ambassador Bremer ordered the closure of Sadr's incendiary newspaper, *Hawza,* but with no operational plan in place to strike against the more dangerous elements of the radical cleric's organization. Sadr then reacted by ordering his followers to rise up against the occupation. A few days later, on April 2, coalition forces arrested a top Sadr aide, Mustafa al-Yaccoubi, and Sadr then unleashed a full-scale insurgency in the Shiite south, seizing for a time control of Najaf, Karbala, and many other strategic sites and forging tactical cooperation with Sunni insurgent elements that had taken control of Fallujah. In the subsequent weeks, after conceding control of Fallujah to a hastily constructed local militia that promised to reassert order, U.S. forces finally went to war on the al-Mahdi army, evicting it from most of the urban sites and strategic centers it had seized, and killing or arresting many of its leaders. American troops fought with skill and effectiveness in this counterinsurgency campaign, largely defeating the al-Mahdi army. But Sadr remained at large, mocking the coalition's demand that he give himself up for arrest, and Shiite leaders who had been alarmed by his attempt to seize power now sought to incorporate him into the future political game. The result was not pacification but rather a second and even more devastating uprising by Sadr's forces later in the summer of 2004.

Not only did the fighting in April and May 2004 fail to extinguish Sadr's forces, it also did nothing to counter Iraq's other heavily armed militias attached to various political parties and movements. These included not only the battle-hardened Pesh Merga of the two principal Kurdish political parties (which numbered an estimated 75,000 fighters), but also the large and well-armed militias of the two most important Shiite religious parties, SCIRI (the Supreme Council for Islamic Revolution in Iraq) and Da'wa al Islamiyya (the Islamic Call Party). At the beginning of 2004, the CPA began negotiating with these and other significant militias a comprehensive plan for disarmament, demobilization, and reintegration (DDR) of their fighters into the new Iraqi police and armed forces and the civilian economy (although the plan was officially called a transition and reintegration [TR] plan). To succeed, any DDR plan has to rely heavily on positive incentives (jobs, pensions, status in the new armed forces) for those militias that agree to cooperate, and force to demobilize those militias that will not. The al-Mahdi army clearly fell into the latter category. Action was needed against it not only to reassure the other Shiite parties and movements that they no longer had to arm for self-defense, but also to warn them that the coalition would confront those forces that did not cooperate. The TR plan drawn up by the CPA was intelligent and comprehensive in design. But the Kurds, understandably wary of any new Iraqi central government, given their history of oppression, would not agree to more than a superficial integration of their forces (with command structures intact) into the new Iraqi armed forces. As for the other large militias, it was always unclear whether they would truly demobilize and disarm, rather than warehouse their heavy weapons while taking up positions, temporarily, in the new armed forces. The TR plan was supposed to have been finalized and announced on May 1, but it was set back seriously by the outbreak of the twin insurgencies in Fallujah and the Shiite south in April. With U.S. forces having to rely to some on extent on the cooperation (or at least forbearance) of the SCIRI and Da'wa militias to evict and defeat the al-Mahdi army, the CPA's bargaining leverage was sharply reduced. The plan was finally released in early June, but with little time left for implementation and enforcement by the occupation authorities before the transfer of power. Following the handover of power on June 28, 2004, the TR plan fell victim to bureaucratic and personal rivalries within the Iraqi Interim Government and was never effectively implemented.

As the new Iraqi state began to emerge from the shadow of occupation, it became trapped in a Catch-22. To be viable, it had to build up its armed forces as rapidly as possible. But the readiest sources of soldiers and police were the most powerful militias, especially the Pesh Merga and SCIRI's 15,000-man Badr Organization. It was thus unclear to whom the new Iraqi armed forces would owe their ultimate loyalty, and unlikely that in the electoral struggle for power, they would act as a neutral force, willing to confront and contain political abuses by their sponsoring parties and coalitions. Although this problem was relatively muted in the January 2005 elections for a transitional government, for which the American forces provided the backbone of security, it threatens to become much more serious in future elections.

Closing the Legitimacy Gap

Just as decent governance was not possible without some minimal level of security, so it was that the security situation was not going to improve without significant progress on the political front. This conundrum was true in several respects. First, although some of the terrorist violence—in particular the suicide car bombings—was organized by external jihadists, particularly al-Qaeda, it appears that the bulk of the roadside bombings, killings of contractors, and other forms of sabotage was committed by Iraqis (mainly Sunnis) who turned against the occupation because they believed it was excluding them politically. Second was the danger of a renewed urban-based insurgency by disaffected young Shiite men, whose lack of access to jobs and opportunity rendered them vulnerable to the appeals of militants like Muqtada al-Sadr. Third, political tensions raised the worrisome prospect of violence between Iraqi Kurds and Arabs, both on the volatile boundaries of the Kurdistan region, especially Kirkuk—where militant Kurds wanted to expel Arabs who had settled there during Saddam's campaign of "Arabization"—and in the larger struggle over the future shape of Iraq. And fourth, the challenge of demobilizing the militias while building up the new Iraqi armed forces had substantial political elements. On all these fronts, containing violence required not only a strong and adept military response, but also a sustained political effort to construct a broad-based, inclusive system with which all major Iraqi groups could identify.

The United States, however, lacked an effective political strategy for postwar Iraq, as became clear almost immediately after the invasion, when former General Jay Garner's ill-fated Office of Reconstruction and Humanitarian Assistance took charge in Baghdad. Part of the problem was that both Garner and Bremer failed to comprehend how Iraqis perceived them—and the entire occupation. Throughout the occupation, the coalition lacked the linguistic and area expertise necessary to understand Iraqi politics and society, and the few long-time experts present were excluded from the inner circle of decisionmaking in the CPA. Indeed, the administration of the occupation was highly centralized under Bremer personally, in a manner that impeded the flow of analysis and knowledge from the field, elevated a small circle of political appointees, and marginalized those with vast stores of knowledge and understanding about Iraq—not just the career U.S. diplomats, but also well-informed British experts, as well as Iraqis and Iraqi-Americans not tied to any specific political interest. This same centralization plagued the challenge of postwar reconstruction. Most of the funds were controlled by the CPA in Baghdad or went to large American companies in megacontracts. But often the most rapid and effective means of generating development and reconstruction activity (and therefore jobs) in Iraqi towns and neighborhoods was through the local provincial and regional coordinators and the local military commands, which accomplished a lot quickly through disbursements by the Commanders' Emergency Reconstruction Program. More money and authority should have been devolved to these commanders and officials in the field.

Because of these structural flaws and knowledge deficits, the coalition never realized that, although most Iraqis were deeply grateful to have been liberated from a brutal tyranny, this gratitude was mixed with deep suspicion of the real motives of the United States (and of Britain, the former colonial ruler); humiliation that it was not Iraqis themselves who had overthrown Saddam; and high, indeed unrealistic, expectations for the postwar administration, which they assumed could deliver them rapidly from all their problems. For the majority of Iraqis, the military action was not an "international intervention," but an invasion and occupation by Western, Christian, essentially Anglo-American powers that evoked powerful memories of previous subjugation and of the nationalist struggles against Iraq's former overlords.

The CPA also failed to grasp that Saddam was not without a base of popular support in Iraq. Although he brutalized plenty of Sunnis, much of the Arab Sunni population either supported him (more or less) or opposed his ouster for fear that regime change would cost them—a 20 percent minority of the population—their historic monopoly over the state and its precious resources. So the U.S. intervention faced the seriously underestimated danger of dedicated resistance from a portion of the population that saw itself losing its preeminence.

The occupation compounded its original errors of analysis with two strategic miscalculations imposed shortly after Bremer's arrival in Baghdad in May 2003. First, it launched a de-Ba'athification campaign that was much too broad, excluding from any meaningful role in the future state anyone who had held any kind of higher-level position in the Ba'ath Party, regardless of whether they were directly involved in serious crimes. And it put the most aggressive and politically ambitious advocate of radical de-Ba'athification, the controversial exile returnee Ahmed Chalabi, in charge of the program.

Second, as one of his first official acts, Ambassador Bremer ordered the dissolution of the Iraqi Army. The Iraqi Army had already collapsed and scattered at the end of the invasion, and as one of the pillars of Saddam's state, it could not have served the cause of democratic reconstruction without intensive vetting of its officer corps in particular. Still, by formally dissolving it, the CPA lost the opportunity to reconstitute some portions of it to help restore order, and it left tens of thousands of armed soldiers and officers cut out of the new order and rendered prime candidates for recruitment by the insurgency. Indeed, the American occupation created a context in which former Ba'athists, mainly Sunnis, not only feared the loss of their previous dominance, but also expected exclusion from any proportional share of power and resources. Some of them who might have been co-opted into the new system were instead drawn toward the violent resistance, viewing it as a rational strategy to drive away the Americans or at least change the terms being offered.

The United States also faced a more pervasive political problem. Deep Iraqi suspicions of American motives combined with the memory of Arabs' historical confrontation with Western colonialism and their resentment of the U.S. stance in the Israeli-Palestinian struggle to generate a massive legitimacy gap for the occupation. The United States needed to take two actions to bridge this gap. First, it needed to solicit and permit more international participation in the political administration of the country. However, the international community was deeply wary of such participation, for fear of blessing what it viewed as an illegal and unjustified military intervention. And second, the occupation needed to put legitimate Iraqi leaders in visible, meaningful governance roles as soon as possible. Much of the 14-month history of the CPA involves the frustrating quest, through a succession of plans and strategies, to set up an Iraqi political authority that Iraqis would view as legitimate.

The most straightforward way to establish such a national authority would have been to hold elections for a transitional government. This course was what Grand Ayatollah Ali Sistani, the most revered and influential Shiite religious leader in Iraq, wanted from the beginning. In fact, because he viewed the occupation authority as illegitimate, he steadfastly refused to meet with any of its officials, creating a profound and persistent communication problem that undermined one transition plan after another. However, the experience of other postwar transitions counseled strongly against a rapid move to national elections. With no electoral register, no administrative framework to organize balloting, no electoral rules, and no time or opportunity for new political parties to emerge and mobilize, early national elections (any time within the first year of occupation) could well have precipitated a disastrous slide toward violence and polarization—even civil war. Moreover, early elections would likely have been swept in the south by Islamist parties, which enjoyed the huge and unfair advantage of the financing and political and military organization they had built up either underground or in exile (in Iran).

The occupation pursued a variety of other strategies to fill the legitimacy void, with varying degrees of success. In each of Iraq's 18 provinces and in most of its cities and larger towns, local coalition military commands, sometimes working with U.S. civilian contractors, formed representative councils through a mix of consultative and deliberative processes. In a few cases, particularly in the far south under British civil and military administration, rough and ready elections were organized using the crude method of the ration card system, which registered only Iraqi households, not individuals, but was believed to have covered about 90 percent of the population. Officials in Basra province (containing the country's second largest city) wanted to experiment with direct elections for local councils, but this and similar initiatives for local and provincial popular elections were vetoed by CPA headquarters, which feared that any such example would undermine the CPA's insistence that direct elections could not be organized in the near term. There was also a fear of what elections would produce. As one British official lamented to me, the "CPA [officials] didn't want anything to happen that they didn't control—and this has been impossible to hide from the Iraqis."

The most intractable and debilitating problem with the local and provincial councils, however, was not their lack of an electoral mandate. Indeed, CPA teams worked energetically and sincerely in late 2003 and early 2004 to "refresh" these councils, removing the most corrupt and unrepresentative figures and bringing in new faces commanding public support and respect, as evidenced in popular consultations. In many cases, this process amounted to meaningful indirect elections. Rather, the biggest problem with the councils was their evident powerlessness and lack of resources—to the point that many of them had to wait for months even to receive their salaries, and most of them felt frustrated by their impotence. In failing to invest these councils with real resources and authority and to give them an opportunity to perform in regenerating development at the local level, the occupation in most parts of Iraq missed a real opportunity to improve its legitimacy.

After 3 months of costly delay, in July 2003, the occupation did constitute an indigenous national authority, albeit only an advisory one: the

Iraqi Governing Council (GC). This body included representatives of some obviously weighty Iraqi constituencies and political forces, including the two main Kurdish parties (the Kurdistan Democratic Party, or KDP, and the Patriotic Union of Kurdistan, or PUK), which had ruled the autonomous Kurdish region since its effective liberation from Saddam's tyranny in 1991; two major Shiite Islamist parties, SCIRI and Da'wa; and some other established parties (including the predominantly Sunni Iraqi Islamic Party and the Iraqi Communist Party). Also included were actors close to Ayatollah Sistani, and representatives of Iraq's other social forces, including its crucially important tribes.

The GC was not bad as a first step, but it was hobbled by serious flaws. First, the GC had an image problem because the body was so heavily weighted with returning Iraqi exiles and placed controversial exiles, particularly Chalabi, in such prominent and powerful roles. Second, the CPA failed to move rapidly enough toward the creation of an Iraqi body that, in its composition and means of selection, would be more representative and legitimate, and in its powers, more truly a "governing" council. And third, the GC members themselves failed to reach out and develop constituencies. It was not uncommon for most of them to be out of the country traveling at any given time. Few Iraqis ever saw any of them in their towns and communities. As a body, the GC members did not distinguish themselves.

The occupation had a serious legitimacy problem with the international community as well. Having invaded without U.N. Security Council authorization or the support of many other democratic publics in the world, the United States was unable to draw in the broader international participation in governance that might have blunted suspicions of American motives and led Iraqis to see the action as something more than an American bid to get control of Iraqi oil and establish permanent military bases on Iraqi soil.

Even with that handicap, however, the United Nations did set up a fairly significant mission in Baghdad with the arrival on June 2, 2003, of Sergio Vieira de Mello—one of the United Nations' best, most experienced peace-builders (who was highly regarded for his leadership of the transitional mission in East Timor). Despite the United Nations' questionable reputation in Iraq, a legacy of its involvement with the debilitating and corruption-ridden sanctions regime, Vieira de Mello and his team were respected in Iraq, and they quickly grasped the need for much more substantial Iraqi participation in postwar governance, including the need to establish an Iraqi interim government early on.

Unfortunately, the impact of the United Nations on the occupation never extended beyond a few cosmetic changes. This failure was due in part to the tragic events of August 19, 2003, when terrorists blew up the poorly protected U.N. headquarters in Baghdad, killing Vieira de Mello and more than a dozen other U.N. staffers and causing the United Nations to draw down its international staff in Iraq from more than 600 employees to less than 100. Following a second bombing of its headquarters on September 22, the United Nations essentially withdrew from Iraq. The August 19 bombing (which killed 22 people in all and wounded more than 100) was one of the worst tragedies the institution has ever suffered and will shape its future thinking about and engagement in conflict settings for many years to come.

Even before the attack, however, Washington—and Bremer in Baghdad—proved unwilling to surrender any significant measure of control. The CPA leadership did not see a real need for the U.N. mission, other than to issue an occasional supportive press release. Even when Vieira de Mello, after meeting at length with Ayatollah Sistani, warned Bremer in mid-June that a political bomb was about to explode—in the form of a fatwa from Sistani insisting that any constitution-making body for Iraq had to be popularly elected—Bremer dismissed the warning.

The obsession with control was an overarching flaw in the U.S. occupation, from start to finish. In any postconflict international intervention, there is always a certain tension between legitimacy and control. Because it started with such gaping legitimacy deficits within Iraq and internationally, the American-led occupation needed to be especially sensitive to this problem, which could only have been overcome by either surrendering a good measure of control to a more collaborative structure, or by rapid and decisive progress to reconstruct the country and hand it fully back to Iraqis. Such a rapid transformation was not in the cards; the situation was too intractable, and the United States, in any case, lacked the wisdom and was unwilling to commit the resources to bring it off. Still, for most of the first year of occupation, the American administration opted for control over legitimacy whenever the trade-off presented itself.

The pattern began to change only when the Bush administration's November 15, 2003, "agreement" for political transition quickly unraveled, and the administration finally turned to the United Nations for help. But it should have done so earlier and more sincerely. In fact, the political and economic reconstruction of Iraq probably would have proceeded much more rapidly and successfully—with far less violence—if the United States had accepted U.N. appeals to transfer power early on to a broad-based Iraqi interim government chosen through a process of inclusive participation and transparent consultation. Instead, the Bush administration opted in May 2003 for a full-blown political occupation of Iraq, with no clear plan or timetable for transferring governing authority to Iraqis.

Building a Government

The Bush administration does deserve credit for adjusting its posture dramatically in the face of two important developments in the final two months of 2003. The first development was the rapid implosion of the new political transition plan that the United States had announced on November 15, 2003. Shifting gears from Bremer's original plan—to transfer sovereignty only once a permanent constitution had been written and a new Iraqi government was democratically elected—Washington had announced on that date a complex and ambitious new timetable that called for the adoption of an interim constitution, the Transitional Administrative Law (TAL) by February 28, 2004; the indirect election (through a tiered system of caucuses) of a transitional parliament in the spring; and the election by parliament of a government that would receive sovereignty on June 30. By mid-March 2005, a constituent assembly would be directly elected to write a permanent constitution, which would be submitted to a referendum by August, followed by direct elections for a new government by the end of the year.

The plan was an important step forward in that it recognized the need to accelerate the transfer of power to Iraqis by a date that was visible on the political horizon. However, from the very start, Ayatollah Sistani denounced the plan, because the transitional parliament would not be directly elected. Most Arab Iraqis (Sunni and Shiite) outside the GC were also deeply suspicious of the proposed indirect elections, a ponderous and opaque tiered system of caucuses that seemed to give far too much initial power to groups (the GC and the various local and provincial councils) that the CPA had appointed. The CPA was never able to overcome Ayatollah Sistani's principled objections, which resonated with the Iraqi public and put the United States in the awkward position of favoring a distinctly slower and less democratic method for political transition in Iraq than that proposed by the Shiite religious establishment of the country.

In the face of Sistani's criticism, the CPA was initially inclined to move forward anyway, on the theory that one man should not be allowed to veto a process. The GC supported the plan (after all, it would have had a significant role in selecting the caucus participants), as did other Iraqi groups working with the CPA. This was not the first time, and it would not be the last, that the CPA's inability to engage Sistani and his following and its isolation from the broader range of Iraqi elite and mass opinion would land the occupation's transition plans into serious trouble. A political confrontation began building over the plan, and it became clear that the United States could not referee a dispute involving itself. Fortunately there emerged a face-saving means of resolution.

In early December, National Security Advisor Condoleezza Rice (who had recently been given overall authority to coordinate policy on Iraq) and her top National Security Council deputy on Iraq, Robert Blackwill, were advised that it might be possible to persuade the United Nations to reengage in Iraq in some kind of mediating or facilitating role. Even better, they heard that Lakhdar Brahimi, an Algerian diplomat who was then completing a successful U.N. constitution-building mission in Afghanistan, might be recruited to lead this effort. Rice and Blackwill greeted this prospect with genuine enthusiasm, and they soon initiated negotiations with the United Nations. In January, the parties agreed that the United Nations would return to Iraq in early February, initially in the form of a small mission led by Brahimi.

Bremer had initially wanted to narrow the United Nations' involvement in Iraq to deliberations on how to modify or improve, rather than scrap, the caucus method for choosing a transitional parliament. But he gradually accepted a broader mandate for Brahimi's mission, and ordered the entire CPA staff to give the U.N. team its full cooperation and to refrain from trying to shape or interfere with its work on the ground. This enabled Ambassador Brahimi and his circle of advisors (some of whom, like Jamal Benomar, had gotten to know the new Iraqi political landscape well while working under Vieira de Mello) to negotiate a breakthrough compromise by the end of their visit on February 13. Brahimi persuaded Sistani, through patient and methodical discussion, that "reasonably credible elections" simply could not be organized by June 30, and that it would take at least 8 months to achieve them once administrative preparations began. This realization led Sistani to accept the famous compromise, which was affirmed by Security Council Resolution 1546 adopted on June 8. Elections for a transitional parliament (and thus for the prime minister and cabinet as well) were postponed until December 2004 or not later than January 31, 2005. Meanwhile, the ponderous caucus system for choosing a government was scrapped. An unelected Iraqi Interim Government with limited powers would receive power on June 30, and Brahimi and his U.N. team would return to consult widely with Iraqis to identify a means for choosing that government.

In the end, with time running out and an interim government needing some weeks to get established before the transfer of power on June 30, the only method of selection that proved viable was appointment by the U.N. special envoy, Brahimi, in consultation with the CPA, the GC, and a wide range of other Iraqi constituencies. In this case, the interaction between the United Nations, the Americans, and the Iraqis did not proceed so smoothly. Ambassador Blackwill favored a straightforward handover of transitional power to the GC (perhaps with another 25 members to be added to make it more inclusive), despite that body's widely apparent lack of public support and confidence. Brahimi, having grasped the low esteem in which the GC was held in the country, favored a truly new government, with a prime minister from outside that body who would lead a technocratic, caretaker government. The members of the GC wanted to elevate themselves to positions of power, and jockeyed intensively for the top jobs. In the end, each side got part of what it wanted. The Bush administration got its choice for prime minister, the most powerful position: Iyad Alawi. Brahimi largely got the cabinet he thought best for Iraq, including a number of new and very competent and respected Iraqi ministers while retaining those Iraqi ministers who were widely considered to have been honest and effective. Significantly, six of the 31 ministers were women. Powerful forces on the GC were not pleased, however. Having demanded the post of prime minister or president in what they viewed as a bi-national Arab-Kurdish state, the two Kurdish parties had to settle for the posts of deputy premier and deputy president. Da'wa and SCIRI, which had also coveted the top slots, were given the other deputy presidency and the finance ministry, respectively. Brahimi failed to persuade Adnan Pachachi to accept the interim presidency after the GC rallied behind the weaker and less experienced figure of Ghazi al-Yawer, who was ultimately given the post.

Constitutional Conundrums

One of Bremer's—and the Bush administration's—highest priorities was to leave Iraq with an interim constitutional framework that would provide a strong and hopefully enduring framework for democratic government and the protection of individual rights. The drafting of the TAL was thus a crucial element of the November 15 plan. Adnan Pachachi, chairman of the GC's constitutional drafting committee, shared the liberal values and aspirations of the United States for this document, and so, quite passionately, did the Iraqi and Iraqi-American legal specialists he tapped to do the initial drafting. From late December 2003 through early February 2004, they worked, alongside CPA advisors, to craft a document that became much more of a full-blown interim constitution than some observers (including the United Nations) thought necessary or appropriate.

Both the Iraqis and the Americans agreed that the document needed strong and explicit protections for individual rights, and the extensive bill of rights that was drafted did not prove controversial. More problematic was how to structure the government, how to divide power between the center and the regions and provinces (in particular, the Kurdistan regional government), what role to give religion, and what process to endorse for adoption of the final constitution. These issues exposed the deep political and social cleavages in contemporary Iraq—between Islamist and more secular forces, between Shia and Sunni, and between Iraqi Arabs and Kurds. The drafters produced a document that assured freedom of religion and that nodded toward Islam without establishing a state based largely or exclusively on Islamic principles. For the time being, this seemed an acceptable compromise. Similarly, the formula for a government headed by a prime minister but with some powers of appointment, supervision, and legislative veto retained by a three-person presidency council, also proved broadly acceptable. Indeed, this was a formula more or less mandated by the GC from the beginning.

One of the toughest sets of issues concerned the vertical division of power and the place of Kurdistan within the Iraqi nation and its political system. Iraqi Kurdish leaders insisted emphatically from the beginning that Kurdistan needed to retain the autonomy that it had exercised during the years since the end of the first Persian Gulf War. Having suffered terrible oppression and discrimination from the central government in Baghdad, they were determined to protect themselves in the future. Moreover, many Kurds—particularly younger ones, who had reached maturity after 1991 without speaking Arabic or identifying with the Iraqi state—favored outright independence, and their leaders worried that if the new system did not preserve Kurdish autonomy, demands for independence might become unstoppable. Thus the Kurds pressed for a highly decentralized— almost confederal—system, while also indicating that they would settle (as their bottom line) for a federal system preserving their regional autonomy and granting them veto powers at the center over key issues. The TAL thus required that all decisions of the Presidency Council (which, presumably, would have one Kurdish member) be unanimous; continued the Kurdistan regional government within its existing borders (deferring the volatile question of the disputed city of Kirkuk until later); and granted that regional government powers far beyond those exercised by the 18 provincial governments. In the final, round-the-clock GC negotiations to complete the document in early March, the Kurds also made a new demand—that any three provinces (and Iraq has three predominantly Kurdish provinces) get the right, by a two-thirds vote in each province, to reject the final constitution in the referendum. To prevent a Kurdish walkout, this provision was inserted into the TAL as Article 61c.

Although the constitutional bargain gave the Kurds the minimum they insisted on, it left many Iraqis, particularly Iraqi Shiites, disaffected. When he learned of these provisions, Ayatollah Sistani raised strong objections, particularly to Article 61c, which he and other Shiites felt would eviscerate the Shiites' power as the demographic majority in the country. These objections led to a last-minute crisis in which most of the Shiite delegates temporarily withdrew from the final negotiations and went down to Najaf to consult with Sistani. Although they finally returned and signed the document, giving it unanimous GC consent, they did so only ambiguously, pledging to amend it (and particularly Article 61c) later.

At this point, the CPA faced a serious dilemma. The negotiations over the TAL had already stretched beyond the February 28 deadline in the November 15 plan. If the country was going to achieve sovereignty on June 30, this first big step had to be completed so that the process could move on to the remaining steps. But by rushing to complete the document without a national debate and the forging of a sustainable national consensus, the GC and the CPA papered over deep divisions that quickly boiled to the surface. Although happy with a number of the document's features, including those providing for individual rights and an independent judiciary, many Iraqis complained that it granted too many privileges and veto powers to the Kurds and other minorities. Lacking an understanding of federalism, many Iraqis worried that the document would be a formula for the breakup of the country and complained it was unfair that one section of the country was given "special rights" (although the TAL permitted any other three provinces to form a region that would have similar rights and autonomy). In particular, anger quickly mobilized over Article 61c as the one provision that extended beyond the transitional period, granting a minority veto of the permanent constitution. Numerous Iraqi Shiites and Sunnis, including key advisors around Ayatollah Sistani, read the document with alarm as an effort to impose, undemocratically, a permanent constitution on the country and thus declared it unacceptable. Sistani subsequently gave a strong warning to the United Nations not to accept or acknowledge the TAL, and significantly, any mention of the document was omitted from Security Council Resolution 1546, distressing the Kurds.

The CPA had long been planning a campaign to sell the TAL to the Iraqi people once it was adopted. But before the lumbering machinery of CPA's Strategic Communications office could launch its public education campaign, crude leaflets hit the streets of Iraq's cities, denouncing the TAL as unfair, unrepresentative, and undemocratic, "a dictatorship of the minorities." These denunciations—particularly over Article 61c and the lack of public discussion and debate of the draft document—caught on with the Iraqi public and largely neutralized the CPA's expensive public relations effort before it ever got off the ground. All of this reflected rather poignantly the cumbersome inefficiency of CPA's public outreach efforts, and its distance from the Iraqi people.

I encountered the popular discontent firsthand in March at public lectures and smaller seminars held in Baghdad, Tikrit, Balad, Basra, Nasariya, and Hilla, where I tried to explain the key principles of the TAL and to stimulate discussion. There was plenty of discussion, but almost all of it was critical. Many Iraqis—provincial and local council members, clerics, sheikhs, civic activists, and other opinion leaders—arrived with the leaflet in hand, and even quoted from it, as they passionately denounced the document. Repeatedly I was asked, how could such a document be adopted without public debate? Why was one section of the country given so much power? The discussions showed that Iraqis wanted democracy, but they had a very partial and majoritarian understanding of what it entailed; that Iraqis wanted more voice and participation in governance; and that the CPA and the GC were widely distrusted and held in low esteem.

Can Iraq Become a Democracy?

I have presented here a largely critical account of the American occupation and of the CPA's effort to design and foster a democratic transition in Iraq. However, there were many other, more positive, aspects to the American-led effort, and these still offer some important foundations of hope for the future. Through various offices and mechanisms, including the U.S. Agency for International Development and the National Endowment for Democracy, CPA designed, funded, managed, or commissioned an ambitious effort to promote democracy in Iraq. Some financial assistance and technical support was delivered very quickly and sensitively to emerging Iraqi civil society organizations, such as women's groups, youth organizations, professional associations, and think tanks working to expand and stimulate democratic participation.

This assistance proved very helpful in some cases, helping the Iraqi Higher Women's Council, for example, to establish a minimum quota (25%) for the representation of women in parliament. As implemented by the Independent Electoral Commission of Iraq (which required party lists to place women at no worse than every third position on each ranked list), the quota worked with extraordinary effectiveness, giving women 31 percent of the seats in the National Assembly and 28 percent of the seats in the provincial assemblies—an outcome without precedent for a contested election in the Arab world.

Training programs were set up to offer nascent Iraqi political parties the skills and tools needed to organize and mobilize for the coming new democratic politics. On the ground in a number of localities, energetic and creative CPA officials channeled assistance, funding, and hope to Iraqi democratic forces. The achievements were particularly impressive in Iraq's south-central region, where millions of dollars were spent to construct a network of 18 Internet-linked local democracy centers (one for human rights, women, and development in each of the six provinces), as well as a regional democracy training center in Hilla that includes a lecture hall, a conference room, two state-of-the art computer rooms, and more than a dozen offices for nongovernmental organization (with men's and women's dormitories on the grounds to facilitate visits for conferences and training programs). This same assistance helped to build a university for humanistic (and democratic) studies in Hilla, in the gleaming former presidential mosque, with a democracy radio station and a vast center for translating works on democracy into Arabic.

Like many CPA officials, I encountered numerous Iraqis with a genuine and deeply moving ambition to live in a decent, democratic, and free society and found them prepared to do the hard work that building a democracy will require. Above all else, Iraqis want security; they want to be free from the terror that disfigured their lives under Saddam and that has continued, in a different form, since the war. But most favor achieving this security through democratic means, not under some "benevolent" strongman. Those who think from afar that the country can be stabilized by another dictator do not grasp the divisions and aspirations in Iraqi society that need democratic expression and negotiation.

The January 30, 2005, elections demonstrated—in most of the country —the promise of democracy for Iraq. Apart from the so-called "Sunni triangle," Iraqis turned out to vote with a vivid, moving aspiration to exercise their rights of political sovereignty and a courageous determination not to be intimidated by the threats of violence. If the election results were depressingly predictable and polarized—virtually all Kurds seem to have voted for the combined Kurdish list, most Shiites voted for the United Iraqi Alliance (dubbed the "Sistani list" because it had the Grand Ayatollah's implicit support), and most Sunni Arabs did not vote—they at least provided the basis for a much more legitimate and representative government. A Shiite candidate of the United Iraqi Alliance, Da'wa leader Ibrahim Jaafari, became prime minister, and a Kurd, Jalal Talabani (longtime leader of the PUK, one of the two major Kurdish parties) became president. These were truly precedent-setting developments.

Having won only about 48 percent of the vote and a bare majority of the seats in the Transitional National Assembly and straddling significant divisions within its Shiite political base, the United Iraqi Alliance will not be able to govern without the quarter of parliamentary seats held by the Kurdish alliance of the PUK and the KDP. This Shiite-Kurdish alliance will face many tensions along the path to governing the new Iraq and writing a permanent constitution for it. But if their political leaders can continue to forge difficult compromises, as they did in the drafting of the interim constitution, and if they can bring in a wider base of Sunni Arab political leaders, then a democracy of sorts could gradually take shape in Iraq.

Because of the failures and shortcomings of the occupation—as well as the intrinsic difficulties and contradictions that any occupation following Saddam's tyranny was bound to confront—it will take a number of years to rebuild the Iraqi state and to construct any kind of viable democratic and constitutional order in Iraq. A key factor determining the success of the transition will be whether the elected transitional government will be able to reach out to Sunni Arab tribal, religious, and political forces that have sympathized with or even given support to the violent resistance, but have done so for tactical and political rather than for ideological reasons stemming from a radical Islamist rejection of the entire democratic project. If these social and political forces in the Sunni heartland—which constitute the majority of Iraqis who have supported or participated in the violent resistance—can be peeled away from the insurgency, then the latter can be progressively narrowed and de-escalated.

However, this process requires extremely difficult steps that the United States was unwilling to take throughout the period of occupation, including direct negotiations with former Ba'athist elements (not the "most wanted" leaders in the infamous "deck of cards," but military and party elites who still matter) and with leaders in the Association of Muslim Scholars, the principal association of Sunni Muslim clerics in Iraq. In addition, it requires relaxation of the de-Ba'athification policy and a willingness to allow a reformed Ba'ath Party, purged of the influence of Saddam Hussein, to contest future elections. Given that the Ba'ath Party has no chance of returning to power in democratic elections, such concessions would be a small price to pay for a dramatic reduction of, and eventually an end to, the insurgent and terrorist violence. Once these social and political pillars of the Sunni Arab communities are brought into the peaceful political process, they will have an incentive to give up the violent struggle and expel or otherwise evict the foreign jihadists and home-grown radical *Salafists*.

Political inclusion and balance will be necessary in all aspects of the emerging structure of governance in Iraq. If people across the country are going to accept and participate peacefully in the new political order, they must come to see that it represents their interests and offers them the prospect for voice and status. It is not enough to have Sunnis in the transitional government and the constitution-drafting committee, which will be appointed by the transitional assembly. They must be Sunnis who are seen to be representative of their communities and who can pull the latter toward political participation and away from violent struggle.

Increasingly, Iraqis will want to shape their own political future, for better or worse. They want their country back. They want full and complete ownership of the constitution-making process. Winding down the violence will also require a clear commitment from the United States to withdraw militarily once the country achieves stability and an acknowledgment that permanent American military bases will not be acceptable to the majority of Iraqis. In addition, the transition in Iraq is going to need massive international assistance—political, economic, and military—for years to come. The transition is going to be costly and will continue to be frustrating. Yet a large number of courageous Iraqi democrats, many with comfortable alternatives abroad, have bet their lives and their fortunes on the belief that a new and more democratic political order can be developed and sustained in Iraq. The United States and the broader international community owe it to them to continue to help.

CHAPTER 9

Striking Out in Baghdad

How Postconflict Reconstruction Went Awry

Johanna Mendelson Forman

IRAQ HAS BECOME the worst foreign policy problem the United States has faced since the Vietnam War. With a monthly price tag of $4.5 billion, it is also one of the costliest. In spite of the formal end to the American-led coalition occupation of Iraq on June 28, 2004, undoing the errors of the past year will be difficult, if not eventually destabilizing. Many problems stem from a lack of postwar planning, and a hubris that defies explanation, given the experience gained in the past 15 years in what we are again calling "nation-building." This situation, coupled with a "go-it-alone" approach to reconstruction, was doomed to fail, and warnings about the importance of support from the international community went unheeded.[1] Although some successful programs were implemented in support of the reconstruction, the absence of a coordinated strategy undercut these daily victories on the ground.[2]

In a region where U.S. influence is often met with skepticism and where Westerners are not always welcome, the preemptive war with Iraq, coupled with an inability to win the peace, has revealed just how threadbare U.S. capacities for postconflict reconstruction are. Because postconflict reconstruction by its very nature occurs in highly insecure environments, the U.S. military is again emerging as the institution that moves from war-fighting to nation-building, with no civilian agencies capable of making this transition.[3] As former Central Command General Anthony Zinni noted, the U.S. military has become the "stuckees"—the force that gets stuck with all of the clean-up because no alternative exists to fill the emergency gaps. And, even though Condoleezza Rice, President Bush's then national security advisor and current secretary of state, warned that "none of us should be forever using the military forces to do what civilian institutions are doing," Iraq has demonstrated that without U.S. forces on the ground to at least provide security, no postwar reconstruction would have happened in Iraq last year.[4]

In this chapter, I explore why the job of rebuilding Iraq has remained an unachievable objective, despite the unprecedented resources (more than $200 billion) allocated to this effort.[5] A window did exist where the American-led coalition might have had a chance to respond to conditions on the ground that appeared to deteriorate during the summer of 2003. But the window to act was limited by a combination of conditions, including the demobilization of the Iraqi army without a reintegration program and the lack of civilian police to prevent street violence, that could not immediately be undone without a change in the strategic thinking of the civilian leadership in Washington.[6]

In addition, I examine the shortcomings of postconflict reconstruction in Iraq, based on the existing understanding of what is needed to win the peace, and provide specific recommendations for how four key pillars—security, governance and participation, social and economic well-being, and justice and reconciliation—must all be considered in building a framework for action. I also focus on what the key gaps were in applying the lessons learned from other recent reconstruction experiences and explain how these gaps unfolded during the occupation. Failure to set benchmarks for progress, along with specific omissions in required tasks in each of the four reconstruction pillars, created more problems than solutions for the 13 months of occupation. Especially in light of the ongoing debate about whether the United States properly planned for a postwar Iraq, it is important to explore how a reconstruction framework might have guided the American-led coalition forces to a more successful result for the Iraqi nation.[7] Finally, I explore what conditions are needed in the postoccupation period to determine whether it is possible to support Iraq and advance the nation toward a more open, participatory society. Throughout this look at the nation-building experience in Iraq, I discuss whether the presence of the United Nations during the postwar period could have facilitated a smoother and more secure transition.

In its simplest form, nation-building is defined as "the use of armed force in the aftermath of a conflict to underpin an enduring transition to democracy."[8] There are two primary steps to nation-building. First, the country must be stabilized through humanitarian assistance and the immediate establishment of security. Second, self-sustaining and durable economic and political institutions must be created to promote democratic ideals.[9] As experiences in Africa and Central Europe illustrate, subduing warring parties, insurgent fighters, and rag-tag armies is but a small part of the larger goal of rebuilding the state. Whether it is Liberia or Sierra Leone, Bosnia or Albania, ensuring a capable state has often been a long-term and elusive goal. Recent research by World Bank economists shows that more than half of all attempts at rebuilding after war result in renewed fighting rather than a stable state.[10] Based on the recent history of post–Cold War conflicts and the tenacity of internal wars in preventing development from progressing, it is a wonder why in March 2003, when the American-led coalition invaded Iraq, there was no coherent plan to manage the country's reconstruction and stabilization after the invasion.[11]

The lessons of the post–World War II era, including the Vietnam War and the successful end of the Cold War, have provided scholars and policymakers with the "dos" and "don'ts" of nation-building that have been practiced in varying degrees in such distant places as Haiti, Somalia, Bosnia-Herzegovina, and Rwanda. In these and other examples, the nexus between security and development, between adequate security forces and progress in reconstruction, is a requirement. Ignoring the central role of security to any program in reconstruction is to do so at one's own peril—and, indeed, the peril of the operation.[12] Yet it was precisely this oversight—the exclusion of the role of the security sector—that led to the current state of insecurity, civil war, and insurgency that plagues the Iraqi state.

Finally, it is difficult to accomplish postconflict reconstruction anywhere in the world when it is done in the isolation of friends and allies. In all but Iraq, the United States worked with the United Nations and a coalition of states that formed the central core of support, both militarily and financially, to ensure that rebuilding was a shared activity. Iraq broke historical ground when reconstruction commenced without a clear mission for the United Nations and allied states, as well as in the absence of international financial support to undertake the required tasks. And even more evident as Iraq moves from occupied state to sovereign nation is that the United States, as the sole global superpower, has assumed the inescapable role as the world's nation-builder.[13]

A Framework for Reconstruction

Postconflict reconstruction has been the subject of intense study since the end of the Cold War. Many institutions that have a role in development have concluded that rebuilding after conflict has specific, unique dimensions that set it apart from the normal development process. It is driven by the timing and sequencing of specific types of activities and is highly dependent on security, which serves as the principle entry point from which all other types of programming flow. In all postconflict reconstruction, the ultimate goal is to create a minimally capable state in four key areas: (1) security; (2) governance and participation; (3) social and economic well-being; and (4) justice and reconciliation. Each of these distinct yet interrelated tasks constitutes a pillar of efforts to rebuild countries after conflict.[14] All four pillars are necessary to ensure that reconstruction advances, although implementation of each one should follow a unique sequence of tasks proven to optimize the likelihood of success. Throughout the process, multitasking is essential, as are cross-cutting factors, such as resource sharing and functional integration, that make for more effective rebuilding. If the proper but admittedly difficult balance can be struck, then the myriad organizations involved in rebuilding can work effectively and efficiently to ensure a smooth transition.

Thinking of reconstruction in terms of these four interrelated pillars also requires that planners consider how a framework for reconstruction will play out over time. Reconstruction begins with the cessation of violent conflict and ends upon the return to a normal society with functioning institutions. Over the course of this process, the various aspects of reconstruction follow a continuum of three conceptual phases: first, the initial response, in which there is large-scale dependency on outside intervention for all basic services; second, transformation, during which legitimate and sustainable indigenous capacity develops; and third, fostering sustainability, in which long-term recovery efforts come to fruition, precipitating the end of international involvement. Transitions between these phases are conditional and situation-specific; often, certain pillars might be at different stages of development.[15]

For instance, in Iraq, the security pillar remains in an initial phase,[16] whereas socioeconomic well-being, as well as governance and justice, are moving toward transformation.[17] However, all of these pillars, regardless of how far along the continuum they have advanced, are still dependent on getting the security pillar right, which will not be easy. Despite the handoff of power, the interim Iraqi government remains unprepared to assume the large-scale security functions now performed by a multinational force led by the United States and Britain.

What becomes clear from examining this task framework is that U.S. military planners were ill-prepared to respond to the multitude of tasks essential to rebuilding Iraq. This lack of preparation was primarily due to two factors: first, taking too optimistic a view of what the postwar security environment would look like; and second, failing to prepare for the peace in a country that had previously lacked any sort of open political system. Part of the lack of preparations can be attributed to the Bush administration's early decision to ignore the work of the previous administration's coordination mechanisms, namely Presidential Decision Directive (PDD) 56 (reproduced at the end of the Flournoy chapter). Instead, the Bush administration opted for National Security Presidential Directive (NSPD) XXIV, which empowered the administration to put the Defense Department in charge of all Iraqi activities.[18] Had the appropriate framework been adopted in preparation for a postwar situation, many of the errors committed after the fighting stopped could have been avoided and many lives could have been saved. In the absence of any clear roadmap, the American-led coalition attempted to win the peace with neither the right tools nor any clear vision of what lay ahead.[19]

It was not only previous American expertise that was ignored in the postwar planning. The United Nations was, and remains, uniquely situated to play a key role in postwar planning. Of course, every nation-building endeavor is unique to the history, geography, and politics of its respective location, so it is important to understand the lengthy and complex U.N. history in Iraq.

The most prominent component of the United Nations' prewar relationship with Iraq was its efforts to provide humanitarian assistance to Iraqis through the Oil-for-Food program. U.N. agents worked alongside Iraqi ministers to procure and deliver food, medicines, and other life-saving equipment to Iraqi food distribution centers, hospitals, and clinics.[20] As the program evolved, it was managed by Iraq's Ministry of the Interior, making it a highly political undertaking. Food vouchers were often used as barter, and medicines were held back from distribution so that Saddam Hussein's regime could use the outdated medicines for public-relations stunts staged to demonstrate the evil of the United Nations and its member states. The program, however, did provide food and medicines to a majority of Iraqis. And every citizen was required to sign up for a distribution card.

However, Saddam Hussein also carved out channels by which he could garnish large sums of cash from the procurement and illegal sale of Oil-for-Food materials, providing him with the financial means to attempt the purchase of fissile material. Despite the huge profits Saddam gained from this humanitarian program, its effects prevented him from acquiring nuclear materials, thus preventing the development of an Iraqi nuclear weapon.[21]

The U.N. presence in Iraq was most visible in Kurdistan before the war. This was the result of a special provision in the Oil-for-Food program resolutions that gave the Kurds a larger share (13%) of the revenues from the program to support infrastructure, education, electricity, healthcare, and other types of aid. Even though the U.N. presence in northern Iraq was important, fraud and abuse in the distribution of funds also resulted in public distrust of the United Nations in implementing programs. By the time the American-led coalition invaded in March 2003, the average Iraqi blamed the United Nations as the source of their economic problems. They considered the United Nations to be the implementing organization of Oil-for-Food. Saddam's propaganda machine would have it no other way. Thus a program mandated by member states of a multilateral institution became a lightning rod for all that was bad about the United Nations. This negativity also rubbed off on the United States in its planning programs just prior to the war.

U.N. activity in Iraq went far beyond sanctions and Oil-for-Food. Numerous U.N. agencies, including the World Food Program, the U.N. Development Program (UNDP), the U.N. Office for Project Services, the U.N. High Commissioner for Refugees, and the U.N. Children's Fund (UNICEF), were actively engaged in humanitarian efforts in Iraq. Also, prior to the March 2003 invasion, the U.N. Monitoring, Inspection, and Verification Commission (UNMOVIC) was engaged in weapons inspections to ensure Saddam Hussein's compliance with disarmament obligations. UNMOVIC was forced to exit Iraq just before military action commenced in March 2003, much to the chagrin of several member nations serving on the U.N. Security Council.[22]

All of these operations, and the experience that they bestowed, uniquely qualify the United Nations to help with the troubles of the postwar period, and suggest that the organization should have had a much more significant role in designing Iraq's postconflict framework and assisting in its implementation.

After President Bush announced an end to major combat operations on May 1, 2003, the U.N. Security Council passed Resolution 1483, resolving that "the United Nations should play a vital role in humanitarian relief, the reconstruction of Iraq, and the restoration and establishment of national and local institutions for representative governance."[23] This resolution also allowed for Sergio Vieira de Mello to be appointed independent special representative to the U.N. secretary general, who asked Vieira de Mello to take a four-month leave of absence from his position as U.N. High Commissioner for Human Rights to serve as the special representative in Iraq. The resolution outlined numerous ways he was to assist the people of Iraq, a laundry list of tasks that included components from all of the pillars—coordinating humanitarian assistance, promoting the safe and voluntary return of refugees and internally displaced persons, restoring and establishing institutions for representative governance, promoting human rights, promoting economic and infrastructure reconstruction, and other functions.

The provisions of Security Council Resolution 1483 did not, however, clearly define the United Nations' role in securing Iraq or in establishing a new Iraqi government. In the absence of U.N. assistance, the task of creating local governing bodies fell to the American-led occupation forces. Through the Law of Armed Conflict,[24] the military was empowered to establish a governing body for Iraq—the Coalition Provisional Authority (CPA). The CPA held tight reign over all political, economic, and security activities in Iraq.

The CPA's job was overwhelming because it was, in effect, the interim government of Iraq and thus bore the responsibility of occupation, which consisted of not only the day-to-day operation of a country of 25 million, but also of the obligations of international law, including peacekeeping, humanitarian activities, and the nurturing of a politically and socially stable environment. These tasks required far more than an in-depth understanding of the country and region. They demanded closer collaboration with Iraqi and international experts in these fields. This type of international assistance was late in coming, and the United Nations' absence from the reconstruction effort deprived the field of a larger number of international experts who could have worked more effectively than U.S. or U.K. forces alone on the long-term development tasks.

Timing of Postconflict Operations: Keeping the Window Open

In postconflict reconstruction, timing is everything. However, focusing on arbitrary deadlines dictated from the outside rather than on circumstances on the ground leads to inevitable failure. A window of goodwill and flexible expectations is often forgiving of many mistakes made by external actors, provided that there is a sense of hope, a vision for the future, and some tangible evidence that things can improve. Yet it was precisely this kind of disconnect between Washington and the field that set in motion events that ultimately rendered the CPA's work so ineffective from its inception in May 2003 until the handover of sovereignty on June 28, 2004.

For Iraqis, the most important and immediate need was security. But tied to security was the immediate need to restore electricity and other basic infrastructure, like water. Without lights, the streets at night were unsafe. Without electricity and water, the abundant oil in the Iraqi subsoil could not be extracted. And jobs were essential for security, because the fall of the Saddam government led to the collapse of the command economy, which had employed the bulk of Iraqis in offices, factories, and farms.

Hope is difficult to quantify, but it usually comes in the form of small, simple comforts restored—that is, electricity, water, and back-to-work programs that put money into the pockets of those whose livelihoods were disrupted by fighting. After the cessation of hostilities is also a time when accurate information about what is happening in the country is essential. Communications strategies that answer the people's questions can make the difference between success and failure.

Unfortunately, the inadequate prewar planning also put communication to the Iraqis as a secondary priority, thus making accurate and reliable information about the reconstruction scarce. Instead, reconstruction efforts and the occupation became the subject of rumor and, at times, intentionally false reports. Finally, in an attempt to meet deadlines imposed by Washington, faulty decisions were made, such as disbanding the Iraqi Army and relieving thousands of Iraqis from their government jobs without compensation or an alternative work plan—some of the deadliest mistakes made by the CPA.

By the end of August 2003, it was apparent that the window of goodwill was closing and Iraq had reached a tipping point.[25] Violence increased in major cities. Bombings in Najaf, killing Imam Hakim, and car bombs in Baghdad, killing Vieira de Mello along with 21 other internationals, marked the beginning of an insurgency that has only increased in numbers and strength. And as the "furnace" month of August lingered on, there was little sign of the CPA's ability to restore electric power due to the increased incidences of sabotage of electric facilities.[26]

Getting It Wrong in Baghdad

The army has a saying: "Any road will get you there if you don't know where you are going." The postconflict phase in Iraq underscored this phrase as evidence mounted that the prewar period was bereft of any serious planning process.[27] Many avoidable mistakes were made in the early days of the occupation that set the course for trouble as the American-led coalition tried to rebuild Iraq. The troubles were myriad. CPA decisions ultimately affected the ability of the coalition and its Iraqi counterparts to restore security, thus hampering attempts to revitalize the economy. Iraqi citizens in cities and rural communities were unable to participate fully in the formation of local government. And national government was relegated to the Governing Council that was hand-picked by the American-led coalition.

The judicial system under Saddam Hussein, which needed overhaul and a new commitment to fairness, was also inhibited by the presence of foreign lawyers, who flowed into the country to attempt reform. But the most egregious offense came in April 2004, when the ability to work on judicial reform was further compromised by the release of incriminating photographs and the emergence of confessions by U.S. soldiers, showing that U.S. occupation forces had abused Iraqi prisoners at the infamous Abu Ghraib prison. Most of the omissions in security, justice, economic well-being, and governance after the war were factors well known to those studying the conflicts of the post–Cold War world.[28]

A pillar-by-pillar look at how the occupation failed to implement a transition framework can provide a better understanding of how lessons from other reconstruction experiences were not applied in Iraq.

Security

The single most costly error committed by the American-led coalition was the decision to dismiss the Iraqi Army.[29] This decision, made in late May 2003 in Washington by a small group of policymakers working with Undersecretary of Defense Douglas Feith, unleashed a chain of events that led to Iraq's ongoing destabilization.[30] That decision represented one of the clearest examples of how military planners failed to learn lessons from other postconflict experiences of the post–Cold War era.[31]

Demobilization schemes require that an alternative security force is available to replace the army being disbanded and that a scheme to continue payroll and training for those being removed from service be established. By dismissing the Iraqi Army's more than 400,000 men without providing any alternative Iraqi security force or international force ready to fill in, more than their livelihood was at stake. The Iraqi Army comprised approximately 7 percent of the total workforce, and when their families and dependents are considered, this one act resulted in an economic crisis for about 2.5 million people, or 10 percent of the population.[32] The dismissal led some of these soldiers to emerge as spoilers to the reconstruction process later in the year. Dispersing these troops also diminished the capacity of U.S. soldiers to gain important intelligence information, as there were no longer individual contacts remaining in any chain of command.[33]

An additional threat arose as a result of the decision to disband the army: It opened a floodgate for foreign fighters to enter Iraq, taking advantage of the absence of any indigenous security force, and cognizant of the shortfall of troops that the coalition controlled. In spite of the increase in foreign forces, the United States acted as if this threat would go away, which it did not. By January 2004, coalition troops were reporting that one in six persons apprehended in the Sunni triangle area was a foreign volunteer.[34]

While creating a new Iraqi security force was always a goal, realizing it has been a struggle due to the lack of any well-defined plans to accomplish this goal in the wake of the decision to disband the old army. Had the army remained intact, the creation of a new Iraqi security force could have advanced more quickly, and many former Ba'athist fighters could have been tapped to serve in the new armed forces.[35]

Further proof of how disbanding the army undermined the creation of an Iraqi national police can be found by looking at recruiting numbers. When the CPA made its penultimate status report in June 2004, it showed that only 5,857 out of 88,039 Iraqi police had received any serious academy training. Similarly, the new Iraqi National Guard, created to replace the old security forces, was also far behind, with approximately 2,362 men out of 39,128 actually in training as of June 2004.[36] Today, only 84,327 Iraqi police officers have been trained and equipped for the desired 142,190 positions. In addition, of the nearly 100,000 Iraqi needed for the armed forces and the National Guard, only 67,584 are operational.[37]

Social and Economic Well-Being

Second only to the dismissal of the Iraqi Army in May 2003 in its devastating effect was the sweeping de-Ba'athification order, a primary cause of unemployment in postwar Iraq. By the stroke of a pen, the CPA forbade thousands of mid-level party civil servants, including doctors and teachers, from participating in public life.[38] The purging of former regime officials suspected of committing human rights violations—known as *lustration*—is a common technique used to build a trusted leadership in postconflict societies.[39] But this policy ignored the fact that Saddam Hussein's brutal dictatorship made loyalty to the Ba'ath party a prerequisite for state employment. A de-Ba'athification Commission, part of the CPA-appointed Governing Council and led by Ahmed Chalabi, purged more than 30,000 civil servants in the occupation's first months. There were plans under way to remove another 30,000 workers, but in June 2004, just before the handover, the original order was rescinded.[40]

The aftermath of these decisions left Iraq without teachers, professors, doctors, or town administrators to support the reconstruction process. Not only did it create hostility toward the occupying forces, it also paved the way for increased support and sympathy for insurgents. The CPA did leave more than half a million Iraqis on the payroll of many state-owned enterprises through the year, which helped maintain government employment levels.[41] However, fewer than 25,000 Iraqis were employed by the CPA—less than 1 percent of the country's workforce—to work on reconstruction, further undermining any sense of local ownership in the state's rebuilding.[42]

A third mistake was actually a series of blunders that left the CPA unable to provide adequate electricity to Iraqis from the war's "end" to the handover in June 2004. Before the invasion in March 2003, Iraq produced 4,500 megawatts of electricity on demand.[43] At the end of the occupation, Iraq's electricity generation hovered at 4,000 megawatts, which equals less than 9 hours of power a day for most Baghdad homes.[44] Nearly 2 years later, the situation has not improved, and Iraqis are only receiving roughly 3,600 megawatts of electricity.[45]

This electricity shortage had a particularly devastating political impact for the occupation. First, the absence of any proper means of national communication left the coalition incapable of letting citizens know when they had power. Even in the well-off neighborhoods, there were only 12 hours of electricity per day, with rolling black-outs.[46] Second, Iraqi expectations for the coalition to restore such basic infrastructure as the power grid far exceeded the contractors' capacity for repairs. Third, the power grids were highly susceptible to sabotage, and the paucity of security forces for this type of protection clearly took its toll as daily bombings of power lines were a major setback to the larger task of turning on the lights. Fourth, the oil industry, the largest source of revenue for Iraq after international support, was totally dependent on electricity to pump the water needed to harvest underground oil supplies. Thus, in a country with the world's second largest petroleum reserve, there was very little ability to meet the minimum number of barrels per day needed for export, further slowing Iraqi economic recovery.[47]

Justice and Reconciliation

Over its 35-year existence, Saddam Hussein's regime compiled one of the worst human rights records in modern times. The alleged atrocities range from war crimes and crimes against humanity to ongoing violations of civil and political rights, including summary executions and torture. When the occupation began, restoration of an independent judiciary was one of the CPA's highest priorities.

Unfortunately, despite efforts to begin an assessment of the rule of law and the reorganization of the judicial system, two events called into question the ability to establish public confidence in the legal system. First, the creation of a special tribunal upon the capture of Saddam Hussein in December 2003 raised questions about the impartiality and fairness of such a body in terms of providing justice and reconciliation for the Iraqi people.[48] Second, the revelation of improprieties in the management of the prison system under the occupation—specifically at the Abu Ghraib prison—called into question both the CPA's capacity and credibility in this area. In May 2004, revelations of prison guard misconduct and prisoner abuse cast a dark shadow over the coalition, which had preached a mission of democracy and human rights as grounds for the war against Saddam.[49]

On December 10, 2003, the Iraqi Governing Council announced the creation of an Iraqi special tribunal, with a mandate including genocide, war crimes, and crimes against humanity committed from July 17, 1968—when Saddam came to power—until May 1, 2003, the official end of major coalition combat operations.[50] But this tribunal has been criticized on several fronts as lacking impartiality and transparency. In addition, Salem Chalabi (nephew of ex-Iraqi National Congress leader Ahmad Chalabi) was appointed to head the tribunal, although he was subsequently dismissed. Finally, it was the Iraqi National Congress, Ahmed Chalabi's group, that announced the tribunal's creation, not the Iraqi Governing Council, thus sparking greater concern about the politicization of this important trial body.[51]

After the handover in June 2004, however, investigative judges undertook in-depth inquiries to establish Saddam Hussein's responsibility as a former president over the actors and institutions that carried out atrocities. Other officials may also be brought to trial. But it remains to be seen, as events unfold, whether Iraqi citizens will fully accept this process as legitimate.

The most spectacular error in the administration of justice concerned the restoration of Iraq's infamous Abu Ghraib prison, well known as a torture chamber for the former regime. For the average Iraqi, the mere symbolism of the continued use of this prison served as a reminder that perhaps things may not have changed in spite of the war and the subsequent occupation. In April 2004, when the atrocities committed by U.S. forces against Iraqi prisoners held in that detention center were revealed, the small margin of support the coalition enjoyed evaporated. The Defense Department and the CPA stumbled through the last months of occupation explaining this gap in the judicial system.[52] Detainee abuse by U.S. military personnel may well become the lasting symbol of an occupation flawed by so many other ill-fated decisions. Photographs of the abuse that were viewed worldwide are a legacy of warfare in the early twenty-first century that may continue to haunt U.S. relations in the Arab world for decades to come.

What compounds the tragedy of Abu Ghraib is that an investigation led by U.S. Army Major General Antonio M. Taguba found that "systematic and illegal abuse of detainees occurred from October to December 2003 within the prison run by the 800th Military Police Brigade."[53] Not only did this report acknowledge that bad things were happening, it also underscored the breach of international law that the American-led coalition was engaged in under its responsibilities to protect detainees as set forth in the Third and Fourth Geneva Conventions.[54]

There is a close relationship between security, law enforcement, and justice. The increasing destabilization of Iraq in the postwar period underscored the precarious balance that existed between the need to protect Iraqi citizens while intercepting the insurgents, who were now infiltrating the entire country. In the raids and dragnets set up by the American-led coalition in the early days of the occupation, many innocent civilians were caught up in postwar chaos that frequently resulted in their arrest or incarceration.[55] The absence of indigenous Iraqi police and the continued reliance on coalition military police made it hard for citizens to distinguish between the war itself and the postconflict environment.

Governance and Participation

Reestablishing sovereignty is central to rebuilding a state. Two entities were charged with providing guidance on governance toward a sovereign Iraq during the occupation. The CPA established the duties of one administrative entity. At its inception in July 2003, the CPA was tasked with leading and overseeing the reconstruction and was vested with executive, legislative, and judiciary power in Iraq. Broadly, its mission was to disarm the Iraqis and to coordinate humanitarian assistance for them. To accomplish these goals, it had to decide where and to whom to appropriate funds.[56]

The second entity, the United Nations, established guidelines for the CPA's conduct and mission through U.N. Security Council Resolution 1483.[57] But the United Nations was also given an ambiguous, ill-defined mission by the Security Council, despite reference to its vital role in the reconstruction. In retrospect, the failure to define a clear role for the United Nations at the outset put the effectiveness of the international organization at risk. Whereas the United Nations has always been considered a neutral interlocutor for the different parties in other postconflict operations, in Iraq, it was considered a collaborator of the occupying powers.[58] Furthermore, before the sanctions were lifted following the resolution's passage in May 2003, the United Nations suffered from a negative image because of its role as coordinator of the Oil-for-Food program. Iraqis considered the United Nations to be a source of their hardship.[59] It did not take long for the spoilers and the growing body of insurgents who were determined to destroy the Western infidels to target the United Nations as part of its strategy to destabilize postwar Iraq. Some observers argue that the insurgents lacked a "grand strategy" for their operations, other than to destroy anyone working with the coalition. In Iraq, these fighters may be considered nationalists who are defending Iraqi honor.

In the absence of U.N. assistance, the task of creating local governing bodies devolved to the American-led occupation forces. Under the Law of Armed Conflict,[60] the military established the CPA as the governing body for Iraq. In turn, CPA Order 71 then empowered the Iraqis to establish their own government.[61] U.S. Army captains and majors served alongside Iraqi locals to create a new political order. The martial nature of this type of arrangement was not lost on Iraqis, with the symbol of military men working on candidate selection a clear part of the mission in Iraq.[62]

In July 2003, Ambassador L. Paul Bremer appointed the Iraqi Governing Council to serve as a transition government, even though more than half its members were Iraqi exiles. Additionally, the body was subject to the guiding hand and veto of the CPA. For those two reasons, its legitimacy as a governing entity was in question from the outset.[63] With the assassination of two of its 26 members during the occupation, the council suffered greatly. Over the course of its short life, however, the Governing Council did draft the Transitional Administrative Law (TAL), which laid the governing foundation for Iraq until the promulgation of a new constitution in 2005. The TAL created the general framework for national legislative elections to take place by the end of January 2005.

The Role of the United Nations

The desire to destroy partners of the coalition was demonstrated on August 19, 2003, when a truck bomb destroyed the U.N. mission in Baghdad. From this tragedy, it became clear that the coalition's approach to rebuilding Iraq would never succeed. Yet it took another 6 months for the United Nations to reengage in the political process in Iraq. In February 2004, Secretary General Kofi Annan appointed his most trusted senior aide, Lakhdar Brahimi, to be a special envoy to Iraq. Brahimi's mission set the course for the transition that occurred in June 2004.[64] By establishing a timetable for national and regional elections and bringing together the various factions, Iraqis saw in the United Nations some hope for an end to the American-led occupation.

On June 28, 2004, the Governing Council officially dissolved, and a new interim Iraqi government was sworn in. Although it was still not an elected body, according to Brahimi, it was the reflection of extremely difficult negotiations that included realistic compromises in a country where bloodshed and violence had dominated the first year of occupation.[65] A little more than a month after the June transition, in August 2004, the Iraqis held a national conference for political parties. This meeting laid the foundation for wider regional and tribal representation. It represented the first real step toward local ownership of the political future of Iraq.

The TAL created the framework for the National Assembly elections that took place on January 30, 2005.[66] The newly elected assembly will draft a permanent constitution that will be put to a national referendum for approval by a majority of Iraqis by October 2005. A permanent National Assembly will then be elected no later than December 31, 2005. The United Nations will provide technical assistance for this process.[67]

Although the role given to the United Nations in postwar Iraq was limited, the international body contributed significantly to the organization and implementation of Iraq's first open elections. It provided support for the formation of the Independent Electoral Commission of Iraq (IECI) and the recruitment and training of 900 IECI staff. A U.N. electoral team of more than 50 staff members in Baghdad, Amman, and New York engaged in a wide range of activities to provide the Iraqi-administered IECI with the technical, logistical, financial, and administrative assistance necessary to conduct successful national elections. In addition, U.N. election experts, both inside and outside of Iraq, trained more than 8,000 Iraqi electoral workers to assist the IECI in conducting a fair and free election. The United Nations also helped to recruit and train up to 148,000 poll workers for the estimated 5,578 polling centers around Iraq.

The future role of the United Nations will be crucial in supporting the government in building capacity, and in laying the foundation for local government, rule of law, and other reconstruction needs. The United Nations' experiences in previous nation-building undertakings provide it with a unique body of expertise.

Today, 23 different agencies and organizations from the greater U.N. family are helping to coordinate aid and reconstruction in Iraq; 46 different projects have been approved, receiving total funding of more than $490 million. One such project is going on in Basra, where the UNDP is providing $15 million in spare parts to rehabilitate the Hartha power station. In Fallujah, UNICEF is leading a group that has distributed 7 million liters of potable water to more than 70,000 people displaced from their homes in recent fighting. The United Nations and the World Bank also set up the International Reconstruction Fund Facility for Iraq to fund activities in Basra, Fallujah, and elsewhere. This fund has gotten 24 donors to come forward with more than $1 billion in support for these activities.

Ironically, the United Nations, spurned by the United States in the early days after the war, became the central element in an exit strategy for the occupation authority. The successful outcome of the January 2005 elections demonstrated that the United Nations could perform its technical support role in the most adverse of environments. Iraqis were jubilant in celebrating their first-ever free election, despite the insecurity and risk that voting posed.

Nevertheless, the U.S. failure to muster broad-based international support for the reconstruction process is evident even after a new U.N. Security Council Resolution, voted on by member states on June 8, 2004, that calls upon the international community to support and protect election workers and requests countries to contribute soldiers to the multinational operation.[68] In spite of the United Nations again being mentioned by U.S. leaders as the institution of choice to advance the reconstruction process, little progress has been made in increasing the number of coalition members. Washington's inability to convince its European counterparts (who were quite engaged in their own right in both the Balkans and Afghanistan) to contribute troops or police, not to mention provide other types of assistance, has underscored how isolated the United States has become among the community of nations with regard to rebuilding Iraq.

Ramifications of U.S. Policy

Iraq is a long-term commitment for the American-led coalition and the United Nations. With taxpayers doling out a billion dollars a week to underwrite U.S. operations in a now-sovereign Iraq, it is clear that the reverberations of this war will impact the U.S. economy for the next decade or more. But the mistakes made in the occupation of Iraq have made—and will undoubtedly continue to make—the postconflict reconstruction program more difficult. And certainly, the immediate insecurity that resulted from uninformed decisionmaking is still costing the American public, in terms of U.S. soldiers' lives as well as public distaste for a war whose original purpose—disarming Iraq of its cache of weapons of mass destruction—can no longer be sustained.

What may result from this war gone awry is a new foreign-assistance capacity that can finally respond to international crises. Iraq has brought home to many in Congress what the policy community had been saying for years: the civilian foreign-assistance capacity is broken, and it must be fixed if the United States is to be responsive to the demands of its role as the world's sole superpower. But to be effective, the United States will have to abandon its Cold War approach to foreign assistance and replace government agencies such as the U.S. Agency for International Development (USAID) with new, more agile and appropriate institutional mechanisms to respond to crises with the entire complement of U.S. national power.[69]

Even though this was the first post–Cold War reconstruction effort that was wholly owned by the Defense Department, it was also evident that the war-fighting capacity of our military, although overwhelmingly successful in the operations for which it was designed, was the inappropriate choice for postconflict reconstruction. There are positive signs that new legislation is being considered to address the gaps in postconflict reconstruction.[70] This part of the larger security and development agenda must be treated as a full-time program of the U.S. government rather than an orphan function of a few offices at the State Department and USAID. The institutional rearrangement has already begun in Washington, and will no doubt be among the priorities of U.S. leaders in the years to come.

There remains a prominent role for the United Nations in Iraq. As Secretary General Kofi Annan stated in a 2005 op-ed in *The Washington Post,* the United Nations will continue to work with the international community on a common agenda: "to move Iraq from the starting point—its successfully completed elections—to a peaceful, prosperous, and democratic future."[71] The United Nations will continue to offer technical advice for the drafting of the Iraqi Constitution and the organization of a national referendum in October 2005 and parliamentary elections in December 2005. Central to all of these efforts is the United Nations' unique credibility with, and access to, estranged Iraqi groups that must be included if a new political process is to prove viable.

No postconflict reconstruction ever takes place in a vacuum. The United Nations always operates at its best when it has a strong national partner. The United States, along with other member states, can provide the support and leadership to help Iraq become a more stable and open society in a region that remains predominantly undemocratic. Without a multilateral institution like the United Nations to lead the way, it is uncertain who or what would fill this leadership gap.

Iraq represented a "fork in the road" for the United Nations as an institution, according to Secretary General Annan, who described the events leading to the war in early 2003 as a turning point for the role of the organization, and the Security Council in particular, as a peacemaking body.[72] But determining the future role of the United Nations in nation-building has only just begun. Just as the grand bargain that created the United Nations in 1945 is being reassessed, a stronger organization may emerge, whose legitimacy could remain a rallying point for the world community when it comes to rebuilding Iraq.[73]

Notes

Special thanks to Mr. Anton Ghosh, Ms. Hilary Sinnamon, Mr. William Gee, and Colonel Paul Hughes for assistance in the preparation of this chapter.

1. See George Packer, "War after the War," *New Yorker,* November 24, 2003, 59, citing a study written for the Department of State by Andrew Erdmann.

2. In July 2003, a field report was published, at the request of L. Paul Bremer and Donald Rumsfeld, detailing the steps needed for a successful reconstruction effort. It was such a plan or roadmap that the coalition was missing when it entered the reconstruction phase. See John Hamre, Frederick Barton, Bathsheba Crocker, Johanna Mendelson Forman, and Robert Orr, "Iraq's Post-Conflict Reconstruction: A Field Review and Recommendations," Center for Strategic and International Studies and Association of the U.S. Army, July 17, 2003, available at www.csis.org/isp/pcr/IraqTrip.pdf.
3. Brad Knickerbocker, "How Iraq Will Change U.S. Military Doctrine," *Christian Science Monitor,* July 2, 2004, 2.
4. Condoleezza Rice, as cited in "The People's Justice in the Balkans," *Washington Times,* August 6, 2001, A16.
5. Susan Page, "Convergence of Factors Raises Cost of Iraq War," *USA Today,* May 13, 2004, 124.
6. See Hamre et al., "Iraq's Post-Conflict Reconstruction."
7. "Iraq: Were We Wrong?" *New Republic,* June 28, 2004, 8–11.
8. James Dobbins, *Nation-Building: The Inescapable Responsibility of the World's Only Superpower* (Santa Monica, Calif.: RAND, Summer 2003), available at www.rand.org/publications/randreview/issues/summer2003/nation1.html.
9. Francis Fukuyama, "Nation-Building 101," *Atlantic Monthly,* January 20, 2004, 159–63.
10. Jean-Paul Azam, Paul Collier, and Anke Hoeffler, "International Policies in Civil Conflict: An Economic Perspective," December 14, 2001, available at http://users.ox.ac.uk/~ball0144/research.htm.
11. See James Dobbins, Keith Crane, and Seth Jones, et al., *America's Role in Nation-Building: From Germany to Iraq* (Santa Monica, Calif.: RAND, 2003), for an excellent overview of the subject.
12. For examples of this discussion, see Peter Uvin, "The Development/Peacebuilding Nexus: A Typology and History of Changing Paradigms," *Journal of Peacebuilding & Development* 1 (2002): 5–24; and Johanna Mendelson Forman, "Development and Security," *Journal of Peacebuilding & Development* 3 (2004): 81–85.
13. Dobbins et al., *America's Role in Nation-Building,* xv. The United States need not engage in such endeavors alone. The United Nations' role in nation-building, much maligned after the failures of Somalia and the former Yugoslavia, was revived after successful experiences in East Timor and Afghanistan. Through the 1990s, there was a perception that the United States, along with other bilateral actors, had gained expertise and knowledge from work in the field. (But Iraq shattered this image, making those who had worked in U.N. missions long for the return of a U.N. "light footprint" to help move Iraq from a totalitarian state to an open, participatory society.)
14. The Post-Conflict Reconstruction Project, a joint effort of the Association of the U.S. Army and the Center for Strategic and International Studies, created a task-based matrix composed of these four pillars. See Robert Orr, ed., *Winning*

the Peace: An American Strategy for Post-Conflict Reconstruction (Washington, D.C.: Center for Strategic and International Studies, 2004), Appendix 1.

15. Ibid.

16. Although the security response is still in an initial phase, Lieutenant General David Petraeus, tasked with retraining Iraq's security forces, has prepared four battalions to operate alongside coalition forces, and has another three in training. See "Quarterly Update to Congress," Section 2207, The White House, available at www.whitehouse.gov/omb/legislative/2207_exec_summary_final.pdf.

17. Johanna McGeary, "Taking Back the Streets," *Time*, July 12, 2004, 28.

18. On PDD 56, see http://clinton2.nara.gov/WH/EOP/NSC/html/documents/ NSCDoc2.html and www.dtic.mil/doctrine/jel/jfq_pubs/1824.pdf. To view NSPD XXIV, go to www.fas.org/irp/offdocs/nspd/nspd-1.htm.

19. Rajiv Chandrasekaran, "Mistakes Loom Large as Handover Nears," *Washington Post*, June 20, 2004, A1.

20. The Oil-for Food Program was mandated by U.N. Security Council Resolution 986 in April 1995. It represented a compromise by Security Council members, who were asked to alleviate the suffering of ordinary Iraqis hit hardest by the sanctions regime that had been established against Iraq immediately following the 1991 Gulf War. For a detailed description of the program and subsequent investigations, see "Iraq in Transition: Post-Conflict Challenges and Opportunities" (New York and Washington, D.C.: Open Society Institute and the United Nations Foundation, Winter 2004).

21. See George A. Lopez and David Cortright, "Containing Iraq: Sanctions Worked," *Foreign Affairs* 83 (July/August 2004): 90–103.

22. For a more extended discussion of UNMOVIC's role in Iraq prior to March 2003, see Open Society Institute and the U.N. Foundation, "Reconstructing Iraq: A Guide to the Issues," May 30, 2003, available at www.soros.org/ initiatives/washington.

23. Resolution 1483 was adopted by the U.N. Security Council at its 4761st meeting, May 22, 2003. The full text is available at http://daccessdds.un.org/doc/ UNDOC/GEN/N03/368/53/PDF/N0336853.pdf?OpenElement.

24. The Law of Armed Conflict is available at www1.umn.edu/humanrts/instree/ auoy.htm.

25. See the report of the Center for Strategic and International Studies (CSIS)/ Association for the U.S. Army (AUSA)/U.N. Foundation (UNF) team, "Iraq's Post Conflict Reconstruction—A Field Review and Recommendations," in *Reconstructing Iraq: A Guide to the Issues* (New York: CSIS/AUSA/UNF, 2003). The report is based on a field visit to Iraq, June 27–July 7, 2003. The team members were John Hamre, Frederick Barton, Bathsheba Crocker, Johanna Mendelson-Forman, and Robert Orr.

26. See, for example, David Rieff, "Blueprint for a Mess: How the Bush Administration's Prewar Planners Bungled Postwar Iraq," *New York Times Magazine*, November 2, 2003, 28.

27. James Traub, "Making Sense of the Mission," *New York Times Magazine,* April 11, 2004, 32.

28. See, for example, Simon Chesterman, *You the People: The United Nations, Transitional Administration, and State-Building* (Oxford: Oxford University Press, 2004), for a comprehensive look at many postconflict operations.

29. Peter Slevin, "Wrong Turn at Post-War Crossroads: Decision to Disband Iraqi Army Cost U.S. Time and Credibility," *Washington Post,* November 20, 2003, A1.

30. Bob Woodward, *Plan of Attack* (New York: Simon and Schuster, 2004).

31. Johanna Mendelson Forman, "Can the Coalition Transform the Iraqi Security Sector before It Is Too Late?" Bulletin no. 29 (Bonn: Bonn International Center for Conversion, October 2003).

32. Michael Slackman and John Daniszewski, "U.S. Policies Lead to Dire Straits for Some in Iraq," *Los Angeles Times,* June 10, 2003, 1.

33. Slevin, "Wrong Turn at Post-War Crossroads."

34. Anthony H. Cordesman, "Cleaning Up the Mess: The Failures of the CPA and the US Effort in Iraq and What Can Be Done to Salvage Them" (Washington, D.C.: Center for Strategic and International Studies, July 7, 2004), 3.

35. Although there is a great deal of support in the Iraqi Ministry of Defense for reintegrating Ba'athists into the military, there are still some officials who do not want the Ba'athists involved.

36. Cordesman, "Cleaning Up the Mess," 4.

37. Michael O'Hanlon, "Iraq Index" (Washington, D.C.: Brookings Institution, April 7, 2005), 19.

38. Deborah Pasmantier, "Coalition makes U-turn on Baathists," Middle East On-Line, April 23, 2004, available at www.middle-east-online.com/english/?id=9772; briefing by CPA Administrator L. Paul Bremer, "Turning the Page," Coalition Provisional Authority, April 23, 2004, available at www.cpa-iraq.org/transcripts/20040423_page_turn.html.

39. Report by the International Committee of the Red Cross, "Peace and the Laws of War: The Role of International Humanitarian Law in the Post-Conflict Environment," *International Review of the Red Cross,* September 2000, 627–51.

40. Bill Powell and Aparisim Ghosh, "Paul Bremer's Rough Ride" *Time,* June 28, 2004, 44.

41. See Christopher Foote, William Block, Keith Crane, and Simon Gray, "Economic Policy and Prospects in Iraq," Public Policy Discussion Paper, Federal Reserve Bank of Boston, No. 04-1, available at www.bos.frb.org/economic/ppdp/2004/ppdp0401.pdf.

42. Matt Kelley, "Fewer than 25,000 Iraqis Working on Reconstruction Funded by U.S.," *Associated Press,* May 18, 2004.

43. CPA Daily Power Production and Distribution, as of May 19, 2004 at www.iraqcoalition.org/essential_services/electricity_graphics/index.html.

44. James Glanz, "In Race to Give Power to Iraqis, Electricity Lags," *New York Times,* June 14, 2004, 1.

45. O'Hanlon, "Iraq Index," 23.
46. Glen C. Carey, "Gas Lines, Outages are Back," *USA Today,* December 8, 2003, A1.
47. Ibid.
48. Rod Nordland and Babek Dehghanpisheh, "Judgment Days," *Newsweek,* July 12, 2004, 26.
49. Seymour M. Hersh, "Torture at Abu Ghraib," *New Yorker,* May 5, 2004, 42.
50. See "Ensuring Justice for Iraq: Evidence Preservation and Fair Trails," *Human Rights Watch,* September 2003; "Building the Iraqi Special Tribunal: Lessons from Experience in International Criminal Justice," Special Report no. 122 (Washington, D.C.: U.S. Institute of Peace, July 2004).
51. "Tribunal Established without Consultation," Amnesty International press release, December 10, 2003; "Prosecuting Saddam: Tribunals Face Challenges of Legitimacy," Statement of Michael Posner, Executive Director of Human Rights First, December 15, 2003, available at www.humanrightsfirst.org/media/2003_alerts/1215.htm.
52. For a more detailed account, see "The Road to Abu Ghraib," *Human Rights Watch,* June 2004, available at www.hrw.org/reports/2004/usa 0604; Reed Brody, "Prisoner Abuse: What About the Other Secret U.S. Prisons?" *International Herald Tribune,* May 4, 2004, 8.
53. The full text of the Taguba Report is available at www.agonist.org/annex/taguba.htm.
54. The full text of the Geneva Conventions of 1949 is available at http://en.wikipedia.org/wiki/Fourth_Geneva_Convention.
55. Hersh, "Torture at Abu Ghraib."
56. L. Elaine Halchin, "The Coalition Provisional Authority: Origin, Characteristics and Institutional Authorities," Congressional Research Service Report for Congress, April 2004, available at www.usembassy.at/en/download/pdf/iraq_cpa.pdf.
57. U.N. Security Council Resolution 1483, May 22, 2003, available at http://daccessdds.un.org/doc/UNDOC/GEN/N03/368/53/PDF/N0336853.pdf?OpenElement.
58. See James Dobbins, Seth G. Jones, Keith Crane, et. al, *The UN's Role in Nation-Building: From the Congo to Iraq* (Santa Monica, Calif.: RAND, 2005), which documents how the United Nations was able to work successfully in rebuilding countries after the Cold War.
59. Nile Gardiner and James Phillips, "Investigate the United Nations Oil-for-Food Fraud," Heritage Foundation Background Paper, April 21, 2004, available at www.heritage.org/Research/InternationalOrganizations/bg1748.cfm.
60. The Law of Armed Conflict is available at www1.umn.edu/humanrts/instree/auoy.htm.
61. The full text of Order 71 is available at www.cpa-iraq.org/regulations/20040627_CPAORD_17_Status_of_Coalition__Rev__with_Annex_A.pdf.

62. Karen von Hippel, "Back-Pedaling in Iraq: Lessons Unlearned," *Conflict, Security and Development* 4 (April 2004): 83.
63. "Governing Iraq," International Crisis Group Middle East Report no. 17, (Baghdad/Washington/Brussels: International Crisis Group, August 25, 2003), 13.
64. Steve Weisman, "U.S. Joins Iraqis to Seek UN Role in Interim Rule," *New York Times,* January 16, 2004, 1.
65. "UN Envoy Lakhdar Brahimi Announces Iraqi Caretaker Government," CPA transcript, June 1, 2004.
66. See "Transitional Administrative Law," *Washington Post,* March 8, 2004, A39.
67. As this volume went to press, a new Iraqi Constitution had been completed and was being voted on in a national referendum on October 15, 2005. Divisions among Sunni leaders, Kurds, and Shiites about representation and minority rights had the potential to delay the final transition to a freely elected government, since it was unclear that the new charter would be approved by the Iraqi electorate. This situation could further complicate the political environment by deepening the divide among the Sunni minority, the majority Shiites, and the Kurds, who have created a political power-sharing arrangement that would continue to exclude the Sunnis.
68. The full text of U.N. Security Council Resolution 1546 is available at http://daccessdds.un.org/doc/UNDOC/GEN/N04/381/16/PDF/N0438116.pdf?OpenElement.
69. The creation of the new State Department Office of the Coordinator for Reconstruction and Stabilization to address postconflict countries and coordinate the U.S. civilian agencies with the international community appears to be one of the more promising efforts to address this gap in managing crises after conflict. But such an office will only be effective if it is backed by the full support of the Department of Defense and has adequate resources to address the immediate on-the-ground challenges, from security-sector reform to job creation and political development.
70. Johanna Mendelson Forman and Michael Pan, "Filling the Gap: Civilian Rapid Response Capacity," in Orr et al., *Winning the Peace,* 116–25.
71. Kofi Annan, "How to Move Iraq Forward," *Washington Post,* February 12, 2005, A19.
72. Kofi Annan, "Implementation of the United Nation Millennium Declaration," Report to the General Assembly of the United Nations (New York: United Nations, September 2, 2003).
73. Kofi Annan, "In Larger Freedom: Toward Development, Security, and Human Rights for All. Report of the Secretary-General of the UN for Decision by Heads of State and Government in September 2005," March 21, 2005, available at www.un.org/larger freedom.

CHAPTER 10

Learning the Lessons of Iraq

James Dobbins

AMERICA'S FIRST 18 MONTHS in Iraq was marked by a series of unanticipated challenges and hastily improvised responses. All appearances to the contrary, however, the United States is no newcomer to the field of nation-building. Its invasion of Iraq marked the sixth time in a decade that American troops spearheaded international efforts to rebuild shattered nations. Five of those six operations—in Somalia, Bosnia, Kosovo, and Afghanistan, in addition to Iraq—took place in predominantly Muslim societies. Yet America's early performance in Iraq showed remarkably little benefit from its past experience.

If Iraq was not America's first foray into nation-building, neither is it likely to be the last. It is important that the costly and hard-won lessons of this most recent nation-building effort not be lost, in turn, to future American administrations. If the difficulties encountered in the occupation of Iraq demonstrated anything, it is that America needs a proven, tested, empirically based doctrine for the conduct of such operations and a cadre of experts available for such duty when the need arises.

Nation-building can be defined as the use of armed force in the aftermath of a conflict to underpin a transition to democracy. The United States undertook that mission successfully in Germany and Japan at the end of World War II. During the ensuing Cold War, under the pressure of superpower confrontation and the threat of thermonuclear war, American military power was usually used to preserve the status quo, not to change it for the better. American military interventions were infrequent, limited in both duration and in objective. U.S. influence was applied to prop up friendly governments and topple unfriendly ones, whether democratic or not. The criterion for American support or opposition during this period was whether regimes were pro- or anticommunist, not whether they were pro- or antidemocratic.

Superpower tensions and the threat of nuclear war imposed a measure of stability on the international system. Both the Soviet Union and the United States fed proxy wars, but also worked to bolster weak regimes and hold together divided societies, lest any vacuum of power open that the other side might fill or any regional conflict spin out of control in ways that might spark a global confrontation. Such states as Somalia, Afghanistan, and Yugoslavia were each regarded, at one time or another, as important pieces on the Cold War chessboard. With the demise of the Soviet Union, however, one superpower lost its capacity to prop up such regimes, and the other lost its most obvious incentive to do so. In the 1990s, freed from Cold War constraints and abandoned by former sponsors, a number of weak states fragmented or collapsed entirely.

Nation-Building after the Cold War

With the end of the Cold War came an opportunity to terminate several long-running proxy wars in Africa, Central America, and Southeast Asia. No longer was the U.N. Security Council paralyzed by superpower vetoes. No longer were international peacekeeping missions dependent on troop contributions from the smaller or poorer neutral and nonaligned nations. After 1989, the Security Council began authorizing new nation-building missions at an accelerating pace. American, Russian, French, British, and eventually German, Chinese, and Japanese troops began to serve in such operations. The North Atlantic Treaty Organization (NATO) became a major subcontractor, running the United Nations' two largest and most demanding peacekeeping missions.

Both the United Nations and the United States experienced this surge in nation-building demand throughout the 1990s and beyond. During the first 45 years of its existence, from 1945 to 1989, the United Nations mounted a total of 13 peacekeeping operations. In the decade following the fall of the Berlin Wall, it launched 41 new such missions. During the Cold War, American military interventions had occurred on the average of once per decade, in the Dominican Republic, Lebanon, Grenada, and Panama. During the 1990s, the frequency of such American ventures increased to

once every 30 months. As a candidate for president, George W. Bush criticized this trend and expressed opposition to the very concept of nation-
building. Circumstances have led his administration to launch three new
nation-building operations in its first 3 years in office, in Afghanistan, Iraq,
and Haiti.

The United States and the rest of the international community have
intervened in failed, failing, or rogue states in recognition that ungoverned
or misgoverned territory generates unwanted refugees, unbridled crimi-
nality, and extensive human rights abuses. The 9/11 attacks demonstrated
that ungoverned or misgoverned lands could also become breeding grounds
and launch pads for global terrorism.

When nation-building returned to fashion in the 1990s, America's
experiences in Germany and Japan after World War II were too distant in
time to offer much relevant guidance, even assuming that the rebuilding
of those two war-ravaged but highly developed and very homogeneous
nations had much relevance to the challenges presented by post–Cold War
failed states. During the intervening decades, the United Nations conducted a number of peacekeeping operations, but these had generally been
designed to maintain ceasefires and patrol disengagement zones, not to
secure and transform whole societies. After the Cold War, the United States
and the United Nations thus came to their nation-building responsibilities
with, in the case of the United States, no relevant doctrine for the employment of military and civil assets in such missions, and, in the case of
the United Nations, with concepts attuned to quite dissimilar missions.

Not surprisingly, both the United States and the United Nations performed badly in their first joint foray into nation-building in Somalia.
Confused command and control, a gross disparity between the size of the
international force (small) and the nation-building objectives for the international mission (ambitious), and the absence of most civil components
of integrated military, political, and economic effort resulted in setbacks
that led first the United States and then the United Nations to abandon
the effort.

A year later, the United States and the United Nations began redeem-
ing their nation-building reputations through successful collaboration in
Haiti. However, the United States and subsequently the United Nations
terminated that mission before lasting improvement in Haiti's chronic
misgovernance could be effected. In Bosnia, the Clinton administration
committed itself once again to an early exit, an error redeemed by the administration's failure to keep this promise when the time came.

In Kosovo, the United States and the United Nations avoided many of
their earlier mistakes. Along with NATO, they fashioned the most robust
of the decade's nation-building missions. Unfortunately, whereas previous

nation-building operations had been marred by unrealistically tight departure deadlines, the Kosovo mission suffered from an absence of any exit
strategy whatsoever. Nearly 6 years on, the need for such a strategy has become more pressing.

Nation-Building after 9/11

George W. Bush campaigned against the use of the American military
for nation-building. Led by unforeseen circumstances nevertheless to
mount three such operations in as many years, his administration proved
reluctant to learn from the experiences of its predecessor. The consequent
lapse of institutional memory has caused the current American administration to repeat some of its predecessor's early mistakes without, so far,
replicating its later successes. The security situations in Afghanistan and
particularly in Iraq look more like Somalia in early 1993 than Bosnia or
Kosovo half a decade later. Haiti is less secure in mid-2005 than it was almost a decade ago, in the aftermath of the 1994 intervention.

Afghanistan and Iraq are, to be sure, much larger nations than those
the United States sought to rebuild in the 1990s. Both are also more distant and culturally distinct than were Haiti, Bosnia, or Kosovo. Nation-
building in such regions was inevitably going to be a tougher and more
expensive proposition.

Some of the difficulties encountered in Afghanistan and Iraq stem
from this difference in size and from the failure to scale American commitments up (or American expectations down) accordingly. The record of
Afghan reconstruction to date illustrates that in nation-building, as in
most enterprises, low input tends to produce low output. Anemic international efforts in Afghanistan, measured in military manpower and economic assistance, have yielded low levels of physical security and economic
growth. Afghanistan is, on a per capita basis, the least resourced of any
American-led nation-building mission of the past 60 years. Indeed, the
proceeds from illegal drug production far exceed the total international assistance received. As a result, terrorists, insurgents, bandits, drug lords, and
warlords vie for control over much of the Afghan countryside. Opium production is the principal source of economic reconstruction. Progress toward rebuilding a national administration and the holding of a democratic
presidential election are bright spots in an otherwise unsettled landscape.

Whereas American economic assistance to Afghanistan is, on a per
capita basis, the lowest of any of its nation-building missions to date, Iraq
is at the other end of the scale. Over the first couple of years of these operations, the United States committed 10 times more aid to Iraq than to
Afghanistan, even though the latter is far poorer, needier, and more war-torn.

The United States has also committed 10 times more military manpower to stabilizing Iraq than to Afghanistan. Yet even this substantial military commitment remains proportionately far below the levels of NATO military manpower committed to stabilizing Bosnia and Kosovo.

Given its size, location, ethnic and religious makeup, and legacy of dictatorship, establishing a democratic Iraq was always going to be the most difficult nation-building challenge faced by the United States since the German and Japanese occupations ended four decades earlier. Inadequate planning, flawed strategy, and faulty execution have added to these difficulties.

The Occupation of Iraq

It has been said that the United States went into Iraq without a plan for the post-combat phase. This is not, strictly speaking, true. Both the military and civilian elements of the U.S. government engaged in a good deal of planning for stabilization and reconstruction. Responsibility for such planning was dispersed, however, and the various elements were never drawn together into a coherent whole.

The State Department had for several years prior to the onset of war conducted preliminary planning for stabilization and reconstruction by engaging a wide range of experts, including émigré Iraqis, in detailed consideration of the political, economic, and societal aspects of a post-Saddam Iraq. This work might have formed the basis for a more structured effort, under White House auspices. Instead, responsibility for the civil as well as the military aspects of Iraq's stabilization and reconstruction was assigned to the Department of Defense, an agency that had not handled such matters since 1952, when the German and Japanese occupations came to an end.

Defense planners do not seem to have made great use of the earlier work done at State. Instead, their efforts focused on a number of eventualities that, fortunately, did not occur, including the use of chemical and biological weapons, the destruction of Iraq's oilfields, and the outflow of large numbers of displaced persons. Defense planners failed to anticipate the power vacuum that would emerge upon the collapse of Saddam's regime, the move by criminal and extremist elements to fill this gap, and the unavailability of indigenous Iraqi security forces to prevent them from so doing. The planners also did not foresee the difficulty of displacing such criminal and extremist elements once they had been allowed to establish themselves, consolidate their power, gain confidence, and intimidate both the indigenous security forces and the local population.

Having failed to anticipate the situation U.S. forces would face at the end of conventional hostilities, Defense planners also failed to establish public security as the preeminent residual military task and to deploy the number and type of forces suitable for that purpose. No society as numerous, heavily armed, and internally conflicted as was Iraq could be adequately policed by the number of troops the United States committed to that task, nor had American troops been prepared to make the immediate shift from combat to policing that the situation required.

In congressional testimony weeks before the onset of war, a senior Bush administration official testified that he could not imagine that it would require more military manpower to secure Iraq than it would to conquer it. This failure of imagination was reflected in planning that anticipated American troop levels in Iraq leveling off once high-intensity conflict had concluded, and coming down shortly thereafter.

Such expectations were not based upon American experience in Somalia, Haiti, Bosnia, Kosovo, or Afghanistan. In each of those instances, the military manpower requirements for stabilization had greatly exceeded those for combat. In Somalia and Haiti, American forces gained entry without firing a shot, but in each case, 20,000 soldiers and marines were subsequently deployed to establish security. In Bosnia and Kosovo, airpower alone had sufficed to secure unchallenged access, but then 60,000 and 45,000 NATO soldiers, respectively, had been deployed to establish and maintain security. In Afghanistan, a few hundred Green Berets were sufficient, with the support of the indigenous Northern Alliance forces and American airpower, to chase the Taliban from power, but then nearly 25,000 U.S. and international troops were needed to establish even minimal order and contain the residual insurgency. In every one of these instances, many more troops were needed to hold the territory in question than to seize it.

In Somalia, Bosnia, Kosovo, and Afghanistan, criminal and extremist elements had moved to fill the vacuum left by the collapse of the old regimes. In Somalia, Haiti, Kosovo, and Afghanistan, the former regime's security services had been destroyed, disrupted, or discredited to the point that they offered no effective help in meeting that threat. Based on those experiences, it was reasonable to anticipate the rioting and looting that accompanied the fall of the Saddam regime, and to calculate, at least roughly, the numbers and types of American forces that would be needed to fill the resultant security gap.

If the failure to prepare adequately for the public security mission in the conventional battle's aftermath was the initial misstep, the decision to structure the postconflict phase as a military occupation was the second. American strategy for nation-building in Iraq was fundamentally shaped by the decision to conduct this mission under the laws of armed conflict, rather than as a "peace enforcement" action under the U.N. Charter. This decision reflected the American administration's emphasis on unity of command over broad participation, on undivided authority over extensive burden sharing, and on American control over international legitimacy.

Given the manner in which the war opened—without U.N. Security Council sanction and over the objections of several of America's closest allies—it would have been difficult to have immediately fashioned arrangements for Iraq's stabilization and reconstruction on the multilateral lines of Haiti, Bosnia, Kosovo, and Afghanistan. Nevertheless, in the days immediately following the breathtakingly successful American march on Baghdad, and at a time when there still seemed every prospect of finding weapons of mass destruction, foreign critics of the war seemed more ready to move beyond past differences than did the American administration. Had the United States been prepared to share responsibility for Iraq's governance, as it had been in all of those previous cases, it seems likely that some formula short of outright occupation could have been devised. Unfortunately, at this stage, many American's seemed more inclined to regard Iraq as a prize won than a burden acquired, and the administration was taking steps to minimize any role by such opponents of the war as France, Germany, and Russia in the reconstruction phase.

For Americans, the term *occupation* conjures up relatively benign visions of Germany and Japan after World War II. For the rest of the world, and particularly the Arab world, the term suggests nothing so much as the Israeli occupation of the West Bank and Gaza. By accepting this term to describe its presence in Iraq, the United States magnified opposition within Iraqi society and among neighboring populations. And by assuming near-exclusive responsibility for the management of Iraq's stabilization and reconstruction, the United States dampened interest among other countries to share these burdens.

Setbacks in the occupation of Iraq derived as much from faulty execution of policy as from poor planning or flawed strategy. An early decision to demobilize the Iraqi Army was taken without first implementing any program for the disarmament, demobilization, and reintegration of its members, thereby complicating efforts to rebuild an Iraqi military and creating a large pool of armed, unemployed, and disgruntled young men. A sweeping de-Ba'athification decree was issued without putting in place a mechanism to review and adjudicate cases of individuals not personally guilty of serious crimes or human rights abuses. Six months went by before money for reconstruction was requested of the Congress, during which critical programs to equip and train new Iraqi security forces languished for lack of direction and funding. Unprecedentedly large sums were committed to improving Iraqi infrastructure, but political, social, and even security-related programs received less attention.

Demobilizing superceded security organizations, weeding out abusive elements, administering transitional justice, establishing new police forces, building political parties, promoting civil society, and organizing elections are hardly unprecedented challenges. Over the years, on the basis of its experience in Panama, El Salvador, Haiti, Bosnia, Kosovo, and Afghanistan, the U.S. government had developed methodologies and created bureaucratic competencies to handle such tasks. The United Nations and other international agencies, with an even greater depth of experience upon which to draw, also offer a rich range of capabilities. The failure to expeditiously implement established methodologies and to employ these American and international competencies in Iraq must be attributed to a certain calculated inexperience on the part of American authorities.

Calculated Inexperience

This calculation was exhibited in the administration's choice of the German and Japanese occupations as reference points in designing its nation-building mission in Iraq. From the administration's standpoint, Germany and Japan held several attractions. These nation-building operations were on a larger scale than any of those in the 1990s. They were more unambiguously successful than even the best-managed of the post–Cold War missions. Finally, these more distant models were free of the controversies that had surrounded the 1990s interventions, which leading figures in the Bush administration had criticized so severely while in opposition.

Rather inconveniently, however, Iraq, as a candidate for nation-building, more resembled Yugoslavia in 1996 than Germany or Japan in 1945. Both Germany and Japan possessed highly homogenous societies and first-world economies, and both had been thoroughly defeated and had formally surrendered.

Iraq and Yugoslavia had been carved out of the Ottoman Empire at the end of the First World War. Both were multinational states, and comprised diverse religious, ethnic, and linguistic communities, some of whom probably would have preferred not to live in the same state if they could have avoided it. Both were third- or at best second-world economies. Neither had experienced the sort of devastation that had leveled Germany and Japan after World War II, and in neither case had conflicts terminated in formal surrenders.

The world had also changed greatly since 1945. At the end of World War II, the United States was the only country with the economic capacity to undertake the rebuilding of Germany and Japan. By the end of the

twentieth century, there were many countries with the capacity to participate in such reconstruction efforts. Throughout the 1990s, by a process of
trial and error, an array of institutional arrangements had been built up to
facilitate broad participation in nation-building operations while providing adequate, if not ideal, unity of command. In choosing the occupations
of Germany and Japan for its models, the American administration turned
away from these highly multilateral post–Cold War arrangements in favor
of the earlier, simpler, more unilateral approaches of the 1940s.

Calculated inexperience was also reflected in the transfer of responsibility for the civil aspects of stabilization and reconstruction from the American agencies that had handled such matters in Korea, Vietnam, Grenada,
Panama, El Salvador, Somalia, Haiti, Bosnia, Kosovo, and Afghanistan (i.e.,
from the State Department and the U.S. Agency for International Development [USAID]) to a branch of government that had ceased to exercise
such functions after the end of the German and Japanese occupations in
1952 (i.e., to the Department of Defense). The decision to marginalize State
and USAID and to centralize responsibility for all aspects of the occupation in the Defense Department greatly increased the start-up costs for this
operation, as untried individuals were sent to face what for them were
unfamiliar problems without the experience, training, bureaucratic back-
stopping, budgetary authority, or institutional framework needed to successfully fulfill their new responsibilities.

Institutional Weaknesses

Difficulties encountered during the first year of American nation-
building efforts in Iraq cannot be blamed entirely on calculated inexperience
—that is, on the decision to sideline the State Department, the United Nations, and other multinational institutions and to concentrate all authority within the Department of Defense. Although the State Department had
slowly improved its management of the civil aspects of nation-building
during the 1990s, it had never become particularly good at this task. From
Somalia to Haiti, Bosnia, and Kosovo, each American-led operation had
been somewhat better organized than its predecessor. Despite the intensity of its nation-building engagement over these years, however, the State
Department persisted in treating each new mission as if it were the first encountered, sending largely new teams of people to face old problems. Worse
still, State treated each new nation-building operation as if it would be the
last, making no concerted effort to elaborate a doctrine for the conduct of
such missions, or to develop a cadre of experienced personnel who could
be called on for service in them as the need arose.

This lack of American investment in its peace-building capacity stood in stark contrast to its large investment in war-fighting. In the aftermath of the Cold War, even as the overall size of the American armed forces shrank, successive administrations made major investments in boosting their combat capability. The result, as demonstrated in Gulf War I, Kosovo, and then Gulf War II, has been that progressively smaller American forces have been able to defeat large enemies ever more rapidly.

Despite the increasingly obvious fact that "postconflict" missions have become more time consuming, resource intensive, and demanding than the brief and relatively bloodless conventional combat phase that some-times precede them, no agency of the U.S. government has, until recently, invested in capabilities, civil or military, to conduct such missions. American performance of these tasks consequently lags well behind its improved war-fighting capacity.

Corrective Measures

Since the Clinton administration's 1993 debacle in Somalia, nation-building has been a highly controversial mission, embraced by neither State nor Defense. Setbacks in Iraq have finally caused State, Defense, the White House, and the Congress to reexamine the U.S. government's organization for the conduct of such missions. Secretary of Defense Donald Rumsfeld has directed a review in his department. Former Secretary of State Colin Powell approved the creation of a new office in the State Department responsible for the planning and staffing of future nation-building operations. The National Security Council (NSC) staff has prepared initiatives to strengthen interagency management of these operations. Bipartisan legislation has been submitted in both the Senate and House that would encourage and direct such changes.

Although the details vary, all these various initiatives appear to represent a turn back toward the multiagency and multilateral approaches that were slowly being developed in the 1990s. They all assume that nation-building should be a shared responsibility, between military and civil, State and Defense, the United States and the rest of the international community. And they all recognize that State, Defense, and the international community as a whole will not get better at these tasks unless they begin to invest in developing such capabilities.

We have learned in Iraq that although unity of command is an important factor in any nation-building mission, so are broad participation, extensive burden sharing, and international legitimacy. Within the U.S. government, stabilization and reconstruction of war-torn societies need to be seen not as sequential—first Defense stabilizes then State reconstructs—but as parallel and shared functions involving a partnership between the two agencies from the beginning, and indeed before the beginning, in the planning phase as well. Integrating those two strands of nation-building into a single policy should be the responsibility of the White House, the NSC staff, and its head, the national security advisor.

Neither State nor Defense is likely to make significant investments in their capacity to conduct such operations, however, unless a clear and enduring division of labor between the two institutions is established—one likely to survive successive changes in administration. This need for predictability suggests the desirability of embodying that division of labor in legislation that would enjoy the support of both departments, of the Congress and the administration, and of Republicans and Democrats alike. Just as legislation governs the way America goes to war, establishing distinct roles and responsibilities for the theater commanders; the armed services; the Joint Chiefs of Staff and its chairman, the secretary of defense; and the White House, so could new legislation provide a template for how America wins the peace, assigning comparable roles to State, Defense, USAID, and the NSC staff.

Beyond Occupation

In 2004, the American administration made important course corrections to its approach to Iraq, accelerating the return of sovereignty to an Iraqi government, assigning central responsibility for Iraq's political development to the United Nations, seeking a greater role for NATO in Iraq's stabilization, and returning primacy for the civil aspects of nation-building within the U.S. government to the State Department.

These steps will help increase support both domestically and abroad for the emergence of a united, modernizing, nonabusive and nonthreatening Iraq. Unfortunately, the security situation there had deteriorated beyond the point where even the best-organized peace enforcement operation on the model of Bosnia or Kosovo could suffice to stabilize the situation. Resistance that initially was limited to former regime holdouts and a few foreign fighters metastasized into the beginnings of a nationalist insurgency. Having failed to deploy U.S. and international forces adequate to preempt such a development, the United States will have to depend increasingly upon its Iraqi allies to meet this threat.

American and Iraqi leaders will need to look beyond peace enforcement operations of the past decade for inspiration, turning to British and American experiences of the past half-century in such places as Malaya,

Kenya, Vietnam, and Northern Ireland for help in fashioning an effective counterinsurgency strategy. Study of those prior campaigns suggests the need to closely integrate political and military planning, to give primacy to political objectives (especially winning the support of the population), and to make public security the centerpiece of both the military and civil efforts. The United States and the new Iraqi government will also need to work constructively with all of Iraq's neighbors if they are to have any hope of cutting off external support for the insurgency.

The recently held elections in Iraq will not end the insurgency, but they do offer an opportunity to turn a faltering American-led counter-insurgency campaign into a more successful Iraqi-led effort. By progressively removing American forces from the forefront of the urban battle and transferring those responsibilities to the Iraqi military and police, the United States can diminish the perception of continued occupation and the incitement to resistance it provokes. This policy may not immediately translate into reductions in the overall size of the American force committed to Iraq. Training, equipping, and supporting Iraqi forces; securing Iraq's borders; safeguarding its lines of communication; and guarding its massive arms and ammo dumps—tasks for which U.S. forces have hitherto lacked adequate manpower—could keep large numbers of American troops profitably engaged in Iraq for some time to come. The largest uncertainty, in the aftermath of Iraq's first free election, is whether the winners and losers will be able to come together to form a government that enjoys substantial support even with those elements in the society that did not vote for it.

As noted earlier, the Bush Administration has learned important lessons from its early setbacks in Iraq, taken corrective measures, and begun to institute organizational changes that can make such failures less likely in the future. So far, however, these changes have taken the form of State and Defense Department initiatives, without any overarching presidential guidance. Congressional attempts to craft supportive legislation have been rebuffed. The alternative of an Executive Order establishing an interagency structure and defining agency responsibilities for the management of such operations has reportedly also been rejected. At best, therefore, the new architecture is likely to be formalized in a Presidential Decision Document, the authority of which will lapse with the mandate of the current president. Given the amount of blood and treasure expended upon just this single endeavor, the nation deserves something more enduring in the way of a considered institutional response to the lessons so painfully learned, and in many cases, relearned in Iraq.

Guidelines for Future Nation-Builders

Francis Fukuyama

THE AMERICAN EXPERIENCE in reconstructing Afghanistan and Iraq following the occupation of these countries in 2001 and 2003 adds considerably to the pool of knowledge concerning nation-building. Nation-building has been studied less systematically compared to other types of international activity, although the literature on the subject has grown considerably in recent years. Major comprehensive studies on the subject include Simon Chesterman's *You the People: The United Nations, Transitional Administration, and State-Building;* the two-volume RAND study on the American and U.N. experiences with nation-building; the U.S. Institute of Peace volume *Turbulent Peace;* and the Center for Strategic and International Studies report *Winning the Peace.*[1] Development of such a literature is important in view of the relatively weak degree of institutional learning on the part of the U.S. government concerning approaches to nation-building. As the chapter in this volume by Minxin Pei, Samia Amin, and Seth Garz suggests, the United States has undertaken postconflict reconstruction on numerous occasions during the twentieth century; the chapters by Francis X. Sutton and David Ekbladh point out that the United States has promoted longer-term economic and political development continuously throughout the period after World War II. This experience has not been matched, unfortunately, by a development of doctrine and a systematic effort to analyze the experience on the part of the U.S. government.

Although the United Nations, which has also had extensive experience in nation-building, may have done a bit better in preserving institutional knowledge, it has also suffered from short memory and disorganization at the start of each new effort.

Countries that are the objects of nation-building efforts are usually among the poorest and most troubled, combining low per capita income; weak or nonexistent public authority; large numbers of displaced persons; poor public health, conducive to the spread of disease; and ongoing human rights abuses by officials, militias, and criminal gangs. After 9/11, the United States discovered that such states could also harbor terrorists capable of inflicting massive damage on the American homeland. Public agencies charged with dealing with such states have developed their own vocabulary for describing them—to the World Bank, they are "low-income countries under stress"; to the U.S. Agency for International Development (USAID), they are "fragile states." A large number of failed states emerged after the end of the Cold War.

Nation-building is undertaken in response to state failure. State failure has a number of distinct causes, whose thorough exploration is beyond the scope of the present volume. In most cases, it has been the product of civil war and in some cases, of cross-border conflict that has left the government of the affected country unable to perform such basic state functions as maintaining domestic security and providing public services. The end of the Cold War broke loose a number of frozen conflicts (e.g., those in the Balkans) and led to lack of superpower interest in some cases (e.g., Afghanistan), which permitted a steady deterioration of political conditions. In cases like the degeneration of the West African states of Liberia and Sierra Leone into warlordism, the causes were more complex.[2]

In Afghanistan, the country suffered from a communist coup, a Soviet invasion, and a civil war lasting for more than a generation. Iraq presents a rather different case from the others usually studied, in that state failure was induced by the American-led invasion in March 2003, which undermined Saddam Hussein's government partly inadvertently (by failing to prevent the looting and general disorder that followed the defeat of Iraq's conventional forces), and partly deliberately (in the disbanding of the Iraqi Army).

Components of Nation-Building

There are four separate activities that are commonly lumped under the heading of nation-building, which may or may not become parts of the actual nation-building process, depending on the circumstances of the particular case. These are:

- Peacekeeping;
- Peace enforcement;
- Postconflict reconstruction; and
- Long-term economic and political development.

The first two functions, peacekeeping and, if necessary, peace enforcement, are necessary conditions for performance of the latter functions of reconstruction and development. In the early phases of a nation-building operation, the security-related functions (along with the military command structure) predominate; as the situation is stabilized, they give way to civilian-led operations and the agencies that control them.

Peacekeeping involves international forces interposing themselves when a ceasefire and political settlement to a conflict have already been negotiated. The international peacekeepers provide a symbolic, international ratification of the settlement and, to a lesser extent, deterrence against resumption of hostilities. The most successful U.N. operations, such as those in El Salvador, Namibia, and Eastern Slavonia, were of this sort.

Peace enforcement, however, involves military operations against one of the parties to a conflict that is deemed to be at fault for causing or perpetuating the problem. Peacekeepers can pretend to be neutral, whereas peace enforcers cannot, as most conflicts are not the result of violations equally committed by all parties. The United Nations, for reasons related to its internal decisionmaking mechanisms, has a difficult time taking sides in most conflicts, and therefore has often been unable to move from simple peacekeeping to peace enforcement. Bosnia is a classic case of this difficulty: U.N. peacekeepers did not even have the mandate to defend themselves, much less the Bosniaks who were being victimized by Serbs. In Srebinica, U.N. peacekeepers were consequently taken hostage by Serbian forces. In this situation, as in Sierra Leone, other nation-states acting outside of the U.N. framework had to intervene to enforce peace (in Bosnia, Croatia and the United States intervened; in Sierra Leone, Britain did so).

The problem is not simply the political one of being able to decide to take one side or the other. The rules of engagement for peacekeeping and peace enforcement are quite different; troops used for one function will often not be good at performing the other. Some contemporary armies, such as Canada's, have trained specially for peacekeeping missions, whereas others, such as the U.S. military, train for classical war-fighting. This state of affairs has led to something of an international division of labor in nation-building operations, with the United States and Britain often doing the heavy lifting—combat—and other European forces taking on constabulary and police roles.

There is a conceptual distinction between reconstruction and development as well. Reconstruction involves returning a society ravaged by war or natural disaster back to something like the status quo ante, whereas development involves the creation of new economic or political institutions that will be self-sustaining after the withdrawal of the international community. Such reconstruction functions as providing health care, security, financial services, infrastructure rebuilding, and humanitarian assistance can be done directly by outsiders. Development, however, requires local ownership in the long run. If countries do not develop the indigenous capabilities to provide basic public services, they will remain wards of the international community. It is often the case that extensive international reconstruction can actually impede long-term development, because involvement by the international community can breed dependence and weaken local institutions.

Security

In postconflict reconstruction operations, adequate security is the absolute sine qua non of success. Larry Diamond's chapter on Iraq points out that the single biggest U.S. mistake after the invasion of that country was the failure to anticipate the widespread looting and disorder that occurred and to deploy forces adequate in numbers and configuration to deter it. In Afghanistan, the situation was somewhat more complex: the bulk of the fighting was done by indigenous allies of the United States (mainly the Northern Alliance), which was able to provide security in certain parts of the country. The problem, as the chapters by S. Frederick Starr, Larry P. Goodson, and Marvin G. Weinbaum demonstrate, was in extending the sphere of military control of Hamid Karzai's new central government out of the capital city of Kabul, often at the expense of former allies who had become local warlords. Quite apart from subduing political challengers, both Iraq and Afghanistan faced serious problems of simple crime and banditry, often well organized, that threatened relief organizations and diminished, by its prevalence, the legitimacy of the occupying authority and the new local government.

As noted above, forces have to train differently for war-fighting and for peacekeeping. There are, in fact, two distinct coercive functions that fall short of active combat. The first is performed by constabulary forces, which are usually provided with armored vehicles and some heavy weapons. Their missions include disarmament of local militias and military units, large-scale crowd control, curfew policing, and, at the high end, some types of peace-enforcement operations. The second function is performed by police (the so-called *civ-pol function*) and includes maintenance of law and order, crime prevention, and local intelligence.

Ideally, both constabulary and police follow-on forces should be available during and immediately after the peace enforcement or active combat phase of a conflict. This ideal is extremely difficult to organize, however. Many countries, including the United States and Britain, do not maintain constabulary forces at all, whereas others, like Italy with its *Carabinieri* and Spain with its *Guardia Civil*, do. Virtually no country, however, maintains standing police forces that can be rapidly deployed to a postconflict situation. The United States indeed does not maintain a federal police force except for the Federal Bureau of Investigation. In prior nation-building exercises, civ-pol units have had to be recruited internationally as individuals, which then necessitates a prolonged period of recruitment and training. In Kosovo, despite prior planning, international civ-pol units did not arrive until nearly a year after the ceasefire marking the end of combat.

One of the largest problems in Iraq, as noted above, was the failure to anticipate the need for follow-on constabulary and police forces. Such countries as Spain and Italy that were part of the American-led coalition could (and in Italy's case, eventually did) supply them, but the timetable on which the Bush administration went to war meant that these forces were not available when most needed—that is, in the immediate aftermath of active combat. There was no police force of any sort; the United States began the arduous process of retraining and re-equipping the Iraqi police only in the months after the end of combat.

In the absence of coalition or American forces to take on the constabulary and police functions, the Bush administration could have used regular combat forces to keep order in Iraq. This is not an ideal situation; it is very difficult to get soldiers who have just been in intense combat to change their rules of engagement and shift to a posture designed to minimize casualties among the local population. In Iraq, moreover, U.S. combat forces were exhausted from their 17-day march from the Kuwaiti border to Baghdad. Nonetheless, the United States could either have planned for a larger initial invasion force,[3] or else more thoroughly thought out Phase IV actions, such as the imposition of curfews once combat ended.

After the provision of basic law and order, the most important security-related task in a postconflict situation is disarmament, demobilization, and reintegration (DDR). The former combatants who were the source of conflict have to be made to turn in their weapons, disband as organized units, and be given other functions in the civilian economy so that they no longer have an incentive to fight. The disarmament and demobilization phases are relatively straightforward; reintegration has usually been much more difficult because it requires resources (essentially, a jobs program) to implement.

In Iraq, as the chapters by Larry Diamond and James Dobbins point out, DDR was incompetently carried out, with no evidence that those presiding over it understood how the process had been executed in other postconflict settings. L. Paul Bremer and his Assistant for Military Affairs Walter Slocombe decided immediately upon their arrival in Baghdad to disband the Iraqi Army. They argued that the army had ceased to exist in any case, that rebuilding it would be too difficult in light of Ba'athist influence in the officer corps, and that its continued existence would alienate the Shia community on which a new Iraq would have to be based.

Regardless of whether that political reasoning was correct, the actual process of demobilization was guaranteed to maximize resentment and hostility on the part of former members of the Iraqi armed forces. In earlier DDR operations, demobilization was carried out in a deliberate and systematic manner. Units are normally disbanded one by one and asked to turn over their weapons; soldiers are given the pay needed to tide themselves and their families over until they can be reintegrated into other occupations. None of this happened in Iraq; the U.S. authorities simply announced that the military was being disbanded immediately without provision for reintegration. Many Iraqi soldiers had in fact followed the instructions given them by U.S. psychological operations forces prior to and during the war to simply lay down their arms and leave their units. It is therefore not surprising that many former Iraqi military men felt intensely resentful and went over to the burgeoning insurgency, complete with their weapons.

On a more positive note, one of the more promising innovations to come out of the Afghan reconstruction is the creation of provincial reconstruction teams (PRTs), discussed in the Starr, Goodson, and Weinbaum chapters, that integrate security and civilian reconstruction functions at a unit level. There are precedents for the PRTs in the Vietnam-era Civilian Operations and Revolutionary Development Support (CORDS) program, as noted in the Ekbladh chapter. Consisting of 60–100 personnel, PRTs have their own organic transport and firepower and can thus provide protection to civilian aid workers in areas not under either the International Security Assistance Force or Afghan National Army control.

Reconstruction of Political Authority

After providing initial security for the local population and aid workers, the second most important activity that must take place in a postconflict situation is the reconstruction of some form of legitimate political authority. Reconstituting authority is often very difficult to do, because it has either collapsed altogether (as was the case in Iraq), or else exists in illegitimate or semilegitimate forms (as in the case of the victorious Northern Alliance and the remaining warlords in Afghanistan). In the latter situation, it was these actors who made a ceasefire possible in the first place, and so the international occupation authorities are in some sense beholden to them for providing basic security. (The same was true in Bosnia: the Dayton Accord was hammered out between the warring ethnic parties, but it was precisely these parties that would have to be bypassed to allow a new, nonethnically divided Bosnia to emerge.) If the nascent political order is too dependent on parties to the original conflict, it may be born with a "birth defect" that will undermine efforts to achieve legitimacy subsequently. Starr's chapter suggests that U.S. dependence on the Northern Alliance ran precisely this kind of risk.

In the contemporary world, legitimacy comes primarily, although not exclusively, from democratic elections. Holding elections is therefore critical to establishing a new, legitimate order, but the questions of when, how, and at what level to hold elections are dependent on the specific circumstances of each postconflict situation. A considerable literature is now available on the question of the timing of first elections.[4] There have been several important cases during the 1990s—most notably Angola and Bosnia—in which the first election was held prematurely. Under these circumstances, militias and other armed groups have not yet been disarmed, leading to voter intimidation; new, more genuinely democratic political parties have not yet had time to organize; and the parties to the original conflict are in a position to cement their own positions by running for office.

As the chapter by Diamond indicates, all these considerations initially led the Coalition Provisional Authority in Iraq to postpone direct elections and devise a Rube Goldberg–like system of local caucuses that would allow the United States to exert some degree of control over election outcomes. In addition, holding elections in Iraq so soon after the end of active combat and in the midst of a growing insurgency posed technical problems of considerable magnitude. Balanced against this difficulty was the need for legitimate political actors and the strong demand on the part of Ayatollah Sistani for early direct elections. In the end, the logic of Sistani's position won out: an early election was warranted precisely to create an indigenous Iraqi government to whom sovereignty could be returned, ratifying the rise of the formerly excluded Shiite and Kurdish communities. The election date selected, January 30, 2005, was the earliest possible, given the technical constraints faced by occupation authorities.

Beyond the national elections in Iraq, however, there were other available routes to creating legitimate political authority that were not taken. In his chapter, Diamond argues that the CPA should have permitted local elections (which could have been held in selected areas much earlier than the national elections) well before January 2005. These elections would have created pockets of legitimacy that would have enhanced the authority of local officials and provided building blocks from which the national parties could have assembled coalitions. The CPA chose not to take this route because it did not want to give up control over the political process, a mindset that fails to recognize the importance of local ownership.

Democratic elections also played an important role in legitimating the new government of Hamid Karzai, who was elected president of Afghanistan with heavy voter turnout throughout the country on October 9, 2004. Afghanistan shows, however, that democratic elections are not the only possible route to legitimacy. The Loya Jirga, as a traditional assembly of tribes and ethnic groups from across Afghanistan, was used to ratify the Bonn process and appoint (under heavy U.S. pressure) Karzai interim president. A second constitutional Loya Jirga in January 2004, approved a new draft constitution and paved the way for October's presidential election.

In Iraq, local U.S. commanders have tried to use the authority of tribal leaders to cut deals to pacify specific parts of the country, particularly within the notorious Sunni Triangle. This kind of approach (which would have been very familiar to British colonial administrators nearly a century earlier) solves one problem in the short run, but stores up problems for the future: by empowering traditional, nondemocratic authority figures, an occupation authority strengthens players that will ultimately play unhelpful roles in a new democratic order.

The Importance of Coalitions

One of the clearest lessons that emerges from many of the chapters in this volume, including those by Michèle A. Flournoy, Johanna Mendelson Forman, Diamond, and Dobbins, concerns the importance of coalitions in postconflict reconstructions. Coalitions, in the form of support from a wide range of other countries and international organizations like the United Nations, are important for a number of reasons. Coalitions increase the legitimacy of an occupation, both in the eyes of the country being occupied, and for the broader international community that will be asked to contribute. In this respect, U.N. involvement can be quite important. (The chapter by Mendelson Forman indicates, however, that the United Nation had negative associations in the eyes of many Iraqis due to its role in the prewar sanctions regime, which is perhaps one of the reasons that its Baghdad mission was targeted in August 2003.)

In addition, coalitions help defray the costs of an occupation. During the 1991 Gulf War, the United States actually received slightly more in international contributions than it expended in military and reconstruction operations; the Iraq war and reconstruction, by contrast, have already cost U.S. taxpayers close to $200 billion.

Finally, coalitions exploit an existing international division of labor. The United States today is supremely effective at conventional war-fighting. However, it does not (as noted earlier) maintain standing constabulary or peacekeeping forces, nor does it have a national police reserve that can be mobilized for postconflict duties. Other countries, such as Canada, Italy, and Spain, do. Sanitation engineers, agricultural specialists, and public health experts are scattered across the international community.

The United States made use of a relatively broad coalition in Afghanistan from the start, and the United Nations played a key role in brokering the Loya Jirga process leading to elections. The situation was quite different in Iraq: although President George W. Bush bragged that his coalition was ultimately larger than the one his father created in 1991, it was of much lower quality. No Arab countries were willing to associate themselves with the occupation; many big NATO allies, such as France and Germany, similarly refused to join, and some that did, such as Spain, withdrew under pressure from domestic opinion or terrorist acts. The United States was wary of the United Nations in the weeks and months following the invasion and was not eager to seek a broader role for the organization until its plans started unraveling in late 2003.

American dominance of the nation-building effort in Iraq reflected, of course, the controversy that surrounded the war itself and the strong opposition of many American allies to it. Foreign hostility increased the Bush administration's desire to exert ownership over the whole reconstruction process. But even prior to the war, Defense Secretary Rumsfeld and some of his associates had held a dim view of the usefulness of allies in nation-building efforts. Rumsfeld famously remarked that "the mission should determine the coalition" and not the other way around. Wesley Clark, commander of NATO forces in Kosovo, recounts running into a senior member of the Bush administration in the Pentagon after the 2000 election who told him, "We read your book—no one is going to tell us where we can or can't bomb."[5] Rumsfeld was concerned that coalition politics not only would hamper military operations, but also make it hard for the Americans to withdraw. The desire to maintain American—and indeed, Pentagon—ownership of the reconstruction reflected a misplaced confidence about how easy the process would ultimately be.

• *Francis Fukuyama*

The Problem of Coordination

The single, simple lesson pointed out by many of the chapters in this book relates to the absence in the U.S. government of an institutional mechanism for coordinating postconflict reconstruction efforts and for preserving institutional memory of prior nation-building exercises. Managing a postconflict reconstruction is an enormously complicated task, made more difficult because it is not done often enough to become routine. There is no obvious lead agency to oversee a nation-building operation; although the Defense Department and the U.S. military plays a large role in the early phases, State, USAID, Justice, and other civilian agencies come to dominate as the reconstruction proceeds. The situation would suggest coordination of the interagency process through the White House National Security Council, but that body is small and does not have the staff to perform this irregular function.

The typical solution for most postconflict operations, as related in the chapter by Dobbins, was to create a country team led by the local ambassador and ground forces commander, with two separate chains of authority leading back to State and Defense, respectively. In the past, this configuration has posed problems for unity of command; there was considerable infighting between the military and civilian agencies in Bosnia over such issues as roles, missions, and the rules of engagement for U.S. forces.

The chapter by Flournoy describes how such early confusion led the Clinton administration to try to formalize the coordination process in Presidential Decision Directive 56, which constituted the basis for the interagency coordination of the Kosovo operation. This framework was rejected by the Bush administration, however, which chose instead to put the Defense Department in charge of the Iraq reconstruction as the administration's solution to the unity of command problem. The chapter by Dobbins explains in great detail why this did not work: the Pentagon did not have the administrative capacity to manage the reconstruction, and decided to create an entirely new agency, the CPA, in the field. The CPA, as the chapter by Diamond shows, was overly centralized and set ambitious tasks for itself that it did not have the ability to fulfill. These shortcomings laid the ground for another course reversal, as the Bush administration shifted back to the more typical, country team approach with the return of sovereignty to Iraq on June 28, 2004. The problem of unity of command is clearly not inherent to the country team approach: As the chapters by Weinbaum and Goodson indicate, Ambassador Zalmay Khalilzad and General David W. Barno, the ambassador and combined forces commander in Afghanistan, respectively, have worked together in a highly cooperative manner.

In light of the Afghanistan and Iraq experiences, the Bush administration has moved to some degree to rectify this situation with the creation
of an office of the Coordinator for Reconstruction and Stabilization. This
office will play a very useful role as the nucleus of future reconstruction
operations and the source of institutional memory. Whether it will be used
in that fashion will depend, however, on the politics of the moment and
the interest of the White House in making use of its expertise. Had this
office existed in the lead-up to the Iraq war, it probably would have been
sidelined along with the rest of the Department of State.

Reconstruction and Economic Development

Civilian reconstruction in postconflict operations poses a host of interrelated problems quite apart from how the civilians relate to the forces
providing security. First and foremost is the issue of donor cooperation.
Reconstruction and humanitarian aid projects, and particularly those that
are well resourced, tend to attract numerous outside participants, including
multilateral agencies (e.g., the United Nations, World Bank, International
Monetary Fund), bilateral donors (e.g., USAID, the British Department for
International Development), and a veritable swarm of nongovernmental organizations (NGOs). Many of the programs are duplicative, do not respond
to local needs, and are sometimes at cross purposes with one another.

The single most important problem is one of ownership. Foreign
donors are primarily interested, understandably, in providing immediate
humanitarian relief and services to the long-suffering local population.
They typically do so, however, in ways that undermine the authority of
and strip the capacity from the newly forming indigenous government.
The outside donors come with laptops, satellite phones, and first-world
salaries; they drive up prices and attract talent away from the local government ministries that will ultimately be responsible for governing the
country. The chapter by Starr chapter explains how foreign NGOs began
to undermine the authority of Hamid Karzai's new Afghan government,
leading Finance Minister Ashraf Ghani to demand that foreign funders
channel their support through his ministry. The same counterproductive
process took place to an even greater degree in Iraq, where the CPA's ambition to provide the country with a complete occupation authority cen-
trally directed by Americans marginalized the few local Iraqi players.

Postconflict situations often seem to pose an insoluble conundrum
regarding local ownership: intervention was necessary in the first place because there was no functioning local government, but the outside provision
of government services becomes an obstacle to the creation of new state

institutions that can stand on their own. Nonetheless, it is precisely the creation of self-sustaining local institutions that provides an graceful exit strategy for the outsiders.

Afghanistan provides some examples of innovative ways of encouraging early local ownership of the reconstruction process. Finance Minister Ghani did succeed in forcing at least the large multilateral and bilateral donors to channel their funds through the central Afghan government. He established a National Development Framework and told outside donors that he would not accept funds that did not fit into priorities that the Afghan government had itself set. He established a series of Consultative Groups and trust funds, administered by the Afghan government, through which outside donors had to operate. Although many of them complained that this procedure was slowing down their disbursal of funds, it increased the leverage, authority, and capacity of the new Afghan government. The latter was in effect trading off some short-term assistance for long-term capacity-building.[6]

In addition, the Kacamatan Development Project, developed first by the World Bank in Indonesia, was brought over to Afghanistan and replicated broadly throughout the country as the National Solidarity Program (NSP). Donor money for public works was channeled through the central government but then block-granted to individual villages, which had to determine their own development priorities. The NSP aimed at increasing the demand for government services at a local level, organizing villagers in ways that gave them leverage against local warlords and hopefully providing a long-term sense of ownership over the project. This and other so-called "community-driven development" projects may not finally solve the problem of local ownership, but they at least acknowledge the problem as being central in the transition from reconstruction to the development of self-sustaining institutions.

Resources

The authors of this volume disagree to some extent on the question of resources, and the manner in which they should be deployed in post-conflict situations. Dobbins, Weinbaum, and Goodson are all extremely critical of the low level of resources provided to Afghanistan, when measured on a per capita basis and compared to other reconstructions. The authors of the chapters on Iraq (Diamond, Mendelson Forman, and Dobbins) have criticized the Bush administration for failing to provide adequate force levels to stabilize that country in the aftermath of active combat. I, by contrast, argue in the introductory chapter that the Afghan light-footprint model builds early local ownership and is more sustainable on the part of foreign donors and taxpayers. Flournoy notes the importance of maintaining long-term political support for nation-building operations, which is always easier to do when taxpayers do not believe they are financing open-ended development projects. Sometimes fewer soldiers and less lavish resources force the outside players to think creatively about using locals or leveraging allies to get the job done. Starr is extremely critical of the way in which outside NGOs, numbering between two and three thousand, bypassed the Afghan government and undercut its authority. Starr and I both refer to the state-building benefits of funneling donor money through the central government, at least when a competent finance minister like Ashraf Ghani was in place. Goodson, however, argues that Afghanistan's reconstruction and humanitarian needs were so great that the NGOs played a critical role in getting aid into the field.

This divide among the volume's authors reflects the trade-off that exists between the immediate provision of humanitarian aid and relief services and the demands of long-term institution building. The choice that was made in Afghanistan, as noted above, was in favor of long-term institutional development over reconstruction; with less competent governments or different local priorities, this might not have been the right choice. On the question of the level of resources, it is hard to argue that the trickle of U.S. and other donor funds that went into Afghanistan between the Bonn Conference and mid-2003 was adequate, even under a light-footprint model; this situation had largely been corrected by 2004–5. When U.S. forces took Baghdad in April 2003, they were exhausted and stretched so thin that they would have been hard-pressed to maintain order throughout the country, much less seal borders and guard weapons depots. Arguments that they should have had fewer resources at their disposal are unconvincing.

Most discussions of postconflict reconstruction end at the moment that the reconstruction phase winds down, the international community begins to withdraw (after having hopefully stabilized the situation), and the focus shifts to long-term economic and political development. As pointed out in the introductory chapter, however, the manner in which the reconstruction phase is approached will strongly affect the target country's prospects for institutional development. In the longer run, the United States needs to confront not just the problem of postconflict reconstruction, but the problem of long-term development as well. The excessive optimism—described by Ekbladh and Sutton in their respective chapters—that characterized American development efforts in the 1950s and early 1960s has been replaced today by a high degree of pessimism that donor countries can do much to promote development. And yet surprising success stories abound. The Republic of Korea was written off, after all, as a basket case at the end of the Korean War. The Bush administration has at least begun to rethink development through such initiatives as the Millennium Challenge Account; it should not give up on the task.

In the wake of the costly effort to remake Iraq, it is not clear what appetite the American public has for new nation-building projects. Conservatives who have traditionally opposed this type of activity are now on board, and it is the Democrats who have called for a rapid exit, but whether this peculiar reversal of political positions will survive the end of the Iraq intervention is an open question. The need for postconflict reconstruction will not end, however, with the end of the Afghanistan and Iraq missions. That is why it is especially important to learn what lessons we can now, rather than waiting for the next contingency, so that we can, once more, reinvent the wheel.

Notes

1. Simon Chesterman, *You the People: The United Nations, Transitional Administration, and State-Building* (Oxford: Oxford University Press, 2004); James Dobbins, Keith Crane, Seth Jones, et al., *America's Role in Nation-Building: From Germany to Iraq* (Santa Monica, Calif.: RAND, 2003); Chester A. Crocker, Fen Osler Hampson, and Pam Aall, *Turbulent Peace: The Challenges of Managing International Conflict* (Washington, D.C.: U.S. Institute of Peace, 2001); Center for Strategic and International Studies, *Winning the Peace in Afghanistan, Failed States* (Washington, D.C.: Center for Strategic and International Studies, 2002).
2. William Reno, *Warlord Politics and African States* (Boulder, Colo.: Lynne Rienner Publishers, 1999).
3. Secretary of Defense Rumsfeld did indeed note that the United States planned for a larger invasion force in the shape of the 4th Infantry Division, which was supposed to enter Iraq from the north, but was prevented from doing so by the Turkish refusal to join the coalition. This explanation merely shifts the planning failure from a military to a political one and does not explain, in any event, why there was not better Phase IV planning.
4. See, for example, Krishna Kumar, *Postconflict Elections, Democratization, and International Assistance* (Boulder, Colo.: Lynne Rienner Publishers, 1998).
5. This quote is in the preface to the paperback edition of General Clark's Kosovo memoir, Wesley K. Clark, *Waging Modern War: Bosnia, Kosovo, and the Future of Combat* (New York: Public Affairs Press, 2002), xxvi–xxvii. He was, of course, upset at this interpretation of his book.
6. I owe this formulation to Hugh Riddell.

Contributors

Samia Amin was a junior fellow at the Carnegie Endowment for International Peace during 2003–4. She received her B.A. from Middlebury College and is now a graduate student at the Kennedy School of Government at Harvard University.

Larry Diamond is a senior fellow at the Hoover Institution, co-editor of the *Journal of Democracy,* and co-director of the International Forum for Democratic Studies of the National Endowment for Democracy. He is also professor of political science and sociology (by courtesy) at Stanford University and coordinator of the Democracy program of the new Center for Democracy, Development, and the Rule of Law at Stanford's Institute for International Studies. From January to April 2004, he was a senior advisor on governance and political transition to the Coalition Provisional Authority in Baghdad. During 2001–2, Diamond served as a consultant to the U.S. Agency for International Development and is a contributing author to its report, "Foreign Aid in the National Interest." He is the author of *Squandered Victory: The American Occupation and the Bungled Effort to Bring Democracy to Iraq* (Times Books, 2005), *Developing Democracy: Toward Consolidation* (The Johns Hopkins University Press, 1999), *Promoting Democracy in the 1990s: Actors and Instruments, Issues and Imperatives* (Carnegie Corporation of New York, 1999), and *Class, Ethnicity, and Democracy in Nigeria: The Failure of the First Republic* (Macmillan, 1988). Larry

Diamond received his B.A. in 1974, an M.A. in 1978, and a Ph.D. in sociology in 1980, all from Stanford University.

James Dobbins directs RAND's International Security and Defense Policy Center. Ambassador Dobbins has held State Department and White House posts, including assistant secretary of state for Europe, special assistant to the president for the Western Hemisphere, special adviser to the president and secretary of state for the Balkans, and ambassador to the European Community. He has handled numerous crisis management and diplomatic troubleshooting assignments as the Clinton administration's special envoy for Somalia, Haiti, Bosnia, and Kosovo, and the Bush administration's first special envoy for Afghanistan. He is principal author of RAND's two-volume history of national building, *America's Role in Nation-Building: From Germany to Iraq* and *The UN's Role in Nation Building: The Congo to Iraq* (RAND, 2005). Dobbins has been repeatedly tapped for sensitive diplomatic troubleshooting assignments, handling the withdrawal of American forces from Somalia, the American-led multilateral intervention in Haiti, the stabilization and reconstruction of Bosnia, and the NATO intervention in Kosovo. In the wake of 9/11, Dobbins was designated as the Bush administration's representative to the Afghan opposition and tasked with identifying and installing a broadly based successor to the Taliban regime. Dobbins graduated from the Georgetown School of Foreign Service and served 3 years in the U.S. Navy.

David Ekbladh is visiting assistant professor of history at American University in Washington, D.C. He is completing a book on the evolution of development as an instrument in U.S. foreign relations during the twentieth century. His research explores how nongovernmental groups and various international organizations, along with the American state, have structured critical elements of development in concept and practice. His articles have appeared in *The Wilson Quarterly, World Affairs, Diplomatic History,* and *Prologue.* From 1999 to 2001, he worked with the Carnegie Corporation of New York on conflict prevention and international affairs issues. He has also helped administer the Joint Research and Exchange program of the Tokyo Foundation. Ekbladh holds a Ph.D. in history from Columbia University, where he was Pacific Basin fellow at the East Asian Institute.

Michèle A. Flournoy is senior adviser in the Center for Strategic and International Studies International Security program, where she works on a broad range of defense policy and international security issues. Previously, she was a distinguished research professor at the Institute for National Strategic Studies at the National Defense University (NDU), where she founded and led the university's Quadrennial Defense Review working group, which was chartered by the chairman of the Joint Chiefs of Staff. Prior to joining NDU, she served as principal deputy assistant secretary of defense for strategy and threat reduction and deputy assistant secretary of defense for strategy. She was awarded the Secretary of Defense Medal for Outstanding Public Service in 1996, the Department of Defense Medal for Distinguished Public Service in 1998, and the Chairman of the Joint Chiefs of Staff's Joint Distinguished Civilian Service Award in 2000. She is a former member of the Defense Policy Board and a current member of the Defense Science Board, the U.S. Strategic Command Strategic Advisory Group, the Council on Foreign Relations, the Aspen Strategy Group, and the Executive Board of Women in International Security. In addition to several edited volumes, Flournoy has published numerous articles and reports on a variety of international security issues. She holds a B.A. in social studies from Harvard University and an M.Litt. in international relations from Balliol College, Oxford University.

Francis Fukuyama is Bernard L. Schwartz Professor of International Political Economy at the Paul H. Nitze School of Advanced International Studies (SAIS) of the Johns Hopkins University. As of July 1, 2005, he is also the director of the International Development program at SAIS. Dr. Fukuyama has written widely on issues relating to questions concerning democratization and international political economy. His book, *The End of History and the Last Man* (Free Press, 1992) has appeared in over twenty foreign editions. He is also the author of *Trust: The Social Virtues and the Creation of Prosperity* (Free Press, 1995), *The Great Disruption: Human Nature and the Reconstitution of Social Order* (Free Press, 1999), and *Our Posthuman Future: Consequences of the Biotechnology Revolution* (Farrar, Straus, and Giroux, 2002). His most recent book is *State-Building: Governance and World Order in the 21st Century* (Cornell University Press, 2004). Dr. Fukuyama is a member of the President's Council on Bioethics. He holds an honorary doctorate from Connecticut College and Doane College and is a member of advisory boards for the National Endowment for Democracy (NED), the *Journal of Democracy,* and The New America Foundation. As an NED board member, he is responsible for oversight of the endowment's Middle East programs. He is a member of the American Political Science Association, the Council on Foreign Relations, the Pacific Council on International Policy, and the Global Business Network.

Seth Garz was a junior fellow at the Carnegie Endowment for International Peace during 2003–4. He received his B.A. from Washington University and is now an analyst at Goldman Sachs.

Larry P. Goodson holds the General Dwight D. Eisenhower Chair of National Security at the U.S. Army War College, where he also serves as professor of

Middle East studies in the Department of National Security and Strategy. From March to August 2004, he was the U.S. Central Command (CENTCOM) Fellow, where he conducted research and advised General John Abizaid, the CENTCOM commander. Professor Goodson's special area of scholarship is the modern politics of Afghanistan and Pakistan, and he has lived and traveled there extensively since 1986, most recently having made three trips to the region in 2004. He also served as international monitor and technical advisor for elections at the Loya Jirga for the U.N. Assistance Mission to Afghanistan. Prior to joining the War College faculty in the summer of 2002, Dr. Goodson taught at Bentley College, the University of the South, the American University in Cairo, Campbell University, the University of North Carolina at Greensboro, and the University of North Carolina at Chapel Hill. Dr. Goodson is the author of the *New York Times* best-seller *Afghanistan's Endless War: State Failure, Regional Politics, and the Rise of the Taliban* (University of Washington Press, 2001). He contributes frequent journal articles and op-eds on Afghanistan and nation-building, and his forthcoming book, *The Talibanization of Pakistan: Transformation of a Society* (St. Martin's/Palgrave), is scheduled to appear in late 2005. Professor Goodson studied at the University of North Carolina at Chapel Hill, where he received his B.A. in political science and economics in 1980, his M.A. in political science in 1984, and his Ph.D. in political science in 1990.

Johanna Mendelson Forman has served as senior program officer for peace, security, and human rights at the U.N. Foundation since 2002. Dr. Mendelson Forman's work focuses on security and development issues, with a special emphasis on civil-military issues, arms proliferation, internal security, and peacekeeping. Most recently, she participated in a review of the postconflict reconstruction effort of the Coalition Provisional Authority in Iraq as part of a team headed by the Center for Strategic and International Studies. The report she co-authored served as the baseline study for reconstruction in Iraq. Her research has also focused on the implications of HIV/AIDS on security and peacekeeping. Her extensive publications on civil-military relations, security sector reform, and democracy in Latin America include *Political Parties and Democracy in Central America*, with Louis W. Goodman and William Leogrande, editors (Westview Press, 1992); *Lessons from the Venezuelan Experience*, with Louis W. Goodman, Moises Naim, Joseph Tulchin, and Gary Bland (The Johns Hopkins University Press, 1994); and *The Military and Democracy: Civil-Military Relations in Latin America*, with Louis W. Goodman and Juan Rial (Lexington Books, 1989). Dr. Mendelson Forman holds an M.A. in international affairs with a certificate of Latin America studies from Columbia University, a Ph.D. in Latin American history from Washington University, and a J.D. from Washington College of Law at the American University.

Minxin Pei is a senior associate and director of the China program at the Carnegie Endowment for International Peace in Washington, D.C. Before coming to Carnegie, he was an assistant professor of politics at Princeton University from 1992 to 1998. He is an expert on U.S.-China relations, the development of democratic political systems, the politics of economic reform, the growth of civil society, and legal institutions. He is the author of *From Reform to Revolution: The Demise of Communism in China and the Soviet Union* (Harvard University Press, 1994) and *China's Trapped Transition: The Limits of Developmental Autocracy* (Harvard University Press, 2006). His research has been published in *Foreign Policy, Foreign Affairs, The National Interest, Modern China, China Quarterly,* and *Journal of Democracy* and includes such articles as "China's Governance Crisis," *Foreign Affairs* (September/October 2002); "Re-Balancing United States–China Relations," Carnegie Policy Brief No. 13 (2002); and "Future Shock: The WTO and Political Change in China," Carnegie Policy Brief No. 3 (2001). His op-eds have appeared in *The Financial Times, The New York Times, Asian Wall Street Journal, The Christian Science Monitor,* and other major newspapers. Dr. Pei received his Ph.D. in political science from Harvard University in 1991.

S. Frederick Starr is chairman of the Central Asia–Caucasus Institute at the Johns Hopkins University (SAIS) in Washington, D.C. His research has resulted in twenty books and two hundred published articles. Dr. Starr was educated at Yale, Cambridge University, and Princeton. Before coming to the Central Asia Institute, he was founding director of the Kennan Institute for Advanced Russian Studies at the Wilson Center in Washington, D.C., president for 11 years of Oberlin College, and president of the Aspen Institute. He founded the Greater New Orleans Foundation and is a trustee of the Eurasia Foundation. Dr. Starr has been closely involved with U.S. policy toward Russia and Central Asia for 30 years and has advised four U.S. presidents. He maintains close ties with government leaders and independent figures in politics and culture from all the states he studies. Dr. Starr is the recipient of five honorary degrees and is a Fellow of the American Academy of Arts and Sciences.

Francis X. Sutton worked at the Ford Foundation from 1954 to 1983, first as a program officer and then as the representative for the East and Central Africa region, deputy vice-president and acting vice-president for the International Division, and finally as a consultant. His career has spanned a variety of fields, from philanthropy to higher education, the social sciences, and international affairs. He is author (with others) of *The American Business Creed* (Schocken Books, 1956) and *Ideology and Social Structure* (Garland, 1991) and editor of *A World to Make: Development in Perspective* (Transaction, 1990). In December

2003, he was given the honorary degree of doctor of humane letters from Aga Khan University in Karachi. Dr. Sutton received his Ph.D. in sociology from Harvard University in 1950.

Marvin G. Weinbaum is professor emeritus of political science at the University of Illinois at Urbana-Champaign and served as analyst for Pakistan and Afghanistan in the U.S. Department of State's Bureau of Intelligence and Research from 1999 to 2003. Professor Weinbaum received his Ph.D. in government from Columbia University in 1965, and he joined the Illinois faculty in the same year. At Illinois, he served for 15 years as the director of the Program in South Asian and Middle Eastern Studies. After retiring, Professor Weinbaum has been an adjunct professor at Georgetown and George Washington Universities and lectures regularly at the U.S. Foreign Service Institute. He is currently a scholar-in-residence at the Middle East Institute in Washington, D.C. Dr. Weinbaum's research focuses on the issues of national security, democratization, and political economy. He is the author or editor of six books, including *South Asia Approaches the Millennium: Reexamining National Security,* co-edited with Chetan Kumar (Westview Press, 1995) and *Pakistan and Afghanistan: Resistance and Reconstruction* (Westview Press, 1994). Dr. Weinbaum has written more than 70 journal articles and book chapters, mostly about Pakistan, Afghanistan, and Iran, but also on Egypt and Turkey. Among his recent publications are book chapters for edited volumes dealing with human rights in Turkey, Iran, and Afghanistan, the history of modern Afghan-U.S. relations, reconstruction politics in Afghanistan, and an essay on Afghanistan for the *Encyclopaedia Britannica.*

Index

Abdullah, Abdullah, 111
Abizaid, John, 90
Abu Ghraib prison, 204, 207–8
Acheson, Dean, 23, 77
Advisory Committee on Postwar Foreign
  Policy, 77, 82
Afghan Interagency Operating Group (AIOG),
  138
Afghanistan, 3, 4, 6–9, 10, 19–20, 36, 43, 65,
  67, 86, 88, 89, 92, 93, 107–24, 125–44,
  145–69, 188, 211, 218, 220, 231, 234,
  236–38, 244; accomplishments in, 115;
  accountability in, 141; "birth defects" in
  strategy toward, 115, 120, 237; broad-based
  government concept for, 158; calculated
  inexperience in, 226; coalitions in, 108–10,
  239; during the Cold War, 219; coordination
  of operations in, 240–41; drawbacks of central authority in, 140–41; elections in (see
  under elections); federalism considered for,
  111–12, 114, 124, 157; first phase of nation-
  building in, 110–12; future challenges in,
  141–44, 161–64; impediments to rebuilding,
  128–34; influence of regional powers in, 134;
  international involvement required in, 140;
  investment encouraged in, 130, 132–33; Iraq
  compared with, 126, 132, 135, 137, 142,
  143, 144, 146, 147, 155, 156, 164, 221–25;
leadership needs in, 128; legacy of previous
  conflicts in, 107, 125, 145; legitimacy in (see
  under legitimacy); national myths needed in,
  127–28; occupation of, 12–14; organized
  crime in, 162; overview of nation-building
  efforts, 66; ownership in, 242–43; regional
  and ethnic divisions in (see under regional
  and ethnic divisions); requisites for rebuilding, 126–28; resources in, 131; security in
  (see under security); separatism/secessionism
  not supported in, 109, 111–12, 113–14, 124,
  143; sovereignty in (see under sovereignty);
  Soviet Union and, 107, 109, 126, 128, 134,
  139, 142, 147, 160, 162, 232; state failure in,
  145, 146, 157, 232; strategic shift in U.S. policy, 119–21, 124, 137, 146, 151; tolerance for
  ambiguity in, 141, 161; transition of power
  in, 135, 161
Afghanistan New Beginnings Program, 150
Afghan National Army, 118, 129, 136, 149–50,
  152, 236
Afghan Reconstruction Group (ARG), 137–38
Africa, 2, 6, 26, 59, 60, 97, 198, 219; Ford
  Foundation and, 49, 51, 54, 57, 58; independence movements in, 44, 45, 49, 57
after-action reviews, 87, 101
agricultural development: in Afghanistan, 115,
  116, 127, 154; Ford Foundation and, 52–56

Agriculture Department, U.S., 129
Aideed, Mohammed Farrah, 93
AIOG. *See* Afghan Interagency Operating
  Group
Alawi, Iyad, 14, 189
Alliance for Progress, 27
American embassies: in Afghanistan, 120, 136,
  165; in Iraq, 178; in Panama, 75, 82
Americans for Democratic Action, 23
Amman, 210
amnesty, in Afghanistan, 141
Anabar Province, 173
Angola, 64, 237
Annan, Kofi, 209, 212
Arabization campaign, 181
Arabs, 181, 183, 187
ARG. *See* Afghan Reconstruction Group
Argentina, 51
Aristide, Jean-Bertrand, 69, 70–71, 72–73
Army, U.S., 22, 23
Army Reserve, U.S., 166
Army War College, 102
Asia, 21, 27, 43, 44, 60
Asian Development Bank, 131, 155
Asia Society, 25
Association of Muslim Scholars, 194
Atomic Energy Commission, 26
authoritarian regimes, 67
authority, delineation of, 88, 89–91
Ayub Khan, 57

Ba'ath Party (Iraq), 182–83, 194, 205, 236
Badr Organization, 181
Baghdad, 178, 181, 182, 192, 210, 235, 239;
  bombings in, 203, 209; central government
  in, 190; U.N. headquarters in, 185, 186; U.S.
  capture of, 224, 243
Bagram, 149
Balad, 192
Balkans, 10, 64, 108, 211, 232
Bangladesh, 97
BAPPENAS, 51
Barclays Bank, 29
Barno, David W., 151, 165, 240
Barton, Frederick, 215n25
Basra, 184, 192, 210
Bechtel Corporation, 26
Bell, David, 56
Benomar, Jamal, 188
Berkeley mafia, 51, 60
Berlin Conference, 131, 136, 156, 164
Berlin Wall, fall of, 219
Bhutto, Zulfikar Ali, 58
Biden, Joseph, 93, 104
bilateral donors, 241, 242
bill of rights (Iraqi), 189

Bin Laden, Osama, 148, 164
Bin Sayeed, Khalid, 52
Black, Eugene, 30
black special operations forces, 138–39
Blackwill, Robert, 188–89
Bonn Accords, 12, 136, 146, 157, 158, 161,
  165, 238
Bonn Conference, 109, 110–12, 114, 115, 120,
  135, 243
Bosnia, 5, 7, 8, 9–10, 35, 64, 67, 83n2, 86, 146,
  166, 198, 218, 224, 225, 228; calculated inexperience in, 226; coordination problems
  in, 240; military force population in, 174;
  missed exit deadline in, 220; NATO forces in,
  97, 222, 223; peace enforcement failure in,
  233; security in, 222, 237
Botswana, 49, 51, 52
Bowles, Chester, 27, 53
Brahimi, Lakhdar, 12, 188, 189, 209
Brazil, 25
Bremer, L. Paul, III, 11, 13, 90, 137, 175, 183,
  187, 209, 213n2, 236; constitution of Iraq
  and, 189; failure to understand Iraqis,
  181–82; refusal to surrender control, 186;
  sanctions against Sadr, 179; U.N. involvement and, 188
Bremer Plan, 137
British Department for International Development, 241
broad-based government, 158
Bundy, McGeorge, 56
bureaucracy, 44; of Afghanistan, 126, 132, 133,
  135; of India, 47–48; of Japan, 77, 78
Bureau of International Narcotics and Law
  Enforcement, 137
Burma, 43, 48, 53
Bush, George H. W., 74, 76
Bush, George W., 89, 241, 244; Afghanistan
  and, 67, 143, 147, 164, 165; attitude toward
  nation-building, 1, 36, 86–87, 220, 222; Iraq
  and, 9, 10, 11, 12, 90, 91, 94, 174, 175, 178,
  186, 187–89, 197, 200, 201, 223, 225, 229,
  235, 239, 242; PDD 56 rejected by, 8, 166,
  240
Business Development Council (Haiti), 73

calculated inexperience, 225–26
Calderon, Ricardo Arias, 74
Cambodia, 66, 67
Canada, 129, 233, 239
capacity-building, 7, 52, 60, 122, 160–61, 167
Caribbean, 2, 8
Caribbean Community, 71
Carnegie Corporation, 24, 26–27, 42
Carnegie Project, 26–27
censorship, 79

Center for International Affairs, 51
Center for Strategic and International Studies, 231
Central America, 2, 219
Central Intelligence Agency, 112, 167
Chalabi, Ahmed, 10, 13, 14, 175, 183, 185, 205, 207
Chalabi, Salem, 207
chemical and biological weapons, 14, 211, 222, 224
Chesterman, Simon, 231
Chile, 64
China, 24, 43, 45, 54, 80, 219
Chung-hee, Park, 15n8
Civil Censorship Detachment, 79
civilian forces: delineation of authority in, 88, 89–91; enhancing capability of, 88, 91–93; funding for rapid deployment of, 95; planning capacity enhancement in, 94–95
Civilian Operations and Revolutionary Development Support (CORDS) program, 28, 236
civil service, 51, 57; of Afghanistan, 120, 122, 124; of Africa, 49; of India, 47–48; of Iraq, 205–6; of Pakistan, 58; steel frame of, 48
civil society, 116, 122, 126, 127, 176
civ-pol function, 11, 235
CJTF. *See* commander of the joint task force
Clark, Wesley, 239
Cleveland, Harlan, 26
Clinton, William, 8, 67, 86, 87, 88, 89, 96, 166, 240; Bosnia and, 220; Haiti and, 70; Somalia and, 227
Coalition Provisional Authority (CPA), 11–12, 13, 14, 36, 90, 175, 182, 183, 191–93, 208, 237, 240, 241; constitution and, 189, 191–92; credibility problems of, 207; elections and, 184, 187, 238; end of tenure, 174; expenditures by, 176; miscommunications with Iraqis, 177–78; Order 71, 209; overwhelming responsibilities of, 202; Strategic Communications office of, 191; U.N. and, 188; unemployment caused by, 203, 205–6; violence toward, 177
coalitions, 108–10, 238–39
Coast Guard, U.S., 71
Cold War, 19–20, 21, 25, 27, 35, 36, 45, 67, 77, 87, 97, 155, 218–21; failed states emerging from, 232; Japan during, 80, 83; lessons from, 198; nation-building following, 2, 219–21, 227
Colombia, 25, 26, 49, 51, 133, 150
colonialism, 26, 43–45, 46, 47, 59, 60
Combined Forces Command–Afghanistan (CFC-A), 165
commander of the joint task force (CJTF), 90–91, 103–4

Commanders' Emergency Reconstruction Program, 182
Common Market, 71
communism, 2–3, 219; in Afghanistan, 125–26, 133, 141, 160, 232; Ford Foundation versus, 43, 46; Japan and, 83; in Vietnam, 67
community-driven development projects, 242
complex contingency operations, 97, 98, 102–3, 166. *See also* Presidential Decision Directive 56
Comprehensive Development Framework, 36
Congo, 59
constabulary forces, 234–35, 239
constituent assembly (Iraq), 187
constitutions: Afghan, 125, 128, 142, 143, 157, 159, 238; Iraqi, 187, 189–92, 194, 210, 212; Japanese, 79, 80
Consultative Groups, 242
coordination problems, 240–41
CORDS. *See* Civilian Operations and Revolutionary Development Support program
corruption, 121–22, 124, 133, 150, 154
Council on Foreign Relations, 29, 61
coups, 64, 71, 72, 76, 77
Cowles, John, 50
CPA. *See* Coalition Provisional Authority
Croatia, 233
Crocker, Bathsheba, 215n25
crop substitution, 155
Cuba, 66, 67
cultural factors, 87
cultural neutrality, 46, 47
currency, 115, 126, 130

Dari, 114
Da'wa al Islamiyya, 180, 185, 189
Dayton Accord, 7, 237
DDR. *See* disarmament, demobilization, and reintegration
de-Ba'athification policy, 182–83, 194, 205, 224
Decade of Development, 27, 31
Defense Department, U.S., 87, 94, 96, 212, 226; Afghanistan and, 136–37, 147, 148, 167; Iraq and, 9, 11, 90, 200, 207, 222, 227, 228, 229, 240
democracy, 3, 68; Afghanistan and, 127, 135; India and, 47; Iraq and, 12, 189, 192–95, 222; Japan and, 77, 78–81, 83; mixed record on achieving, 65–67; Panama and, 73–75, 77
Democratic Revolutionary Party (Panama), 77
dependency theory, 30
Deputies Committee, 99, 100, 101
development: classical ideology of, 45–46, 57; crisis of, 29–30; Ford Foundation and, 44, 45–47; as nation-building, 45–47;

development (*cont.*)
  in post–World War II era, 20–27, 29–30;
  reconstruction versus, 4–8, 234
Development and Resources (D&R), 26, 29,
  33–34
development community, 24–27
development house concept, 30
Diet (Japanese), 79
disarmament, demobilization, and reintegration
  (DDR): in Afghanistan, 127, 149, 150, 152,
  156, 162, 163, 164; in Iraq, 180, 224, 235–36
Dodge, Joseph, 80
Dominican Republic, 66, 219
donor countries, 241; Afghanistan and, 117,
  122, 127, 131, 133, 140, 149, 152–53, 154;
  Haiti and, 72
donor fatigue, 29
Dost, Ramazan Bashar, 117
Dostum, Abdul Rashid, 152, 159, 160
D&R. *See* Development and Resources
drought, 154, 155
drug production and trafficking, 2, 116, 117,
  121–22, 127, 131, 135, 136, 138, 148, 149,
  152, 161, 167, 221; failure of measures
  against, 150; increase in, 162–63; as percentage of GDP, 150, 155; possible responses to,
  133–34, 155

East Asia, 2, 6
Eastern Europe, 11, 146
Eastern Slavonia, 86, 233
East Timor, 4, 11, 35, 86, 135, 146, 185
Eban, Abba, 44
Ebtehaj, Abolhassan, 51
Economic Bureau (Iran), 51
Economic Cooperation Administration, U.S., 23
Economic Cooperation Agency, U.S., 27
Economic Recovery Steering Group for Haiti,
  72, 73
economy: of Afghanistan, 126–27, 130–31,
  143, 154–55, 162; development strategies
  for, 241–42; of Haiti, 72–73; of Iraq, 176,
  205–6; of Japan, 80; of Panama, 75–76
education, 53, 55, 56
Egypt, 51, 58
800th Military Police Brigade, 208
Eikenberry, Karl, 165
Eisenhower administration, 23, 24, 27
elections: in Afghanistan, 109–10, 114, 115,
  119, 122, 123, 125, 126, 128, 137, 142–43,
  151, 157, 158–60, 161, 163–64, 167, 168n17,
  238; in Haiti, 70–71; in Iraq, 173, 183–84,
  187, 188, 193–94, 209, 210, 211, 212, 229,
  237–38; in Japan, 79; in Panama, 74, 77.
  See also parliamentary elections
El Salvador, 225, 226, 233

embassies, American: in Afghanistan, 120, 136,
  165; in Iraq, 178; in Panama, 75, 82
employment, 154. *See also* unemployment
Endara, Guillermo, 74, 76, 77, 82
Ensminger, Douglas, 54–55, 59
environmentalism, 30
European Bank for Reconstruction and
  Development, 122
European Union, 122
executions, 206
Executive Committee (ExCom), 88–89, 99,
  100, 101
Export-Import Bank, 73, 83

failed states, 2, 4, 87, 145, 146, 157, 220, 232
Fairbank, John King, 21, 24
Fallujah, 179, 180, 210
famines, 89, 91, 154
Farah, 152
federalism: Afghanistan and, 111–12, 114, 124,
  157; Iraq and, 190, 191
feminism, 30. *See also* women
Finland, 129
Finn, Robert, 136–37
Fischer, Joschka, 112
Food and Agricultural Organization, 23
food production, 54, 55–56
Ford, Edsel, 42
Ford, Guillermo, 74
Ford, Henry, Sr., 42
Ford Foundation, 5, 24, 30, 42–63; agriculture/
  rural development and, 52–56; assistance
  strategies of, 47; endowment of, 42; expenditures on development, 43, 57, 62n10;
  national planning and, 50–52; relationship
  with governments, 47–52; retreat from
  nation-building, 55–59; world peace promoted by, 46
Ford Motor Company, 42
foreign aid, 241–42; to Afghanistan, 125, 127,
  131, 133, 136, 152–53, 155–56, 164; donor
  fatigue and, 29; to Haiti, 72–73; to Iraq, 155,
  156; to Japan, 80, 81; new directions in,
  31–35. *See also* donor countries
Foreign Operations Administration, 27
4th Infantry Division, 244n2
fragile states, 232
France, 108, 219, 224, 239
Franks, Tommy, 9, 11, 161
Fulbright, J. W., 32
Future of Iraq project, 9, 175

Gaither, Rowan, 48
Galbraith, John Kenneth, 24
Gandhi, Indira, 62n16
Garner, Jay, 9, 11, 16n18, 181

Gellner, Ernest, 44
Geneva Conventions, 208
genocide, 207
Germany, 108, 219; Afghanistan and, 13, 122,
   129, 136, 138, 149, 150; Iraq and, 224, 239;
   postwar nation-building in, 4, 5, 43, 166, 218,
   220, 222, 224, 225, 226; West, 65, 66, 67
Gerschenkron, Alexander, 24
Ghana, 51
Ghani, Ashraf, 116, 122, 241, 242, 243
Gide, André, 58
Gopal, Sarvepalli, 53, 55
Gorgon, 55
Governing Council (GC). *See* Iraqi Governing
   Council
Grant, James, 30, 32
Great Society, 31
Green Revolution, 24, 56, 57
Green Zone, 177
Grenada, 65, 66, 219, 226
Grew, Joseph, 77
gross domestic product (GDP), 6, 60, 134, 150,
   155
ground troops, 65
Guantanamo Bay military base, 72
Guatemala, 65

Haiti, 8, 35, 67, 68, 78, 81–82, 83, 86, 87, 146,
   166, 198, 220; calculated inexperience in,
   226; as case study of failure, 69–73; complex
   contingency operations in, 97; embargo im-
   posed on, 72; lessons learned in, 223, 224,
   225; overview of nation-building efforts, 66;
   security in, 222
Haitian National Police, 71
Hakim, Iman, 203
Hamre, John, 215n25
*Handbook for Interagency Management of Com-
   plex Contingency Operations,* 101
Hannah, John, 32–33
Harrod-Domar growth model, 6
Hartha, 210
Harvard Development Advisory Service, 50, 57
Harvard University, 42, 50, 51, 52
Hasan, Eduardo Herrera, 76
Hawza (newspaper), 179
Hazaras, 111, 115, 118, 127, 158, 159
Heald, Henry, 55–56
heavy footprint model, 12–14, 160–61
Herat, 122, 134, 152, 159
heroin, 148, 150, 152, 155
High Representative (Bosnia), 7
hijab, 179
Hill, Forrest, 48, 56
Hilla, 179, 192, 193
Hilliard, John, 51

Hirohito, Emperor of Japan, 77–78
Hoffman, Paul, 42–43, 45, 47, 48, 50, 53, 55
Homeland Security Department, U.S., 167
humanitarian interventions, 1, 67, 197, 241,
   243; in Afghanistan, 131, 136, 140; in the
   Balkans, 64; in Iraq, 97, 200–201, 202, 208
human resources, 132–33
human rights, 5; in Afghanistan, 136; Ford
   Foundation and, 58; in Iraq, 193, 201–2,
   206–7
Hussein, Saddam, 2, 11, 12, 14, 36, 89, 175,
   183, 185, 193, 194, 200, 201, 203, 205, 222,
   223, 232; Arabization campaign of, 181;
   capture of, 206; human rights violations by,
   206–7; judicial system under, 204; popular
   support for, 182

IADP. *See* Intensive Agricultural Districts
   Program
IATF. *See* interagency task force
Idea of India, The (Khilnani), 3
IECI. *See* Independent Electoral Commission
   of Iraq
Ignatieff, Michael, 2
illiteracy, 155
Independent Electoral Commission of Iraq
   (IECI), 192, 210
India: Afghanistan and, 134; Ford Foundation
   and, 47–49, 50, 51, 53–55, 56; Partition of, 3,
   44, 53
Indian community development, 50, 53–55, 57
Indian Planning Commission, 50, 52
Indochina, 45
Indonesia, 43, 45, 48, 50–51, 52, 60, 242
infant mortality rates, 154
infrastructure: of Afghanistan, 127, 154, 155;
   of Iraq, 176, 202, 225; of Vietnam, 32
initial response phase of reconstruction, 199
Institute of Economic Planning (Egypt), 51
Institute of Peace, U.S., 231
institutional memory failure, 8–12
Intensive Agricultural Districts Program
   (IADP), 54
interagency and coalition training centers,
   95–96
interagency planning and execution, 88–89, 94
Interagency Planning Group, 165
interagency planning teams, 95
interagency task force (IATF), 90, 95, 103–4
interim government: in Afghanistan, 110, 157,
   158, 162; in Iraq, 173, 175, 177, 180, 188,
   199, 209–10
Interim Police Security Force (IPSF) (Haiti),
   71–72
International Bank for Reconstruction and
   Development. *See* World Bank

International Cooperation Administration, 27
International Criminal Investigative Training
  Assistance Program, 72
International Monetary Fund, 72, 130, 241
International Organization for Migration, 72
International Reconstruction Fund Facility,
  210
International Rice Research Institute, 24, 56
International Security Assistance Force (ISAF)
  for Afghanistan, 129, 136, 149, 151, 161, 164
International Voluntary Service (IVS), 25, 33
Iran, 26, 67, 143, 175; Afghanistan and, 134;
  Afghan refugees in, 132, 159; in Cold War
  era, 20; Ford Foundation and, 48, 51, 52, 54,
  55; Iraq supported in, 178
Iraq, 1, 6–12, 19–20, 36, 43, 64, 65, 67, 86, 88,
  89, 91–93, 97, 136, 138, 151, 167, 173–95,
  196–217, 218–29, 231, 234, 235–39, 244;
  Afghanistan compared with, 126, 132, 135,
  137, 142–44, 146, 147, 155, 156, 164,
  221–25; assassination of government officials
  in, 177, 209; assassination of translators in,
  178; calculated inexperience in, 225–26;
  casualties in, 174; coalitions in, 239; consequences of miscalculations in, 174–75; coordination problems in, 240, 241; corrective
  measures in, 227–28; elections in (*see under*
  elections); electric power in, 202, 203, 206;
  federalism desired in, 190, 191; Ford Foundation and, 48, 54; governance and participation in, 197, 199, 208–9; institutional weak-
  nesses in, 226–27; justice and reconciliation
  in, 197, 199, 206–8; legitimacy in, 173, 176,
  181–86, 238; occupation of, 12–14, 222–25;
  overview of nation-building efforts, 66; prisoner abuse in, 204, 207–8; ramifications of
  U.S. policy in, 211–12; regional and ethnic
  divisions in, 180, 181, 190, 191, 193–94;
  resources in, 242; revolution (1958) in, 48;
  security in (*see under* security); social and
  economic well-being in, 197, 199, 205–6;
  sovereignty in, 13, 173, 191, 193, 208, 240;
  state failure in, 232; strategic shift in U.S.
  policy, 187; transition of power in, 173, 175,
  186–89, 199, 202; weapons inspections in,
  201
Iraqi Army, 183, 203, 204–5, 224–25, 232, 236
Iraqi Central Criminal Court, 178
Iraqi Communist Party, 185
Iraqi Governing Council (GC), 12, 177, 185,
  187, 188, 203, 207; constitution and, 190,
  191, 192; dissolution of, 209; lack of esteem
  for, 189; purges by, 205
Iraqi Islamic Party, 185
Iraqi special tribunal, 206–7
Ireland, 229

ISAF. *See* International Security Assistance Force
  for Afghanistan
Islam: in Afghanistan, 111, 127, 128, 132, 143,
  146, 149, 150, 160, 162; in Iraq, 178, 179–
  80, 184, 190, 194. *See also* Shiite Muslims;
  Sunni Muslims
Islamabad, 134
Islamic Call Party. *See* Da'wa al Islamiyya
Israel, 183, 224
Istanbul Conference, 151
Italy, 108, 129; Afghanistan and, 136, 138, 149,
  150; constabulary forces in, 235, 239; in
  post–World War II era, 5
IVS. *See* International Voluntary Service

Jaafari, Ibrahim, 193
Jalal, Masooda, 160
Jalali, Ali, 121
Japan, 6, 9, 219; Afghanistan and, 136, 138,
  149, 150; Korea occupied by, 15n5, 22;
  Malaya occupied by, 45; as model of success,
  77–81; overview of nation-building efforts,
  66; postwar nation-building in, 4, 5, 21, 43,
  65, 67, 68, 77–81, 82, 83, 166, 218, 220, 222,
  224, 225, 226; rearmament, of, 80–81
Japan-U.S. Security Treaty, 81
JDG. *See* Joint Development Group
jihads, 128
Johns Hopkins University, 28
Johnson administration, 28–29
Joint Chiefs of Staff, U.S., 93
Joint Development Group (JDG), 29, 33
Jordan, 51
judicial/legal institutions: in Afghanistan, 126,
  141, 143, 150; in Iraq, 204, 206–8
Justice Department, U.S., 9, 11, 72, 75, 240

Kabul, 12, 92, 139, 152; central government
  in, 109, 113–16, 118, 120–22, 124, 127, 131,
  140, 143, 158, 163, 234; destruction of, 141;
  meeting on NGOs in, 117; Northern Alliance
  forces in, 111, 112; security in, 128, 129, 149
Kabul-to-Kandahar highway, 10, 154
Kacamatan Development Project, 242
Kandahar, 149
Karachi, 46, 50
Karbala, 179
Karzai, Hamid, 12, 14, 110, 111, 113–15, 135,
  138, 157, 160, 161, 165, 234, 238; appointees
  of, 163; counterinsurgency operations and,
  139; drug traffic and, 133, 155; economy
  under, 130; foreign attempts to undermine,
  134, 241; increased support for, 121, 143–44;
  Khan dropped as VP candidate by, 150; negotiations with former foes, 122; NGOs and,
  116; percentage of vote won by, 159;

regional/ethnic tensions and, 132, 158; as
sole elected representative, 164; U.S. pro-
gram for, 120; weakness of, 118
KDP. *See* Kurdistan Democratic Party
Kennan, George, 43
Kennedy, John F., 25, 27, 30
Kenya, 49, 51, 52, 229
Khalilzad, Zalmay, 137, 138, 143, 164, 165, 240
Khan, Akhter Hameed, 60–61
Khan, Amanullah, 152
Khan, Ismail, 122, 150, 152, 159
Khan, Liaquat Ali, 46
Khan, Mohammad Fahim, 111, 112, 115, 121,
150, 159, 160
Khilnani, Sunil, 3, 48
al-Khoei, Ayatollah Majid, 178
Kirkuk, 181, 190
Knaus, Gerald, 7
Kochis, 163
Korea, 15n5, 22, 64, 226. *See also* South Korea
Korean War, 15n8, 80, 244
Kosovo, 2, 5, 8, 67, 86, 135, 146, 166, 218, 224,
225, 227, 228; benefits of experience in,
220–21; calculated inexperience in, 226; civ-
pol units in, 235; coordination of operations
in, 240; NATO forces in, 220, 222, 223, 239;
Russia and, 111
Kuhn, Thomas, 121
Kurdistan, 16n18, 181; constitution and,
189–90; regional assembly for, 173; U.N. in,
200–201
Kurdistan Democratic Party (KDP), 185, 193
Kurds, 173, 200–201, 237; alliance with Shiites,
193–94; Arabs versus, 181, 190; constitution
and, 190, 191; political parties of, 185, 189;
transition and reintegration plan and, 180
Kuwait, 11
Kvashnin, Anatoli, 111

Lagos, 49
land-grant colleges, 25
land reform, 79, 80
Latin America, 35, 49, 51, 52
Lavalas party (Haiti), 70–71
Law of Armed Conflict, 202, 209, 214n24,
217n60
lead donor nation model, 149, 152–53
Lebanon, 219
legitimacy, 81; in Afghanistan, 9, 108–23, 126,
127, 128, 142–43, 238; balancing reconstruction with, 82; in Iraq, 173, 176, 181–86, 238;
in Panama, 76–77
Lenin, Vladimir, 45
lessons: from Afghanistan experience, 123–24,
139–41, 164–67; from Iraq experience,
218–29; of the 1990s, 88–94; of post–World

War II era, 198; recommendations based on,
94–96; unlearning of, 86–88
Lewis, John P., 58
Lewis, W. Arthur, 24
Liberal party (Japan), 79
Liberia, 232
Libya, 64
life expectancy, 60, 154
light footprint model, 12–14, 134–35, 140,
147, 148, 160–61, 242–43
Lilienthal, David, 26, 29, 30, 33–34
Lithuania, 129
local councils (Iraq), 184, 187
looting, 14, 75, 82, 175, 223, 234
Loya Jirga, 110, 112–18, 119, 135, 157, 158,
238, 239; erosion in aftermath of, 115–18;
mixed messages from, 112–15
Lugar, Richard, 93, 104
lustration, 205

MacArthur, Douglas, 4, 9
macroeconomic policies, 115, 130, 154
al-Mahdi army, 178, 179, 180
Malaya, 45, 228
Mao Zedong, 45, 54
Marshall Plan, 21, 23, 42–43, 80
Martin, Felix, 7
Mason, Edward, 30, 50, 51
Massachusetts Institute of Technology (MIT), 51
Mass Education Council (Burma), 53
Massoud, Ahmed Zia, 160
maternal mortality rates, 154
McNamara, Robert, 35
Mekong River, 29
Mendelson-Forman, Johanna, 215n25
Meshrano Jirga, 157, 163
Michigan State University (MSU), 25, 32, 34
microeconomic policy, 154
military forces: in Afghanistan, 12, 92, 139,
153, 165–66, 222; delineation of authority
in, 88, 89–91; enhancing capability of, 88,
91–93; in Haiti, 70–72; in Iraq, 92, 174–75,
222; in Panama, 74–75
Millennium Challenge Account, 244
Ministry of Defense (Afghanistan), 111
Ministry of Foreign Affairs (Afghanistan), 111
Ministry of the Interior (Afghanistan), 111, 129
Ministry of the Interior (Iraq), 200
miracle seeds, 56
mission creep, 92
MLAT. *See* Mutual Legal Assistance Treaty
MNF. *See* Multinational Force
modernization, 21, 26, 27–28, 30
Mogadishu, battle of, 91, 93
Mohammed Zahir Shah, King of Afghanistan,
112

Mohaqiq, Haji Mohammad, 159, 160
Mongul Empire, 3
Mossadeq administration, 48
MSU. *See* Michigan State University
Muhammad, Atta, 152
mujahidin, 126, 160
multilateral donors, 241, 242
multilateral operations, 66, 67, 139, 154
Multinational Force (MNF): in Haiti, 69, 70, 71, 72, 81; in Iraq, 179
Mutual Legal Assistance Treaty (MLAT), 76, 82
Mutual Security Administration, 27
Myrdal, Gunnar, 24

Najaf, 179, 191, 203
Nambia, 233
narco-Mafia state, 133–34
Nasariya, 192
Nathan, Robert R., 23, 24, 26, 29
Nation, The, 33–34
National Advisory Council on International Monetary Affairs, U.S., 80
National Assembly (Afghanistan), 158
National Assembly (Iraq), 173, 192, 210
National Congress (Iraq), 10, 207
National Defense University, 96, 101
National Development Framework, 242
National Endowment for Democracy, 192
National Foreign Affairs Training Center, 96, 101–2
National Foundation for Overseas Operations, 27
National Guard (Iraq), 205
National Guard (U.S.), 166
National Institutes of Health, 55
National Liberation Front (NFL; Viet Cong), 28
National Movement of Afghanistan, 160
national myths, 127–28
National Science Foundation, 55
National Security Act of 1947, 166–67
National Security Council (NSC), U.S., 80, 91, 99, 101–2, 104, 240; Afghanistan and, 137, 138, 167; Iraq and, 188, 227, 228; planning office recommended for, 94–95
National Security Presidential Directive XX (NSPD XX), 89, 94
National Security Presidential Directive XXIV (NSPD XXIV), 200
National Solidarity Program (NSP), 242
nation-building: components of, 232–34; criteria for, 64–65; defined, 3, 197, 218; number of U.S. attempts in, 64, 65; in post–World War II era, 43–45; principles of, 81–83; requisites of successful, 68–69; return of, 35–37; two primary steps in, 197–98

Nations and Nationalism (Gellner), 44
NATO. *See* North Atlantic Treaty Organization
Nehru, Jawaharlal, 46, 48–49, 50, 53, 55
neoclassical growth model, 6
Nepal, 57
Netherlands, 129
New Deal, 5, 20–21, 22, 23, 29, 34
New Delhi, 46
New Directions policy, 31, 32–33, 34
New York Times, 70
New Zealand, 129
NGOs. *See* nongovernmental organizations
Nicaragua, 64, 66, 67
Nigeria, 49, 51
Nixon, Richard, 31, 32, 35
Nixon Doctrine, 31
nongovernmental organizations (NGOs), 5, 7, 19, 33, 120, 241; Afghanistan and, 114–17, 123, 130, 133, 135, 140, 146, 151, 152, 154, 156, 161, 241, 243; Haiti and, 73; Iraq and, 20; Korea and, 23; in post–World War II era, 22, 25, 27, 36; problems caused by, 115–17; shift in U.S. relations with, 34–35
Noriega, Manuel, 73, 74, 75, 76, 77
North Atlantic Treaty Organization (NATO), 94, 219, 220; Afghanistan and, 12, 115, 129, 144, 151; Bosnia and, 97, 222, 223; Iraq and, 228, 239
Northern Alliance, 13, 14, 114, 115, 121, 147, 149, 223, 234, 237; broad-based government and, 158; de facto rule by, 111–12; elections and, 159
Northern Ireland, 229
Norway, 129
NSP. *See* National Solidarity Program
NSPD. *See* National Security Presidential Directive
nuclear weapons, 200
Nuhzat-i-Milli Afghanistan, 160

OAS. *See* Organization of American States
occupation: of Afghanistan, 12–14; of Iraq, 12–14, 222–25
OEF. *See* Operation Enduring Freedom
Office of Reconstruction and Humanitarian Assistance (ORHA), 9, 11, 181
Office of the Coordinator for Reconstruction and Stabilization, 93, 95, 166, 217n68, 241
Office of the Undersecretary of Defense for Policy, 10
Office of Transition Initiatives, 95
oil, 185, 202, 206
oilfields, destruction of, 222
Oil-for-Food program, 200–201, 208, 214n20
Operation Enduring Freedom (OEF), 110, 149, 151

Operation Iraqi Freedom, 146
Operation Just Cause, 75
Operation Promote Liberty, 73, 75
Operation Provide Comfort, 16n18, 97
Operation Sea Angel, 97
Operation Support Hope, 97
OPIC. *See* Overseas Private Investment
   Corporation
opium, 127, 131, 133–34, 135, 148, 150, 152,
   155, 162–63, 221
Order 71, of CPA, 209
Organization of American States (OAS), 71, 72
organized crime, 162
ORHA. *See* Office of Reconstruction and
   Humanitarian Assistance
Orr, Robert, 215n25
Ottoman Empire, 225
Overseas Development Council, 30
overseasmanship, 26
Overseas Private Investment Corporation
   (OPIC), 73, 83
ownership, 241–43

Pachachi, Adnan, 189
Pakistan, 5, 165; Afghanistan and, 109, 134,
   143, 152, 162; Afghan refugees in, 132, 159;
   Ford Foundation and, 48, 50, 52, 53, 55,
   57–58
Palestine, 183
Panama, 11, 65, 68, 78, 81, 82, 83, 219, 225;
   calculated inexperience in, 226; mixed success in, 73–77; overview of nation-building
   efforts, 66
Panamanian Defense Force, 74
Panamanian Public Force, 76
panchayati raj, 55
Panjshiris, 113
Panjshir Valley, 111, 132
parliamentary elections: in Afghanistan, 125,
   126, 143, 160, 161, 163–64; in Iraq, 187,
   192, 212
Pashtunistan, 143
Pashtuns, 111, 112, 113, 114, 115, 118, 127,
   132, 138, 157, 158, 162; calls for separate
   state in, 143; security issues and, 130
patriotic societies, 78
Patriotic Union of Kurdistan (PUK), 185, 193
PDD 56. *See* Presidential Decision Directive 56
peace-building capacity, 227
Peace Corps, 25, 26, 27, 34
peace enforcement, 233, 235
peacekeeping, 219, 220, 233, 234; in Afghanistan, 129, 139, 153, 164; in Bosnia, 64; in
   Iraq, 202
Peceny, Mark, 68
Pedram, Latif, 160

Pentagon, 8; Afghanistan and, 9, 119–20,
   136–37, 148, 149, 164; Iraq and, 10, 13,
   174, 175, 177, 239, 240
per capita income, 6, 72
Persian Gulf War (first), 190, 227, 239
Persian Gulf War (second), 227
Pesh Merga, 180, 181
Petraeus, David, 214n16
Phase III plan, 148
Phase IV plan, 11, 148
Philippe, Guy, 71
Philippines, 8, 24
planning: enhancing capacity in, 94–95; Ford
   Foundation and, 50–52; in Haiti, 68–69; interagency, 88–89, 94; interagency teams for, 95;
   in Panama, 75–76; of reconstruction, 82–83
Point Four declaration, 22, 46–47
Poland, 179
police force, 235; in Afghanistan, 119, 126,
   129, 137, 138, 150, 152; in Haiti, 71–72;
   in Iraq, 177, 180, 205; in Panama, 76
Police Reserve (Japan), 78
policy oversight, 88, 93
political administration, 65
political-military implementation (pol-mil)
   plan, 100–101, 102–3
poppies, opium, 127, 131, 133–34, 135, 138,
   150, 155, 162–63
population control, 56
Post-Conflict Reconstruction Project, 214n14
post–World War II era, 4, 5, 19–41, 59, 218,
   220, 231; consensus during, 19–20, 24, 35,
   37; development during, 20–27, 29–30; lessons from, 198; new nation-building during,
   43–45, 52–53. *See also* Germany, postwar
   nation-building in; Japan, postwar nation-
   building in
poverty, 32, 33, 154–55
Powell, Colin, 227
Presidency Council (Iraq), 190
Presidential Business Mission (Haiti), 73
Presidential Decision Directive 56 (PDD 56),
   8, 86, 88–89, 94, 96–103, 166, 200, 240;
   after-action review, 101; agency review and
   implementation, 102; background of, 97–98;
   components of pol-mil plan, 102–3; Executive Committee (*see* Executive Committee);
   intent of, 98–99; interagency pol-mil rehearsal, 100–101; pol-mil plan, 100; purpose
   of, 96; training, 101–2
Preval, Rene, 71, 72–73
Price, Don, 48
Progressive party (Japan), 79
provincial councils (Iraq), 173, 184, 187
provincial reconstruction teams (PRTs), 10,
   129–30, 138, 151, 164, 165, 168n8, 236

public support, 68, 88, 91
PUK. *See* Patriotic Union of Kurdistan
purges: in Iraq, 205; in Japan, 78–79, 80
Putin, Vladimir, 111

al-Qaeda, 12, 135, 139, 140, 144; drug smuggling by, 149, 152; Iraqi terrorism organized
by, 181; persistence of, 152; preoccupation
with eradication of, 113, 115, 119, 148, 164
Qanooni, Younus, 159, 160
Qawliyya, 179
al-Qizwini, Sayyid Farqad, 179

Rabbani, Burhanuddin, 111, 160
railroads, 134
Ramparts magazine, 34
RAND, 2, 231
ration card system, 184
Reagan administration, 5
reconstruction, 233, 241–42; in Afghanistan,
10, 134–40, 153–57, 161, 164, 221, 237; balancing legitimacy with, 82; case study of,
134–39; development versus, 4–8, 234; economic, 176; in Haiti, 72–73; in Iraq, 176, 177,
182, 196–217, 224–25, 237, 239; in Japan,
78–81; planning, 82–83; political, 176,
236–38; of post–Civil War South, 8; security
relationship with, 139–40, 156; social, 176
refugees: Afghan, 132–33, 153, 155, 159; Iraqi,
201
regime change, 64–65
regional and ethnic divisions: in Afghanistan,
109–10, 111, 114, 118, 119, 120, 124, 127,
131–32, 141, 143, 157–58, 159, 163, 167; in
Iraq, 180, 181, 190, 191, 193–94
regional assembly (Kurdistan), 173
religious freedom, 136, 190
Republican Palace, 12, 177, 178
Republic of Korea. *See* South Korea
resistance, overcoming, 69
resources, 131, 242–44
revolutionary development program, 28
Rice, Condoleezza, 188, 197
Ring Road, 10, 154
Rockefeller, David, 30
Rockefeller Foundation, 24, 30, 42, 55, 56
Roosevelt, Franklin D., 42, 82
Rostow, Walt, 27, 50
Rothkopf, David, 73
rules of engagement, 71, 153, 174, 233, 240
Rumsfeld, Donald, 9, 10, 13, 174, 213n2, 227,
239, 244n3
rural development, 52–56
Rural Electrification Administration, 29
Rusk, Dean, 27
Russia, 24, 111, 134, 219, 224

Rwanda, 198
Ryukyu Islands, 25

Sadat, Anwar, 51
al-Sadr, Muqtada, 178–80, 181
Salafists, 194
Salim, Ezedine, 177
San Francisco Peace Treaty, 81
SCAP. *See* Supreme Command of the Allied
Powers
Schlesinger, Arthur, Jr., 21
SCIRI. *See* Supreme Council for Islamic
Revolution in Iraq
SEADAG. *See* Southeast Asian Development
Advisory Group
secretary of defense, U.S., 93
security, 234–36; in Afghanistan, 128–30,
139–40, 148–53, 156, 161, 164, 166–67, 222,
234, 236; in Iraq, 148, 174, 176–81, 193, 197,
198, 199, 202–3, 204–5, 208, 222, 223, 224,
234, 235–36; post–September 11, 87; reconstruction relationship with, 139–40, 156
security sector reform (SSR), 149, 150, 152, 162
Self-Defense Force (Japan), 78
separatism/secessionism, 109, 111–12, 113–14,
124, 143
September 11 terrorist attacks, 2, 8, 89, 111,
113, 145, 146, 147, 148, 166, 167, 220, 232;
nation-building in aftermath of, 221–22;
security in aftermath of, 87
Serbs, 2
shari'a courts, 179
Shidehara government, 79
Shiite Muslims, 111, 173, 181, 183, 236; alliance with Kurds, 193–94; constitution and,
190–91; elections and, 187, 193–94, 238; political parties of, 185; Sadr and, 178, 179–80
Shinseki, Eric, 174
Sierra Leone, 232, 233
Singapore, 45
single, nontransferable vote (SNVT) system,
160, 163
Sistani, Grand Ayatollah Ali, 183, 185, 186,
187, 190, 191, 193, 237
Sistani list, 193
Slocombe, Walter, 236
Snowbound (Whittier), 61
SNVT. *See* single, nontransferable vote system
social capital, 176
Somalia, 4, 6, 8, 35, 83n2, 86, 198, 218, 227;
calculated inexperience in, 226; during the
Cold War, 219; complex contingency opera-
tions in, 97; lessons learned in, 87, 89, 91,
93, 96, 166, 220, 223; security in, 222
Southeast Asian Development Advisory Group
(SEADAG), 25, 29, 34

Southern Command, U.S., 75
South Korea, 2, 15n5,8, 20, 22–24, 23, 26, 29, 244
South Vietnam, 2, 20, 25, 27–29, 31–34; ineffective use of aid in, 31–32; overview of nation-building efforts, 66; U.S. commitment to, 28–29
sovereignty: in Afghanistan, 9, 12, 107–14, 116, 118–19, 120, 121, 123, 142, 158, 160–61; in Iraq, 13, 173, 191, 193, 208, 240; in Japan, 81, 82; in Panama, 76. *See also* transition of power
Soviet Union, 4, 21, 26–27, 45, 146; Afghanistan and, 107, 109, 126, 128, 134, 139, 142, 147, 160, 162, 232; demise of, 35, 59, 219; Japan and, 80, 83
Spain, 129, 179, 235, 239
Srebinica, 233
SSR. *See* security sector reform
Stabilization and Reconstruction Civilian Management Act of 2004, 104
state-building, 3, 5; in Afghanistan, 151, 157–61, 164; in Iraq, 176–77, 187–89
State Department, U.S., 87, 96, 226, 240; Afghanistan and, 9, 119, 120, 129, 136, 137, 138; Haiti and, 72; Iraq and, 9, 10, 11, 175, 212, 222, 227, 228, 229; Japan and, 77; Office of the Coordinator for Reconstruction and Stabilization, 93, 95, 166, 217n68, 241; Panama and, 75
state failure, 2, 4, 87, 145, 146, 157, 220, 232
strategic hamlets program, 28, 38n25
sub-Saharan Africa, 2, 6, 49, 58
Sudan, 59
suicide bombings, 181
Sukarno, 45, 51, 60
Sunni Muslims, 173, 179, 181, 183, 194–95; constitution and, 190, 191; elections and, 187, 193; political parties of, 185; support for Hussein in, 182
Sunni triangle, 193, 205, 238
support, public, 68, 88, 91
Supreme Command of the Allied Powers (SCAP), 78–80
Supreme Council for Islamic Revolution in Iraq (SCIRI), 180, 181, 185, 189
survivability, 64–65
sustainability, 199
Syria, 175

Taguba, Antonio, 207–8
Tajikistan, 165
Tajiks, 111, 113, 114, 118, 121, 127, 132, 143, 158, 159, 160, 162
TAL. *See* Transitional Administrative Law
Talabani, Jalal, 193

Taliban, 3, 8, 12, 67, 107, 110–11, 126, 129, 132–34, 136, 139, 146, 147, 151, 155, 158, 161, 162, 223; amnesty for participants, 141; drug smuggling by, 149, 152; election disruptions threatened by, 159; jihad against, 128; negotiations with leaders of, 122; persistence of, 116, 118, 152; preoccupation with eradication of, 113, 115, 119, 148, 164; revival of feared, 113
Tannenbaum, Frank, 49
Tanzania, 49, 51
taxes, 113, 116, 118, 120, 122, 126
Technical Assistance Program, 22
Technical Cooperation Administration, 27
Tehran, 134
Tennessee Valley Authority (TVA), 5, 21, 26, 29
terrorism, 87, 232; Afghanistan and, 12, 136, 138–39, 144, 146, 167; Iraq and, 173, 175, 177, 181, 186, 194; war on, 1, 136, 165. *See also* September 11 terrorist attacks
Thatcher administration, 5
Thurman, Maxwell R., 75
Tikrit, 192
Tokyo Conference, 122, 131, 136, 155, 156
torture, 206
TR. *See* transition and reintegration plan
trade, 23; Afghanistan and, 130, 154; Haiti and, 72, 73; Japan and, 80
transformation phase of reconstruction, 199
Transitional Administrative Law (TAL), 187, 189–92, 209, 210
Transitional Authority (Afghanistan), 110, 157
Transitional National Assembly (Iraq), 193
transition and reintegration (TR) plan, 180
transition of power, 88, 94; in Afghanistan, 135, 161; in Iraq, 173, 175, 186, 187–89, 199, 202. *See also* sovereignty
Treasury Department, U.S., 11, 72
Truman, Harry, 22, 46–47, 53, 61, 80
Turbulent Peace (U.S. Institute of Peace), 231
Turkmen, 143, 159
TVA. *See* Tennessee Valley Authority

Uganda, 51–52
UNDP. *See* United Nations Development Program
unemployment, 72, 75–76, 154, 203, 205–6
UNICEF. *See* United Nations Children's Fund
unilateralism, 66, 67
United Iraqi Alliance, 193
United Kingdom / Great Britain, 219, 235; Afghanistan and, 109, 129, 136, 138, 149, 150; India and, 3, 48–49; Iraq and, 174–75, 182, 184, 199, 202; Sierra Leone and, 233
United Nations (U.N.), 31, 42, 46, 60, 90, 94, 220, 231, 232, 233, 241; Afghanistan and,

United Nations (*cont.*)
12, 13, 67, 108, 109, 110–11, 112, 119, 120, 133, 146, 154, 157, 158, 239; bombing of headquarters, 186; crisis of development and, 29; Haiti and, 67, 69–70, 71, 72; Iraq and, 9, 185–86, 188, 189, 191, 198, 200–202, 208–11, 212, 213n13, 226, 228, 238–39; Korea and, 23, 24; in post–World War II era, 22, 27; Somalia and, 89, 91, 93; Vietnam and, 29
United Nations Assistance Mission in Afghanistan, 154
United Nations Children's Fund (UNICEF), 30, 201, 210
United Nations Development Program (UNDP), 22, 155, 156, 201, 210
United Nations Educational, Scientific, and Cultural Organization, 23
United Nations High Commissioner for Refugees, 201
United Nations Korean Reconstruction Agency, 23
United Nations Mission in Haiti (UNMIH), 69–70, 71
United Nations Monitoring, Inspection, and Verification Commission (UNMOVIC), 201
United Nations Office for Project Services, 201
United Nations Security Council, 67, 94, 219; Afghanistan and, 151; Iraq and, 185, 201–2, 208, 211, 212, 224; Resolution 986, 214n20; Resolution 1483, 201–2, 208, 214n23; Resolution 1546, 188, 191
United States Agency for International Development (USAID), 29, 30, 34, 104, 226, 232, 240, 241; Afghanistan and, 9, 119, 129, 136, 137, 138, 154; Haiti and, 72; Iraq and, 9, 10, 11, 192, 211, 212, 228; Office of Transition Initiatives, 95; Panama and, 75; pinnacle of influence, 27; Vietnam and, 28, 31–33
United Task Force, 89
universities, 25, 34
University of Texas, 42
UNMIH. *See* United Nations Mission in Haiti
UNMOVIC. *See* United Nations Monitoring, Inspection, and Verification Commission
USAID. *See* United States Agency for International Development
Uzbekistan, 165
Uzbeks, 111, 127, 132, 143, 158, 159

V-AID. *See* Village Agricultural and Industrial Development program
Vieira de Mello, Sergio, 185–86, 188, 201, 203

Vietnam, 226, 229. *See also* South Vietnam
Vietnam War, 2–3, 5, 19, 20, 27–29, 36, 37, 67, 236; changes in foreign aid during, 31–35; Iraq situation compared with, 175, 196; lessons from, 198; strategic hamlets program in, 28, 38n25
Village Agricultural and Industrial Development (V-AID) program, 53

war crimes, 78, 206, 207
warlords, 6, 108, 116, 118, 132, 135, 139, 145, 148, 149, 156, 161, 221, 237; downside of cooperation with, 153; drug traffic and, 133, 152, 167; Karzai and, 122, 143; in Liberia and Sierra Leone, 232; official dealings with, 117; as political candidates, 150; power maintained by, 152; return to leadership roles, 162; security provided by, 128; U.S. negotiations with, 113, 115, 119, 152, 158; U.S. pressure on, 120, 124
war on terrorism, 1, 136, 165
Washington Post, 212
weapons of mass destruction, 14, 211, 222, 224
West Germany, 65, 66, 67
Whittier, John Greenleaf, 61
Williams College, 52
Winning the Peace (Center for Strategic and International Studies), 231
Wolesi Jirga, 157, 160, 163
women: in Afghanistan, 132, 136, 141, 163; in Iraq, 179, 189, 192, 193; in Japan, 79
Woods, George, 30
Woodward, Bob, 11
World Bank, 4–5, 30, 31, 36, 52, 198, 232, 241; Afghanistan and, 122, 131, 155; crisis of development and, 29; expanded role of, 35; Indonesia and, 242; Iraq and, 210
World Council of Churches, 29
World Food Program, 201
World War II, 8, 65, 225. *See also* post–World War II era

al-Yaccoubi, Mustafa, 179
Yale University, 42
al-Yawer, Ghazi, 189
You the People (Chesterman), 231
Yugoslavia, 97, 219, 225

zaibatsu, 77, 79
Zambia, 49
Zia ul Haq, Muhammad, 58
Zinni, Anthony, 196–97